W9-ADJ-538

FACES FROM THE FIRE

Also by Leonard Mosley

Non-Fiction

SO FAR SO GOOD
CASTLEROSSE
DOWNSTREAM: 1939
GIDEON GOES TO WAR: THE STORY OF WINGATE
REPORT FROM GERMANY: 1945
THE CAT AND THE MICE
CURZON: THE END OF AN EPOCH
THE LAST DAYS OF THE BRITISH RAJ

Fiction

NO MORE REMAINS
EACH HAD A SONG
WAR LORD
SO I KILLED HER
THE SEDUCTIVE MIRROR

Faces from the Fire

The Biography of Sir Archibald McIndoe

by

LEONARD MOSLEY

PRENTICE-HALL, INC.
ENGLEWOOD CLIFFS, N.J.

First American Edition

 Library of Congress Catalog Card Number 63-11038.

29871-T

MADE AND PRINTED IN GREAT BRITAIN

CONTENTS

		Page
	PROLOGUE	9
Chapter		
1	TESTING TIME	13
2	LEARNING FROM THE DEAD	30
3	'THE NOSE IS IN THE MIDDLE OF THE FACE'	48
4	THE BATTLE OF BRITAIN	77
5	WARD THREE	93
6	THE DEATH OF HILLARY	115
7	'WE ARE THE GUINEA PIGS'	136
8	'SOMEONE OF IMPORTANCE'	172
9	MCINDOE VERSUS BEVAN	189
10	HAVEN ON KILIMANJARO	216
11	THE GOLDEN HAND	230
12	DOES A DOCTOR KNOW?	246
13	HOW LONG?	256
14	EPILOGUE	259

ILLUSTRATIONS

Facing page

1 Sir Archibald Hector McIndoe (*Photo: P-A Reuter*) 32
2 Archie's mother as she was when he was a boy 33
3 Mrs McIndoe with the portrait she painted of her son (*Photo: East Grinstead Courier*) 33
4 Ken, Archie and John McIndoe 64
5 Archie and Adonia McIndoe with Adonia junior and Vanora in 1938 64
6 Archibald McIndoe with his partners, Sir Harold Gillies, Rainsford Mowlem and T. P. Kilner 65
7 Geoffrey Page at East Grinstead 96
8 Richard Hillary after his operation (*Photo: Topix*) 96
9 & 10 The famous saline bath at East Grinstead 97
11 The original saline bath unit and crew 128
12 The first meeting of the Guinea Pig Club: Tom Gleave, Russell Davies, Geoffrey Page, Peter Weeks, Michael Coote and the Maestro 128
13 McIndoe with Jill Mullins, Clark Gable, airmen, nurses and visitors at Dutton Homestall in 1943 129
14 Another Guinea Pig reunion: Archie McIndoe, John Hunter and Edward Blacksell (*Photo: Sunday Pictorial*) 160
15 The Maestro checking on a patient's progress during a reunion (*Photo: Sunday Pictorial*) 160
16 The Duke of Kent with McIndoe and some of the nurses at East Grinstead 161
17 Digging the first sod for the children's ward with Kay Clemetson 161

Maynard Thomas
Carol Coffer

ILLUSTRATIONS

Facing page

18 & 19 Kay Kendall before and after McIndoe operated on her nose (*Photos: Charles Trigg and P-A Reuter*) 192
20 McIndoe with Jack Penn in Africa 193
21 McIndoe inspecting his African farm 193
22 McIndoe with Queen Elizabeth the Queen Mother when she opened the American Wing at East Grinstead (*Photo: H. Connold*) 224
23 The Duke of Edinburgh with Tom Gleave, the Chief Guinea Pig (*Photo: Ian W. Craig*) 224
24 Sir Archibald McIndoe with Mrs Constance Belchem, who was to become the second Lady McIndoe (*Photo: Planet News*) 225
25 Sir Archibald and Lady McIndoe with Princess Marina (*Photo: Crown Copyright*) 240
26 Archie's daughters, Vanora and Adonia. 240
27 Sir Archibald and Lady McIndoe returning from Spain 241

PROLOGUE

IN THE YEARS BETWEEN 1940 and 1945, the crucial years of the last war so far as the RAF was concerned, 4,500 burned air-crew men were recovered by rescue squads from crashed planes in this country, or parachuted in flames to safety. Of that number, 3,600 sustained burns of the hands and of the face. They were victims of a new disease, a disease of wartime which came to be known as the Airman's Burn. A pilot was hurled like a blazing torch from his plane and sustained burns of the exposed parts of his body; or his plane crashed and he was enveloped in flame, lying unconscious against red-hot material; or he sustained deep burns of the exposed part of his body, together with a greater or lesser extent of the covered parts, depending upon the efficiency of his protective clothing.

Most of these fried, frizzled, grossly mutilated and tormented young men found themselves, sooner or later, looking up through the remains of their charred eyelids at the round, sympathetic face of a surgeon named Archibald Hector McIndoe.

Archie McIndoe was a plastic surgeon. He had started professional life as an abdominal surgeon of great skill and promise, but had turned to the art of skinning and grafting in the hungry nineteen-thirties, when no one would give him a job in England at his speciality. In the years leading up to the war, he had built up a reputation in Harley Street as a man who could bob a nose, lift a face or a woman's pendulous breasts, could remove a scar, an acne, sew up a hare-lip or join a cleft palate—who earned his living, in fact, by making the ugly beautiful.

He had always maintained, however, that there was more, much more, to his profession than mere cosmetic surgery. The meticulous art of cutting, grafting, stitching and reconstituting which he had learned so painstakingly was never meant to be confined to the whims of vain women or the rectification of Nature's mistakes. Plastic surgery—or reconstructive surgery, as he preferred to call it—had a higher, more creative, dynamic than that. It was the art of surgical restoration; not, like ordinary surgery, a skill by which you opened someone up, cut something out, and sewed them up again, but a sculptor's job with human flesh as the material by which you fashioned a face or rebuilt a pair of hands out of a mass of mangled material which some man-made accident had destroyed.

The last war gave him the opportunity—and provided him with the material—to demonstrate the rightness of his belief. As consultant plastic surgeon to the RAF, he received all cases of bad burns among airmen at the headquarters he had established at the Queen Victoria Hospital at East Grinstead. From the Battle of Britain onwards, the charred and the smashed young men of the country poured in upon him. Here were young men who represented the flower of England's youth, at one moment young pilots fighting the Nazi invaders over the Channel and the North Sea, the next scorched and suppurating bodies hovering in agony between life and death.

His problem was not only to save their lives but to make them whole again.

What differentiated Archie McIndoe from all the other fine plastic surgeons who worked on the burned and shattered during the war is not so much that his skill in grafting and mending was greater, though he had no equals in that. It was his supreme conviction that to make a monstrously mutilated young man *whole again* required much more than the twenty, thirty, forty or even fifty operations needed to give him a new nose, eyelids, lips, chin and working hands. It needed a mental and emotional as well as a surgical approach, a relationship between doctor and patient that would clean the wounds from the mind as well as the body.

His technique was revolutionary, and, to some, shocking. He shattered the old convention of surgical secrecy and took his young patients into his confidence. 'It is my practice,' he wrote, 'to describe to the patient the scheme to be followed, announce the exact number of operations it will entail, how many weeks or months will be spent in the hospital and how much time will be required out of the hospital to recuperate, what the patient should do during these off periods, and finally, the approximate date when the face will be completed. Only then can his confidence and above all his intelligent interest be maintained, for assuming that in addition a pair of badly burned hands must be restored the total period of incapacity may be four years.'

He allowed his burned airmen to get up from their beds and go out, to the pub or cinema, and be hanged to the citizens who might be horrified by their appalling faces. He encouraged them to think of themselves not as invalids but as human beings going through a reconstructive phase. He taught them to live with their injuries—and taught outsiders to live with, and learn to love, these injured men too.

As his great colleague and mentor Sir Harold Gillies once said, Sir Archibald McIndoe was truly one of the great heroes of the Battle of Britain. Hundreds of injured airmen have learned to live and thrive because of him, and the Guinea Pig Club—whose members all went through his restorative processes—is his great memorial.

But not only that. In making the faces of so many mutilated men, he changed the face of plastic surgery, transformed it from a half-despised skin-deep craft into a creative surgical art whose future, thanks to his pioneering techniques, has possibilities which would have been thought miraculous before he came on the scene.

Of his part in the struggle to heal the ugly wounds of war, he wrote modestly:

'Eventually there comes the exciting moment when all the tissue required in the repair of an injured face is in position, all major contraction has been overcome and the patient has resolved his scars, softened his grafts, and is ready for trimming. The aim is to produce a face which in sum total is symmetrical in its separate parts, of good colour and texture and freely mobile, so that expression of mood is possible in all its infinite variety. It is not possible to construct a face from one destroyed of which the observer is unconscious, but it should not leave in his mind an impression of repulsion, and the patient himself should not be an object of remark or pity. Only then can the surgeon feel that his work has been faithfully done.'

It is a measure of Archie McIndoe's success that no patient who ever passed through his hands ever feels himself an object of pity.

He went on after the war to beautify many. For, of course, the nose-bobs and the face-lifts and hare-lips came again. But none of them is prouder of his or her appearance than the grossly mutilated pilots and air crews whose shattered faces and downcast minds he restored during the war.

He did faithfully by them all, and faithfully by the art of surgery too.

CHAPTER ONE

TESTING TIME

IT WAS A LUMP of black rock, a hundred feet across, which lay athwart the main channel opposite the little seaside resort of Brighton, eleven miles from Dunedin, on the South Island of New Zealand. At full water all to be seen of it was the turbulence of spray around it as the Pacific rollers wrecked themselves upon it on their way to the shore. But as the tide ebbed, it seemed to eave itself, an oily, igneous stump, out of the waves and float in e swell like a giant raft, half a cable's length away across the nnel.

ach day during their holidays, the two boys would set off for hore, and there was plenty for them to do. The great waves ke on the reefs a quarter of a mile out and spilled on to the ches like giant bottles of fizzy lemonade; and the effervescent f was there to be tossed in or rolled in until you learned to climb crest and ride it back to the shore. At low water, there were ark green pools in the reef to be explored for the crayfish, which they caught, and the giant octopuses with suckered tentacles and slimy grasp which, they told themselves, lurked in the darker depths.

But always, when the tide was out, they came back to the same place, the shoreward side of the channel facing the black and foreboding but nonetheless beckoning slab. They dangled their feet over the edge of the channel and fished for butterfish and greenbone, but their minds were on the rock. It tantalized them. Once a great bird, which Jack said was a cormorant but Nookie swore was an albatross, swooped down and strutted just short of the black ledge, and they envied him the ease of his approach, the calm arrogance of his occupation; and when he took off again, his great wings beating the air with a noise like an unoiled winch,

Nookie at least was ashamed. For the giant bird as it came over them sprayed droppings in the water quite close to them, as if in contempt for their wingless, earthbound helplessness.

That was the beginning of the Christmas holidays in 1912. Before the year was out and the holidays were over, Nookie swore to himself that he would be where the albatross had been. Though he did not tell Jack about it yet.

There were six members of the McIndoe family: John McIndoe and his wife, Mabel, and their three sons and one daughter, John junior (called Jack), Archibald Hector (known as Nookie), Kenneth and Mabel junior. They lived in Dunedin, where John owned a comfortable business as a jobbing printer, and though Archie McIndoe was later on to claim—like many another great man—that he roughed it as a child, their circumstances were secure and stable and they wanted for nothing. Jack was the eldest child and Nookie was eighteen months younger; the other two, bor several years later, were small fry who simply got in their way.

'Father was very fond of horses,' Jack recalls. 'He had buil stable and coach-house in the paddock at the rear of our ho He always kept a cab which he frequently used to ride into ness. While we were still small he bought us a Shetland p called Tim. In the coach-house were two gigs and two sets harness with saddles and bridles for Tim and the cab. We bo were taught how to handle horses, to ride and drive at a very ear age. We were also taught how to handle firearms. Our first were comparatively safe airguns, and I think our best sport arose shooting the mice which frequented the stable and the chaff-house. When we were old enough we each had a ·22 Winchester which we used a great deal shooting rabbits. Archie was a first-rate marksman and later became the champion shot at Otago Boys' High School.'

The nearest Archie McIndoe got to selling papers on the corner in the tradition of the self-made millionaire were the chores which his mother made him and his brother do around the house.

'We had daily and weekly tasks set for us,' says Jack, 'and no play was permitted until these tasks were completed. Archie and I did the daily chores in turn week about. One week he would feed and water the horses and clean out the stable. I would mix the hot mash with the kitchen scraps and feed and water the ducks and hens and gather the eggs. These tasks were carried out at 7 am and 4.30 pm. Then one of us would chop the kindling and the other would brush Father's boots. On Saturday morning we had the grass to cut, the asphalt paths to sweep and the garden to weed, and on Sunday morning we helped father to wash the gigs, clean the harness leather and polish the nickel rings, bits, buckles and stirrups.'

In addition, there was the seaside cottage at Brighton, to which the whole family repaired each weekend, and there it was boating, swimming, fishing and shooting all day long. It more than made up for the blue-striped sailor blouses, the wide striped collars, the long black stockings and black boots, the half-mast pants with elastic at the waist and below the knees, and the button-like caps on close-cropped heads which the two boys were expected to wear for Sunday school and company.

John McIndoe, Archie's father, was a second generation New Zealander whose family had its roots in the Kyles of Bute, where his grandfather had once been provost of the burgh of Rothsey. John's father had come to New Zealand from Scotland to get away from strife in the kirk and because he needed more than the few acres of land he had been allowed to farm at home. He was a tough man of the soil who loved his Bible and fed his family on the milk of the word, but drank other things himself, mostly whisky. He brought his children up to fear God but no man, to remember Scotland with affection but to love New Zealand with passion, and to follow the only calling worthy of a man, on the land.

But the sap which had coursed so strongly through previous generations had been strained by the time it reached John McIndoe's veins. He was a good and kindly man, but lukewarm in spirit, mild in temperament, and not strong in body. The only revolt he ever engineered in life was to break away from the land and set himself up as a jobbing printer in Dunedin, a venture which, in a city which grew rapidly towards the end of the last century, proved solidly if not sensationally successful. It was enough. He did not wish to fight for any more. For the rest of his life, he was content to be managed by his wife. Meanwhile, he ran his business in town, drove his horse-drawn cab until it was outmoded, and then replaced it with the first of the motor cars.

He smoked a pipe and posed as the autocrat of the breakfast table, a pillar of the community, a member of all the societies.

But in truth, Mabel McIndoe ruled him and he was content that she should do so. Mabel was one of those women for whom *self-sufficient* is the only description. She was small in physical stature but big in every other sense of the word, and for the whole of her long life she made it clear to the world that she had no need of anyone. On one occasion, she wrote to her favourite son, Archie:

'I am writing this in bed where I have been for the last five days. This diabolical climate is doing its damndest to finish me but the Lord send I'll cheat it yet. All my bronchial tubes are blocked and I cough incessantly . . .'

But next day she followed it with another:

'I wrote you yesterday when feeling ill and under the strain of considerable emotion. I suppose it relieved my feelings but I should have destroyed the letter instead of sending it to you . . . Destroy it and never mention I wrote to you, if you love me.'

She was seventy years old at the time, and it was probably the nearest to asking for help she ever came in her life.

In truth, she came from a family whose womenfolk have never seemed to need help. She once, for the benefit of her children and grandchildren, wrote the story of her family background, and it is a salty and incisive narrative in which, time and again, the women win out against what might seem today to be desperate trials and conditions.

'My father, Charles Hill, was trained as a hatter,' she wrote, 'and was expected to join the family business in Bristol. But in 1852 he married Eliza Ann Hulbert, daughter of John Burgess, brass founder. He was twenty-one and she was twenty-two. The marriage took place in a registry office and young Charles departed immediately to seek his fortune in Australia. He told me on his deathbed that he left my mother as he found her! Eliza went back to her job as maid and Charles sailed round the Cape of Good Hope landing, I think, at Melbourne.

'In Australia, with a capital of fifteen shillings in his pocket, Charles spurned the hatting trade for the gold rush at Ballarat. He kept alive by playing his violin around the diggings, and it was a year before he came back to Melbourne, picked up a job as an employee in a hatters, and saved enough to send for Eliza and her two sisters. Their first child was born in 1855 and their second a year later, and shortly thereafter Charles Hill decided that he had had enough of Australia. He shipped himself and his family to America, where they settled down with the intention of farming in Kansas.

'But the winter was cold and by the time they arrived there Eliza was pregnant with a third child. She was seven months gone when her husband, restless once more, upped the scanty family sticks and they boarded a sailing vessel, the *Mary Ann*, to sail back to Australia again. The voyage took four and a half months and was a stormy passage. The third son was born at sea, and he was a bonny child despite the fact that his mother was washed down a gangway on to the head of a sailor a few days before he was born.

'She fed the baby herself, as indeed she did all her nine children,' Mabel wrote. 'The next event was an outbreak of scarlet fever on the ship. Charlie and Jack took it but got better, but a kind woman who was helping mother died of it and was buried at sea.'

The Hill family stayed twelve years in Australia this time, in which Eliza bred five more children and lost two of them from 'inflammation of the bowels'. This time it was she who persuaded her husband to make a move. 'She used to say that Australia was not a white man's country,' said Mabel. 'She found the hot, suffocating winds of Melbourne very hard to bear. When her brother, C. P. Hulbert, came to Australia after the Maori War with stories of the benign climate and favourable conditions to be found in New Zealand, the family decided to try their luck in yet another country.'

There, at long last, a hatter once more, Charles settled for good and prospered, and it was there that Mabel Hill was born. She sailed and swam and learned to play the piano. She also began to paint.

'It was agreed on all sides that I ought to go to Paris to study,' Mabel wrote, 'but my emotions got in the way. From the time I was eighteen I had an "understanding" with Harry Mowat, a tall young man from Marlborough, but I did not see much of him because he left before I was nineteen. The engagement went on for four years with me getting steadily more and more tired of it.

Then when I was twenty-two I went to stay with friends in Dunedin. They took me to a bowling match and introduced me to John McIndoe, then about thirty-six.'

Almost at once she made up her mind. She wrote to Harry Mowat and broke off her engagement. She still wanted to go to Paris to study, but John McIndoe's charm and gentle manner touched her heart. 'When, in 1897, my Christmas holidays, I went down to Dunedin and found a new house being built for me, I felt I had to give up Paris in favour of marriage.'

They were married three weeks later in St John's Presbyterian Church, Wellington.

It was a decision which, in later years, when the children started to come, she was often to regret, but she gave no hint of it at the time. Her family and friends all remember, however, her moods of isolation, her need to get away from them on occasion.

'As a wife she was forbearing,' one of them recalls. 'As a mother she could be stern and implacable, but as a person Mabel McIndoe was an indomitable woman whose sense of purpose and inner convictions were so strong that you could almost hear the trumpets blaring offstage as she walked into a room.'

Each day in her life was a fresh adventure, though not necessarily one to be shared with anyone else. Each man or woman was measured and found worthy or wanting according to whether they were weak or strong. She had no time for doubt and indecision in herself and therefore could not understand them in others. 'Savour what joys life gives you and suffer its pains without complaining,' she used to say; and this simple philosophy, together with a supreme confidence in the rightness of her opinions, made her no easy woman to live with and fenced her off from casual intimacies.

Towards her easygoing husband, she was warm and affectionate and it would be unjust to suggest that she had no gentleness in her. She was a woman of drive, but she never drove him. But to a great extent his was a dull world in which she could simulate only a half-interest, and she had one of her own which gave her the colour and excitement, and the dreams, which were her compensation. For she had grown to be an artist of considerable talent, and this was the real love of her life. She painted her sons and she painted the lavish landscapes around her homes in Dunedin and Brighton.

Looked at all these years later, the paintings hit the eye, if not the heart, as more than amateur productions. The portrait of Archie McIndoe as a child captures the suggestion of a smile that was rarely absent from his face, but also traps the determined glint that lurked behind it. In her landscapes, she sometimes seems to be disciplining Nature, as if to rebuke the New Zealand flora for its opulence, but the line is sure, economical, professional, almost surgically clean.

These were the qualities which, by example as well as by blood, put a poker down the back of her most distinguished son, and gave him an iron determination, and, sometimes, a ramrod stubbornness. She loved her children but with a love which was very much this side of idolatry. They were never dandled on her knee (not after the cradle stage, anyway) and they were never kissed or over-fondled. But the brown eyes were always upon them, like a mother bird's on her chicks: and they were never in any doubt that, when the time came, and they were ready, she would not hesitate to throw them out of the nest.

There had to be a practical reason why the channel should be crossed and the black rock gained. By Boxing Day, Nookie had confided his ambition to Jack and by the following morning the whole family knew about it. It was impossible to explain to either his father or his mother that he wished to swim the channel and sit on the rock just because it was there, because it challenged, because an albatross had mocked him. It was Jack who produced the solution. The delicacy at the family luncheon table was greenbone, a fish not unlike a salmon with few bones and firm white flesh, sweet to the taste; but it was expensive in the shops and hard to catch on the line. John McIndoe had recently purchased a two-inch mesh set-net and what better use could it be put to than to stretch it across the channel between the shore and the rock and trap the fish as they swam in with the current and swell? Only, to work it, someone would have to carry the line for the net across the channel to the rock . . .

At first there was a doubtful shake of the head from father and a forthright no from mother.

'You are getting too venturesome in your ploys,' Mabel McIndoe said. (She was fond of the word 'ploy'.) 'The current is too strong and'—to Jack—'I don't think you're a strong enough swimmer yet.'

Jack said, 'It's not me who wants to swim it, Mamma. It's Nookie.'

'In that case,' said their father, 'there's nothing doing. It's too far and you're too young. You're just a shrimp,' he said to Archie, catching him by the arm, affectionately.

The boy shook him off and turned to his mother. 'But it's my New Year resolution,' he said. 'I've got to do it. I promised. And I can't break a promise, can I?'

'Promised whom?' asked his mother.

'Myself, of course! Who else?'

Mabel McIndoe looked at her husband and he, seeing the expression in her eyes, sighed, lit his pipe, and coughed.

'In that case,' he said.

Next day, before low water, the whole family clambered over the rocks to the channel. 'Father carried the net,' recalls Archie's brother, 'Archie a coil of light rope and I a hessian bag. Archie stripped to his bathing trunks, placing his blouse, jersey and pants and a towel in the bag. I tied one end of the rope round his waist and let out some slack. The tide was not quite out and rollers were still breaking partly over the island and sweeping round through the channel, where there was quite a current. The long seaweed was swinging oilily and making sucking, squelching noises. Archie grinned at me as he stood ready to dive. Father gripped his pipe in his teeth. Mother was white in the face. Boss (the family dog) let out a yelp and Archie was in the channel, his arms working like flails as he battled his way across the open water and through the writhing kelp to the other side. He hauled himself up on a ledge as a swell lifted his body, and he was safely across.'

He pulled on the rope and brought the net into position across the channel. Everyone except Archie then sat down to watch. In from the sea swam the fish and first one and then another—greenbone, butterfish, moki—enmeshed themselves in the net and writhed and fluttered, silver flashes in the translucent green.

'It's worked, it's worked!' cried Jack, jumping to his feet.

But for Archie McIndoe it was now anticlimax. He had wandered across the rock to look out across the Pacific. He did not quite strut but his chest was pouting. Who cared about *fish*?

Across the channel, his mother was watching him. For a woman who kept her emotions severely in check the look on her face was surprising. The family had always suspected that Archie, out of all of them, had always been the one who was for her something special, and now they were certain.

That Christmas he was just eleven and a half years old.

Life until the age of fifteen was exciting, adventurous and sumptuously full for Archibald Hector McIndoe, and in after-life, when he was not indulging in his rags-to-riches 'ploy', he would recall it with almost aching nostalgia.

'Do you remember the gymkhana at the Domain at Brighton?' he asked his brothers at a grown-up reunion, and as he said it the years seemed to fall from his face and it became the chubby, grinning ball of his boyhood, eyes almost obscured by the creases of laughter.

That was the year when the boys groomed the pony Tim with curry-comb and brush, trimmed his mane, pinned a jaunty cockade to his ears, and slipped him into a trap which they had decorated with flowers and coloured crêpe. And then Archie climbed aboard and drove pony and trap into the ring. He was something to see, for he wore a costume of his own designing: black face, long red and white striped trousers, white morning coat with red rose in the buttonhole and a white bell-topper.

'Archie's face was coal black, his lips thickened with red greasepaint,' his brother John remembers, 'and he wore white gloves. He drove down to the Domain and entered the arena for the judging at a smart trot. We thought he couldn't miss. He didn't. He won first prize. Not content with this success, he walked round to the shooting tunnel and it wasn't long before I saw him struggling across the grounds carrying half a sheep. He'd cleaned up there too.'

Like his mother, he was small in size, but under her firm and sometimes not so gentle prodding, he pushed his body and the mind inside it to the limits. When he was fourteen, his father bought a motor car, but never got beyond the rudiments of driving. Archie would slip into the stable, where the car was garaged, and jack up the wheels in order to practise the double-declutching necessary on the gears of those days. When he took the car out for the first time, he was too short to see over the steering-wheel. A cushion would have taken his short legs away from brake and clutch, so he drove by peering through the steering-wheel spokes. 'I suppose if I had one virtue as a boy,' he wrote later, recalling his childhood, 'it was the fact that I was a trier. Later on, when I grew up, I sometimes used to think I was bullied into doing things by Mother, but it wasn't really true. Not in the sense that she would say: "Do this" and "do that". What she did do was look at me if I was slack about something in a way that made me look for a mouse-hole to crawl into. I would work myself to the bone in order to avoid that look.'

All the family took lessons in painting and music from Mabel McIndoe. Jack was the most successful as a painter, but Archie developed his mother's quick, clean line in his sketches. He would go with her to the bi-annual theatricals at Otago University, where she would make up the players for the stage, and soon was expert enough to be accepted as her assistant.

'I suppose I did it because I liked putting rouge on pretty girls' faces,' he said. 'But it did teach me one thing which came in useful later on—that you can do all sorts of things to a human face once you learn the knack.'

By the time he was fifteen years old, he could play the piano well. 'Of the four of us,' says his brother, 'Archie was easily the best. He was powerfully built and had broad palms and thick fingers, yet his touch was light and he could play classical music with great expression and entirely from memory.' He had won prizes for shooting and gymnastics and, in his brother's phrase, was 'as strong as an ox'. At school in the same town at this time was a boy named Porritt (later to become Sir Arthur Porritt, President of the Royal College of Surgeons of England) and a rivalry developed between them that was to continue through their lives. It gave Archie McIndoe tremendous satisfaction, which he did not entirely succeed in concealing, to end his schooling in the Upper Sixth of Otago Boys' High School as head prefect, sergeant-major of the cadet battalion, with firsts in most of his scholastic subjects, prizes for shooting and gymnastics and caps for football and cricket. Yet such was his personality that not even his brothers, who had to live with him, were ever jealous of him. No matter how many successes he had and how easily he seemed to achieve some of them, it always was to take a great deal of effort to be jealous of Archibald McIndoe. Though, in later life, some people did succeed in being so.

Abruptly, in 1916, boyhood ended, at fifteen and a half. John McIndoe, who had been ailing for some time, died after a short illness and his widow, Mabel, was left with three boys and a six-years-old daughter on her hands.

It was a crisis which did not daunt her. To some extent, indeed, it was a release, for it opened up prospects for her, once the boys were off her hands, which she had dreamed of for a long time—travel abroad and the long painting holidays which she would never have been able to take had her husband remained alive.

She called her two elder sons into conference with her and discussed the future. Jack had already been working in his father's printing works for some time. 'Now your father is dead,' she said, 'you will naturally take over in his place. But first you must have the experience to fit you for it.'

She had been in consultation with her advisers, she said, and had arranged for a manager to move into the printing works for the time being. Jack would leave at once to learn his craft. He could not go to England because the war was on, but she was sending him to Australia instead. A ticket had been booked on the boat sailing from Auckland next week, and he would go to Sydney where . . .

She turned her bright brown eyes on her second son. 'And now, Archie, let us deal with you.'

It was not on this occasion that he told her he wished to be a doctor; or, if it was, neither his mother nor Archie told Jack about it. The interview was one purely for the purpose of confronting the boy with the family situation and stressing the fact that now was the time to think about his future. And from the remarks his mother made only one sentence can be remembered: '*You can make whatever you like of your life when the time comes, but the preparations for it you must make now.*' Years later, when he was a success, Archie McIndoe used to indulge in gentle mockery of his mother's earnest stimulation and say: 'What if I had said I wanted to be a cat burglar. Would the family advisers have bought me a ladder and a jemmy?' But in fact he took what he was told very much to heart. He had already decided that he wanted to go to university, and for the first time in his life, though not for the last, he decided that he would never get there if he relied upon someone else to pay his fees. He did not play less games and he was still the ringleader of the gang at school who waylaid the local girls and scattered fireworks among them, a gambit which produced an effect known as 'the blue-stocking can-can'. But by night the books came out in his bedroom and he devoured them, murdering sleep to cram down the knowledge he needed for his examinations.

In 1918, just before his eighteenth birthday, he went on a school outing to Wellington, on North Island, and while there fell in with some medical students who filled him full of beer, took him back to their quarters, and tried to put the fear of God in him when he woke from a stupor by propping parts of a skeleton around him on the sofa where he lay. When they came back to him, they found him ostentatiously drinking—or pretending to drink—what remained of the beer from a mug in which he was using a fibula as a stirrer. They promptly hailed him as one of them, and when he got home he cherished the adventure.

A few months later, he confided to this mother that he was going to be a doctor. Mabel McIndoe argued with him at first and pointed out that the family finances were unlikely to stretch to the four or five years at university which would be needed for such a project.

'Oh hell, Mother,' he said, imitating the language of his medical student friends, 'what do I care about the family finances? This is something I'll pay for myself.'

Mabel McIndoe looked at him with an expression that carefully masked the approval from everywhere but her eyes and said:

'In that case, son, it may be possible.' And then sharply added: 'But never use that word hell in this house again, do you hear, unless you are quoting it from the Bible!'

'No, Mother,' he said, meekly, and then added under his breath: *like hell I won't*.

'He never told me why or just when he made up his mind to be a doctor,' recalls his brother John. 'For one thing it never occurred to me to ask him. For another, he was naturally reticent. It was his own decision and there were never any doubts about it as far as he was concerned. Finance appeared to be the only difficulty, but after going into the ways and means, Mother and I agreed that it could be managed.'

This is rather a pompous way of saying that Mabel McIndoe decided that the family business would buy Archie McIndoe's books and give him a small allowance so long as he was in university. The resources of the family were not called upon to produce any money for fees, for he had won a scholarship.

In March 1919 he entered the Medical School of Otago University and from that moment on he was in a world which fulfilled every wish he had ever made. He had no difficulty with any of his examinations. He passed each one almost invariably with high marks. He was the star performer in the college musical sextet, played rugby, went to dances, kept up his shooting.

In 1923 he graduated MB, ChB, but airily passed it off to his family by saying:

'It isn't important. All it gives me is the legal right to sign a death certificate.'

For his final year, he chose as his thesis a subject called *A Survey of a Group of Slum Houses*, the fruit of some intensive days and nights around Dunedin's dock area where he appears to have got close enough to a number of young women to hear the rasp of the lesions on their lungs, and close enough to substratum life to write about the effect of drink and malnutrition on families he had been studying. The style is very much like the young man he was becoming: sharply to the point, uncomplicated and pungent, but also intensely sympathetic and human.

But one thing he was sure about, and his sympathy with the ills of the poor did not alter it. He was determined not to become a general practitioner, hunking a little black bag through the city streets by day or driving out to lonely farms to deliver babies by night. To supplement his small allowance from the family he had been working on the land during his vacations and he had had his bellyful of ordinary medicine. The farmers would call him in to lance boils, bandage sores and administer nostrums for croup, chicken-pox, fever and all the other ills to which the hands, mostly Maori, were subject. He hated it. Later on, when he became a famous surgeon, his friends at a house-party or on a jaunt would come to him with a cut finger or a sprain and ask him what they should do. 'Call a doctor,' he would say.

Besides, at medical school, he had discovered what for him was to be a magic wand—the surgeon's knife. Watching it at work in the operating theatres, guided by the right hand, he would marvel at what it could do; and the first time he wielded one himself, cutting clean through the skin, paring back the gristle and flesh, and then with scalpels probing deep into the body, he knew that medicine would never have any excitement for him unless the part he played in it was that of a surgeon.

'I am having a love affair with the human belly,' he wrote to one of his old schoolmates. 'I have seen what is inside it from my books and from cadavers, but that is like going to a theatre after the play is over and nothing but the scenery is left on the stage. You should go inside when the play is on! I never thought that a liver could act like Godfrey Tearle or a kidney could be as exciting to watch as Marie Tempest!'

In his final year he won the junior medicine prize at Otago Medical School but he also gained the senior clinical surgery medal, and that was far more important. In 1924, he was appointed house surgeon at Waitako Hospital in Hamilton, North Island, New Zealand, but so far as he was concerned, it was only a very temporary stopping place on the way to his target.

The target was England. Only there, he felt, could he learn the skills and gain the experience he would need if he were to become the great surgeon he was determined to be.

But where was the money for a passage to England coming from? The family could not very well be asked to provide it unless he had a place to go to. He sat down to write around for recommendations, and answered all the job advertisements in the medical journals. It did him no good whatsoever when he learned that Arthur Porritt, who had taken up medicine too, had been awarded a Rhodes scholarship and would shortly be going to England, passage paid.

It was at this point that two people came into his life and changed the direction if not the character of his ambition. One was a New Zealand girl named Adonia Aitken. The other was an American named Will Mayo.

To be accurate, Adonia Aitken had been in his life for some time. He had first met her in a cluster of girls laughing and gossiping at the top of the stairs as he came into the assembly hall at a college dance, and by the time he got her down to the dance floor he was in love with her.

This was not surprising. Adonia was eighteen years old, dark-haired, large-eyed, as thin as a wisp and as light as thistledown, and in a community where the girls were apt to gutter comfortably like oil-lamps she shone with a brilliance that was electric. Everyone in Dunedin knew about Adonia. She was a child prodigy who had been winning competitions for pianoforte since she was nine and now, with every diploma possible having been gained, seemed on the brink of a promising career as a soloist. She danced superbly well, graceful, lissome, almost liquidly mobile. She was all nervous energy and tantalizingly full of charm and promise, and she shattered Archie McIndoe. By the end of the evening he was enchanted, and two days later—after they had been for a walk together, to a performance by Maude Adams, who was appearing in Dunedin at the time, and sat down together to play a duet—he was obsessed. It was a mutual obsession. Adonia was unofficially engaged at the time to the scion of a local business house, but she broke it off the morning after she had met Archie McIndoe for the first time. From both their points of view, it was a mad infatuation. It would be years before Archie could afford to keep a wife. Marriage to a penniless doctor would wreck all hopes Adonia had cherished of a career on the concert platform.

Archie went off to his job in Hamilton and Adonia and her family moved to Christchurch, but distance did nothing to cure them. They used to meet for snatched weekends to talk over their dilemma, but at the end of each meeting they both realized that they were hooked.

In the meantime, the younger of the two Mayo brothers, founders of the famous Mayo Clinic in Rochester, Minnesota, had arrived for a visit to Otago Medical School, and the labs and operating theatres had been burnished in his honour. Otago University was proud of its medical school, and rightly, for its standards were high and the doctors who emerged from it by no means of 'provincial' or 'colonial' calibre. Will Mayo was impressed with what he saw, so impressed that he asked the dean,

Sir Lindo Ferguson, what he could do to show his appreciation. The dean and the sub-dean, Professor Hercus, conferred and suggested that the Mayo Foundation might perhaps offer a fellowship to an Otago graduate. At the same time, Professor Hercus wrote to young McIndoe at Waitako Hospital and told him what was afoot. 'This is your opportunity,' he wrote.

Doctor McIndoe did not need to be told that it was indeed. He kept in touch, by letter and telegram, with his old professor while Mayo, the dean and the sub-dean went through the list of possible names. When he heard a rumour that he might be passed over in favour of another graduate, he left Hamilton at once for Dunedin and waylaid Mayo in the hospital grounds. The story has been told that it was his eloquent pleading on this occasion—and no one could plead as eloquently as Archie when he needed something or believed in something—which moved Will Mayo to grant him an extra fellowship. In fact, he need not have worried, for the Otago University archives reveal that 'Doctor Archibald McIndoe was recommended for the first New Zealand fellowship of the Mayo Foundation, and his recommendation was supported by the dean and the faculty.'

Archie went back at once to Hamilton and resigned his position as house surgeon at the hospital, and then wired his mother to meet him in Christchurch. He did not tell her why.

But Mabel McIndoe was, as should already have been made clear, a shrewd and far-seeing woman and she was not surprised when she was met at the station by Archie with a radiant Adonia Aitken hanging on to his arm.

'We are going to get married, Mother,' he said.

'Archie,' she replied, 'you are a fool.'

'I know,' he said. 'But there it is. We haven't any money. We couldn't possibly live on what I shall get from the Mayo. But we're going to get married, just the same.' He added: 'Tomorrow. It's all arranged. That's why I asked you to come.'

Mabel McIndoe said: 'How can you get married tomorrow and still take the fellowship? It specifies particularly that you must be single.'

'That's all right,' Archie said, cheerfully. 'We won't tell 'em.'

'But you can't tell them you're a single man and then turn up with a wife!'

It was at this point that Adonia broke in. 'I shan't be going,' she said. 'I shall stay here and wait until Archie can send for me.' And when Mabel McIndoe was about to speak, she went on: 'I'll wait three years if necessary—until he's finished his fellowship. I don't mind. It's worth it. I'll work here. I'll play and I'll teach the piano, and I'll save and save.'

Mabel McIndoe sighed. 'I still think you are a fool,' she said to her son. 'But it's your life.'

'That's all right then,' said Archie. 'Now let me tell you about the arrangements for the wedding.'

Mabel McIndoe and Adonia Aitken looked at each other, and it would be a mistake to say that there was any warmth in the glances. In those moments, in fact, the seeds were sown of a lifelong antipathy.

The wedding took place quietly in Christchurch the following day, after which Archie and his bride returned with Mabel McIndoe to Dunedin. Two weeks later, like his grandfather before him, he left his bride and sailed alone from Auckland for San Francisco. Not even Adonia realized at the time that he was leaving New Zealand for good.

CHAPTER TWO

LEARNING FROM THE DEAD

THE ATTITUDE OF A medical student towards the human conditions with which he comes in contact during his training is apt, from sheer reaction, to be cynical or tough. Otherwise the shock of those first experiences of illness and injury, the realization of the appalling vulnerability of the human frame, the sight and sound of pain, the reluctant understanding of the processes of mortality, would be hard to bear. The beery antics with the lecture-room skeleton, the bed-pan brawls with the student nurses, the gruesome bonhomie over a cadaver which was only too recently alive—these can be forgiven as part of the hardening process through which every young doctor must pass. The danger for a medical man is to allow the protective skin he grows during training to thicken into rhinoceros hide for the rest of his life. 'There are some doctors, and too many surgeons,' Archie McIndoe used to say, 'who grow so hardened to other people's suffering and so used to death that a body on an operating table is merely the object of a good plumbing job.' When the heart in it ceases to beat 'it is wrong that it should signify not the end of a life but the inconvenient conclusion of a case'.

Though later on in life he could come up with such remarks as: 'I've just met a tumour in Number Four Wing that's an absolute beaut!' he remained always aware that the body from which the tumour had been extracted also contained a heart, in rather more than the medical sense of the word. In one of his first letters home after reaching the Mayo Clinic he wrote:

'I am continually being told that it will do no good to my skill or my peace of mind if I take too personal an interest in the cases I see in the hospital, but it is hard advice to follow. I don't like to see people suffer and I think pain is damnable. I hate it when people die because I think it is unjust if they are young and pathetic if they are old and have not died easily. I shall have to learn how to be a plumber.'

The Mayo Clinic training methods went a long way towards teaching him.

He arrived in Rochester, Minnesota, in the Christmas holidays of 1924 to find holly wreaths on the doors of the Mayo Clinic and a warm welcome awaiting him inside. He met the twin pillars of the Mayo Foundation, the famous Doctors Charlie and Will Mayo, and their right-hand man, Doctor Balfour, and Will brought out the proudest trophy of his recent tour, a Maori's grass skirt which had been presented to him by a Maori queen with whom he had rubbed noses outside Dunedin. But once the festivities were over, he was sent across to the University of Minnesota (with which the Clinic is affiliated) for nine months' study; and for a year after that, his principal field of activity was in the mortuary conducting autopsies on cadavers. In that year he did examinations on nearly six hundred bodies. It was the way to learn, but as he said in a letter home: 'I long for the day when I can be saving life instead of merely confirming the nature of death.'

Even in those days, the Mayo Clinic was far better known, to the world as well as to Minnesota's own citizens, than the small city of Rochester in which it had been built. It rose from the Zumbro valley in a skyscrapered complex which consisted of the Clinic itself and the Kahler Hotel, just across the street. The hotel was connected with the hospital by an underground passage and its guests consisted of visiting doctors and patients either convalescing or awaiting consultations and operations.

'Mayo belongs to Rochester and Rochester is proud of it,' said a slogan painted across a wall of the City Hall. But it had not always been so. One could say that it flourished there in spite of rather than because of Rochester.

It had come into being largely because a tornado swept the city and destroyed a large part of it on Tuesday, August 21, 1883. At that time Doctor William Worrall Mayo was in private practice in the town with his two young sons, Will and Charlie, and they were flourishing. Old Doctor Mayo was a doctor in the old horse-and-buggy tradition, loved and trusted by his neighbours, whose sons and sons' sons he had brought into the world. There was no hospital in Rochester then; patients in need of operations went down to the twin cities of Minneapolis and St Paul, and not even Doctor Mayo himself felt the need of it. The second-generation immigrants from Germany and Scandinavia who peopled the town and the surrounding countryside could, he felt, be adequately dealt with in his own surgery or in their own homes.

August 21, 1883, dawned hot and ominously still, but black clouds were piling up over the alfalfa fields, and all day through they rose like a rampart into the brassy blue sky. Just before seven in the evening they broke, and the wind howled down upon the city. The wooden bridge over the Zumbro River was torn from its moorings; roofs began to fly; and soon the northern part of Rochester, known as Lower Town, was a flattened ruin.

Rescue parties were organized. Men with lanterns shuffled through the shambles for the dead and wounded and brought them to hotels, offices and the nearby convent of the Sisters of St Francis which had been turned into makeshift casualty wards. The doctors of the town got to work; women volunteered as nurses; but before long there was friction.

'The doctors could not agree on what should be done for the patients,' wrote the Mayo Clinic's official historian. 'One of them who had heard somewhere that an emetic should be given the first thing in case of accident ordered that treatment for all the injured. Doctor Mayo was outraged by the idea—and no doubt by the man's crass assumption of authority. When the fellow stubbornly persisted, the Old Doctor issued an ultimatum. "Either he gets out or I do." Clearly someone must be put in command, and the city council named Doctor Mayo to take charge of the hospital.'

The dead were buried in batches. The wounded were tended. The destitute were fed and later rehoused with money from a fund which had been organized. Rochester licked its wounds and slowly forgot about its disaster.

But at the convent of St Francis, Mother Alfred, the Mother Superior, could not forget it. 'Sometime after the temporary hospital was closed,' the official history records, 'Mother Alfred paid a visit to Doctor W. W. Mayo. Did he not think it would be well to build a hospital in Rochester? His reply was quick and positive: the city was too small to support a hospital, it would cost a great deal, and there was not much prospect of its success. But

Sir Archibald Hector McIndoe

Archie's mother (*left*) as she was when he was a boy, and (*below*) with the portrait she painted of him

Mother Alfred had made up her mind. Quietly she overruled the Old Doctor's objections and said that if he would promise to take charge of the hospital the sisters would finance it. When he insisted that it might cost as much as forty thousand dollars, she replied that they would spend more than that if necessary.'

So was St Mary's Hospital, which was the nucleus of the Mayo Clinic, conceived. The misconception that the Mayos were originally responsible for the venture got started early, but Doctor W. W. Mayo in 1904 addressed a letter through the Press insisting that 'the sisters of St Francis are to be credited with its inception and the funds for its building' and that he merely acted as the agent to carry out their wishes.

But from the moment of its inception, four years later, Mayo was the name which animated it, with the Old Doctor as physician-in-charge and his two sons as members of the staff. It was a hospital open to all sick persons regardless of their colour, sex, financial status or professed religion. 'The cause of suffering humanity knows no religion and no sex,' said Mother Alfred; 'the charity of the Sisters of Saint Francis is as broad as their religion.' And she made that clear to the members of her Order a few years later when one of them, a young nun working with Doctor Mayo as nurse, attended the examination of a patient which called for her to see him naked. She returned to the convent in a fury of shame and humiliation and was roundly rated for her feelings by the Mother Superior. Henceforward, the nuns of St Francis learned to live with life as it is and men as they are made.

The citizens of Minnesota, however, did not. These formative years were those when waves of immigrants from Ireland and Italy were pouring into America and religious fanaticism, whipped up by such organizations as the Know-Nothings and the American Protective Association, violently anti-Catholic, was sweeping through the Middle West. These forerunners of the Ku-Klux-Klan campaigned against such organizations as St Mary's Hospital and Doctor Mayo and his sons were vilified for associating with the Papists. The people of the city and State were urged to boycott the hospital. The Mayos, staunch Protestants themselves, ignored the attacks and slowly, as the fires of religious hatred died, the patients began to come to them.

From these beginnings came the Mayo Clinic. It grew with the years and changed its status. After the death of the Old Doctor, Charlie and Will Mayo took over, and they prospered. They poured their wealth back into the hospital and new buildings were erected: a skyscraper hospital, an hotel for patients and visitors, a research unit. The Clinic was formally named, and then the Mayo Foundation was formed in association with the University of Minnesota.

Charlie and Will went out to the world to broaden their minds and their surgical techniques, and they sat at the feet—or, rather, hung over the operating tables—of the foremost surgeons of the western world, learning skills, absorbing new ideas, and making plans, plans, plans, for the extension of their hospital in the Middle West. It had already grown in size. Now it began to grow in prestige. The small city with the Mayo Clinic in its midst became, first for surgeons and then for their patients, a place where people looked for all the new developments in surgery which were taking place in the first two decades of this century. For the Mayo brothers were willing to go anywhere and spend, between them, any amount of time at any amount of inconvenience in order to gain knowledge for their job.

'One of the famous, or notorious, feuds of this vital period,' records the official history, 'was between the conservative New Yorkers and Joseph Price of Philadelphia. Price was introducing into the United States the radical ideas and procedures of the English titan, Lawson Tait, and was reporting such success in abdominal operations, one hundred in a series without a single death, that the diehards simply refused to believe in him. When Doctor Will began to venture beyond ovariotomy in abdominal surgery, he was dissatisfied with his results. His death rate was too high, about seventeen per cent as he later remembered it, so he decided to see Joseph Price.'

From him he learned not only technique but also a broad-minded attitude towards the controversial members of his profession. And later on he said to Archie McIndoe:

'When you hear that a certain celebrated surgeon is a liar, and that you are not to believe what he says, go to see him. Find out whether his trouble is his goodness or his badness. Sometimes a good man is cussed more vigorously than he would be if he were bad.'

The diplomas and the recognition poured in from all over the world, and Rochester became a place of medical pilgrimage. The equipment was first-rate. Doctors queued up for a chance to work there. Provided you were a nurse or a doctor, you could come in and watch all the surgical and medical processes that were going on.

By 1925, when McIndoe arrived, Will Mayo could say: 'To be frank about it, we have accomplished much, my brother and I. But we should have done great things; we were given the opportunity. We were born at the right time and to the right parents. Perhaps no one again will have the opportunity to accomplish as much. That day is gone, except for some genius. We were not geniuses. We were only hard workers. We were reared in medicine as a farmer boy is reared in farming. We learned from our father.'

To this hive of busy surgical skills and dedicated medical enthusiasm came Archie McIndoe with a mind open and avid for enlightenment; and it was in the mortuaries of the Clinic that he got his first experience of it.

A corpse is a dead thing which was once a living being, and what more can you say about it than that? To the layman and to many a visiting doctor, it sometimes seemed that the Mayos had an obsession about cadavers. The American College of Surgeons required of its accredited hospitals, of which the Clinic was naturally one, that autopsies be carried out on at least fifteen per cent of the deaths in them, and that discussions be held on the findings with all the medical staff who had looked after the patient in life. The Mayos, however, insisted that all deaths in the hospital should be subject to examination; and not only that. They had made an arrangement with the managers or superintendents of all hospitals, boarding-houses and hotels in Rochester to telephone the Clinic whenever a death occurred. There was always a fellow on duty in the department of post-mortem pathology at the Mayo (they did twenty-four hours on and twenty-four off) and he at once set off to visit the relatives of the dead person to secure their permission for an autopsy, and then arranged for the body to be shipped to the department. The examination began at once.

Archie McIndoe, called from his cot to go out to collect a body, soon became familiar with the sleazy lodging-houses of the Lower Town where some old drunk had died of cirrhosis of the liver or an old tart from the ravages of her trade, and the ride back in the ambulance through the silent streets followed by a predawn session of cutting and bottling soon became a routine. But he never forgot his first case. It was the police doctor who called him to a large downtown hotel and when he reached the room on the seventh floor he was directed by a patrolman into the bathroom. No one had bothered to empty the bath and it was red with blood. Beside it lay the naked body of a young girl who had killed herself in the classic fashion by cutting her wrists. She had once been very beautiful. 'It seemed such a waste,' he said, later. 'And then, when we got her on the slab, it was strange, and somehow distasteful, the way our pity changed to enthusiasm as we got to work, for here was something we so rarely got—a young and healthy body to explore.'

The chief pathologist under whom McIndoe worked was Doctor Harold E. Robertson, a dedicated and driving seeker after scientific truth. By fellows and surgeons alike, he was a man both respected and feared. To McIndoe he said, at their first formal meeting:

'I want to know everything about everybody you open up. Not just why the patient died. I want a report on the state of the patient's health throughout his lifetime: you can tell that from the lesions of his body. I want his medical record measured against every organ inside him. If a gall-bladder was removed years ago, how did the operation affect his liver? Did he have ulcers? Has he ever suffered from pneumonia? And if he has had an operation, why did he die?'

The work was long and hard and meticulous. In the old days, the specimens were taken out and bottled and a routine report was written by the fellow in charge of the autopsy. But not under Robertson. He insisted on microscopic slides being made and fully detailed reports. After this, when the examination was complete, McIndoe would hand them over to his chief and wait to be called to a conference in the boardroom where the surgeons and their internes had already been summoned. These were the sessions which many a surgeon came to dread, for Robertson was merciless in his analysis and if a mistake had been made, he spared no one. At first, this public discussion of a specialist's failings roused some of the members of the staff to the point of rebellion, for they preferred to publicize their successes and quietly bury their failures; and the test came for Robertson when he superintended a post-mortem by McIndoe on the body of a woman who had died on the operating table of Doctor Will himself. Would Brother Mayo be spared the sometimes blunt criticism to which his staff were subjected by Robertson? They soon had their answer. The microscopic slides went up on the screen, and quietly but incisively Robertson pointed out why the woman had died, where an error had been made, and how she might have been saved. Doctor Will himself was among those present and he was a man who was not accustomed to criticism; those of his staff who had the courage to look at his face saw that he was finding it extremely hard to take. But when it was over, he rose to his feet and said:

'I would like to thank Doctor Robertson for his concise diagnosis of this case. I have learned a lot from it.' And then, turning to the others: 'Now I know what it feels like to have an autopsy done on myself.'

He sent a note to Archie McIndoe later in the day. It was a commendation of his work on the body of the dead woman. 'Doctor Charlie was the tough one of the brothers,' Archie recalled later. 'He had a grim sense of humour. The first time I operated in his presence he gave a running commentary on my technique to a largish audience of doctors and nurses. He must have noticed that I was nervous, because he broke off at one point to whisper to me: "You're doing fine. So long as you don't drop the bits on the floor, I don't mind." But Doctor Will was the gentle and thoughtful one, always ready with a quiet word of encouragement when you were feeling low.'

Not that Doctor Will was without his own brand of medical humour. One of his patients was a woman of ample proportions who was found to have a carcinoma in one of her extremely large breasts. Will Mayo removed the breast. When he visited his patient later she complained bitterly that she had been 'intolerably mutilated' and asked what he was going to do to restore the shape of her bosom.

Doctor Will thought for a minute and then said:

'Well, you might try stuffing a little hay in it.'

For a time Adonia McIndoe stayed with her mother-in-law in Dunedin, but though they both tried hard, it was no use. As personalities they were not compatible. Adonia departed for

Christchurch where she taught the piano and bombarded Archie with letters pleading with him to send for her. But how could he do that? The Mayo brothers had built up their reputation as savers of lives but they also had another, as inveterate savers of money.

The doctors on the staff of the Clinic were under contracts which stipulated that their salaries be approved by the Properties Association which leased its facilities to the hospital. The Association was pledged, in an agreement with the Mayo brothers, never to pay salaries which would eat into capital. The result was that though the staff was adequately paid, and though insurance schemes made sure of their security in old age, they received far less than they would have been able to command in many other US hospitals. 'I am determined,' said Doctor Will, 'that no member of the staff of the Mayo will ever from his work here build up enough capital to keep his children on the beach at Miami when they should be working.' He gathered his surgeons and doctors around him by giving them all the facilities a dedicated doctor might need, by ensuring them of prestige and regard in their profession, and by allowing them to borrow heavily for housing for their families and education for their children. Most of them were heavily in debt to the Properties Association and even if they had wanted to leave—which very few of them did—they could not afford to do so.

But if the salaries of the staff were modest those paid to the fellows were pitifully small. Archie McIndoe, in his three years at the Mayo, received forty-five dollars a week (less than £10 at the prevailing rate of exchange) and from that he not only had to keep himself but also pay for his books. Absorbed as he was in his studies, he could manage; but there was certainly not sufficient to keep a wife. Adonia, however, was insistent. She was lonely and unhappy in New Zealand, and determined to join him. In truth, he was lonely too. It was the heyday of what came to be known later as the Roaring Twenties, and on the occasional trips which he took with some of the other fellows to Minneapolis or Chicago he came in contact with the unbuttoned and uninhibited life of the Middle West, and there were temptations which a young man of twenty-five found hard to resist. Minneapolis and St Paul, brewing centres of the American beer trade, had not taken kindly to Prohibition and were getting their own back on the Government by hard drinking and gay parties. Chicago was wide open. When every girl you meet is filled with the spirit of giving, it's difficult and seems boorish not to take; and Archie McIndoe's colonial conscience troubled him.

He took it finally to Doctor Will and confessed that he had left a wife behind him. Doctor Will told him to send for her. But how could he do that when he would not be able to afford to keep her once she arrived?

'I'll talk to Robertson,' said Will Mayo. 'If she's intelligent enough, we'll find her a job in the pathology department.'

A cable was sent and Adonia was told to pack her bags. But first she did a cram-course of anatomy at Otago, and by the time she arrived in Rochester she at least knew the difference between costal cartilage and a kidney. It was a joyous reunion for both of them. They settled into a tiny flat, with a double bed which came down out of the wall, in downtown Rochester, a few blocks away from the Clinic. Archie, by this time, had begun to take a special interest in abdominal surgery, particularly the diseases of the liver; and, encouraged by Doctor Donald Balfour, he was preparing his first paper on the subject. So even on his days off from the pathology department he would wait for telephone calls, and then he and Adonia would race down to the mortuary and get to work on the liver of the latest cadaver.

'It seems strange now to think how we worked together in those days,' says Adonia. 'In the middle of preparing a meal, I would have to drop everything and down we would go to the Clinic. We were very methodical. He would take out the liver. I would take the knife and slice it for him. And then, after examination, we would stain and bottle it. I got so expert at it, and so unconcerned, that I would sometimes find myself saying: "This is marvellous, Archie. Look, a real case of cirrhosis. Look at the white marks!" And I would forget, at least, until we sat down to supper later on, that I had been talking about part of a man who had been alive only a few hours before.'

Adonia McIndoe was taken into the bosom of the Mayo faculty, where they liked her almost feverish gaiety and unflagging energy. She was a great success at parties and picnics; the faculty were inclined to be cliquey and formed their own social circle into which the fellows, footloose bachelors who had not yet 'arrived', were admitted only on festival occasions, but Adonia's presence subtly changed Archie's status. The wives liked to hear her bright, shrewd and witty chatter, and they fussed over her when she became pregnant.

One of the surgeons who came under her spell was Doctor Donald C. Balfour and it was a conquest of some importance, for it brought Archie to the attention of the third most important influence in the Mayo Clinic, the other two being, of course, Charlie and Will. Balfour was a Canadian who had come down to Rochester in 1907 as a visiting surgeon, but, in the words of one of his associates, 'turned out to be a wonder. He performed a series of more than two hundred operations without a single death.' In a period when a stomach operation was apt to be as final as a crossing of the Styx, he developed and perfected techniques which revolutionized surgery in this most vulnerable region of the human frame. He was asked to join the staff, went on to marry Doctor Will's daughter, Carrie, and became a partner in the Clinic and one of the directors of the Foundation.

Balfour's hobby was playing the organ. He had installed an instrument in the hall of his home on the outskirts of the city, and he loved to sit down and play for hours. One evening, several months after Adonia's arrival, he invited the McIndoes for dinner and afterwards said he would play for them. He had just mastered a new piece of music which was a duet for organ and piano, and he bemoaned the fact that he could not find anyone to play the piano part with him. Adonia said that perhaps she might be allowed to have a try; and reading from sight she gave a performance which delighted the older man.

'But this young woman is far too talented to be working in the labs,' he said to Archie McIndoe. 'We'll have to find her some place where she can play in public.'

He did not have to look farther than the Foundation's own property, the Kahler Hotel, just across the street from the Clinic. The hotel had a sort of palm court orchestra which played afternoons and evenings to the hotel guests and visitors, and two weeks after her demonstration Adonia was installed as resident pianist. She was pretty and vivacious and she played well. Except for the time off she took to give birth to the first McIndoe daughter. Adonia junior, she played there until 1928. Her salary was sixty dollars (about £12) a week, which was more than Archie was earning, and it made a vast difference to their standard of living. They were able to buy a car and move to better quarters.

It was a busy life for both of them. They were up at six every morning, for there were household chores to do, the baby to tend; and still, in the middle of the night, they went over to the mortuary to work together on the mysteries of the human liver.

In 1927, Archie McIndoe received the degree of MSc in Pathology from the University of Minnesota, and his days and nights in the post-mortem theatre were over—officially, at least. Balfour had begun to take a keen interest in him and his work, and recommended that when his fellowship was over in 1928 he should be awarded the William White Travelling Fellowship and afterwards offered a post as assistant surgeon on the permanent staff of the Clinic. His future seemed assured. He could look forward to a steady climb up the rungs of the hospital ladder to the safe, comfortable and prestigious position of staff surgeon (perhaps chief surgeon and even director) of the Mayo; and what young medical man could want more than that?

There was only one snag. Archie McIndoe had come to the United States on a student's visa and to stay in America he would need either a permanent visa and a working permit or citizenship. After talking it over with Adonia, he decided to apply for citizen's papers and filled out the papers. They were sponsored by Doctor Will and Doctor Balfour and he was told that it was a foregone conclusion. But for some reason it was not. The papers did not come through. Doctor Will, on a visit to a conference in Washington, even spoke about it to President Hoover, who promised to look into it. Nothing happened.

With the travelling scholarship which he had been awarded, Archie and Adonia decided upon a visit to England and in the summer of 1928 they sailed from New York. It was to be a working holiday and they carried letters of introduction to some of the most famous surgeons in the country. They took furnished rooms near Russell Square and Archie began a round of the hospitals. It was not a success. After the modern facilities of the Mayo Clinic, he was disappointed and depressed by the gloomy hospitals in London, Liverpool and Manchester. He found the surgeons cool at best and patronizing at worst. 'They treat me like a bloody colonial,' he complained.

As for Adonia, she hated every moment of her stay. She was lonely and bored, and longed to get back to America. Adonia junior caught a cold and a cough; the food was mediocre; the weather was wet and chilly. They went on for a brief stay in Paris, had a quarrel when she wanted to go to the Salle Pleyel and he preferred a visit to the Folies Bergère. They were glad to sail home, back into the warm womb at the Mayo, where everything was clean and safe and secure.

The months that followed saw the apotheosis of Archie McIndoe from a promising young medical man into a surgeon of great skill, perception and forethought. Under Doctor Balfour's protecting wing, he learned to fly and he found the sky a stimulating place in which to soar. To begin with, the young eaglet was well looked after. When some of the senior and more hostile members of the faculty bawled him out in the theatre for clumsy technique, it was Balfour who restored his shattered pride. It was Balfour too who urged him to concentrate on abdominal surgery, appended his name to the papers which McIndoe produced (and so ensured them of attention), and encouraged him to experiment. It was through this kindly mentor that his nocturnal studies of the human liver first bore fruit. He had discovered that the liver has two separate blood supplies and that under certain conditions a carcinoma of the liver might be surgically dealt with, one blood-stream being kept working while the other was cut off. The first time he tried out his theory, the patient, an old man, died and he had to sit through one of the post-mortem sessions of the pathology department in which his temerity was strongly condemned. But as the senior surgeons started to snigger at him, Balfour arose to defend him. He had checked every stage of the operation, he said, and saw no reason why it should not have been a success; the only reason for failure, in fact, had been the neglect in earlier diagnosis, not done by McIndoe, which had failed to reveal that the patient had a cardiac weakness. When Archie McIndoe stopped him in the corridor later to thank him for his advocacy, the older man brushed it aside.

'But next time you do that operation,' he said, 'make sure that the patient isn't already moribund. Operations are for people who are going to live, not for those who in any case are going to die.'

He was allowed to continue his experiments and they succeeded to such an extent that, in 1930, he was asked to demonstrate his technique—now known at the Mayo as McIndoe's Operation—to a convention of surgeons in Chicago. It was a demonstration which was to have two sequels, one profound and one piquant.

His daughter Adonia was now four years old. A new child was on the way. He had won the respect of the Mayos, the affection of Balfour, and the hand in which he held the knife had become firm and confident. So far as the Clinic was concerned, he had no reason to anticipate anything but advancement; and yet he was unhappy, dissatisfied, filled with discontent. This was due partly to his personal life, for his domestic happiness had become tarnished; there were worms crawling through the household woodwork and they were eating into his security. But the truth is that what worried him most was the very stability and predictability of his professional life. The future ahead of him was all too sure and the temptation to accept it as fore-ordained was beginning to get him down. He went on a trip to Minneapolis on one occasion and though he carefully telephoned Adonia to explain his absence nevertheless did not reappear for two days, and it was evident from his appearance and his hangover that he had not been engaged in medical pursuits. Adonia was furious with him and the fragile tempers of both of them cracked beneath the strain.

'I went away,' he said finally, 'because this goddamned place is so dull, dull, dull!'

It was not the first of the rows between them, and far from the last.

The demonstration in Chicago was a success which only increased the itch of discontent in him. It was done before an audience of medical men which included some distinguished visitors. One of them was Lord Moynihan, then President of the Royal College of Surgeons of England, and they were impressed not only by the revolutionary character of the operation he performed before them but by the extraordinary cleanness and economy of his surgery and the swiftness of his technique. Moynihan took a note of his name but did not appear to realize at the time that he was a New Zealander.

About ten days after he returned to Rochester, Archie McIndoe received a telephone call from one of the doctors who had been present at the demonstration. He had a patient, he said, who appeared to be suffering from certain symptoms requiring abdominal surgery and he would be grateful if Doctor McIndoe would accept him as a case. There were reasons, he went on, why it would be unwise to have the operation done in Chicago. His patient was rich and neurotically allergic to publicity, and it would be appreciated if the surgery could be done under the most discreet circumstances. He then named a fee which was at least five times as much as was normally paid by patients at the Mayo. He gave the man's name as Mancini and made arrangements for a consultation two days ahead.

It was no unusual thing at the Mayo Clinic to have these calls from out-of-town doctors and Archie McIndoe entered the details in the hospital records as a matter of routine. He saw the patient in his office and examined him and did not register any particular surprise when three plump and well-dressed men tried to be present while it was taking place. He shooed them out. He was used to the anxious attendance of relatives.

He operated the following week, opening up the man's stomach and extracting from it a piece of metal which had lodged in the tissue and had obviously been causing severe pain. It was not a serious operation and could obviously have been done by any competent surgeon. The three men were in attendance once more and this time they had brought company. In the hospital car-park there were several Cadillacs and one of the fellows came through to report, with some excitement, that one of them was bullet-proofed. In the lounge of the Kahler Hotel, Adonia found herself and her fellow members of the trio playing the 'Indian Love Lyrics' to a group of fidgety blondes who would obviously have preferred the rhythms of the Charleston and Black Bottom.

The armour-plated Cadillac drove away when it was announced to the entourage that Mr Mancini had come through the operation successfully, but it came back two days later. This time a large black ambulance came with it, and Mancini was carried into it under the supervision of the Chicago doctor. McIndoe's protests that the patient was not yet ready for removal were brushed aside. The cavalcade of Cadillacs drove away, but just before it did so one of the plump men emerged from the bullet-proof car and came up to McIndoe.

'Al told me to say thank you for all you did for his kid brother,' he said. 'He asked me to give you this. So long, doc.'

He handed over an envelope. The cars drove away. When Archie opened it, he found inside ten hundred-dollar notes. It was not until several hours later that he realized he had operated on gangster Al Capone's brother.

Lord Moynihan's visit to the Mayo Clinic was less spectacular but its consequences were considerably more far-reaching.

Moynihan was an old friend of Will Mayo and an old admirer of the Mayo Clinic. On the wall of Will's office was a painting by Sir Joshua Reynolds of John Hunter, the great eighteenth century student of gross pathology, which had been given to him by Moynihan, following a visit by the great man (then plain Berkeley Moynihan of Leeds) in 1903. On that occasion Moynihan demonstrated a loop operation with the aid of clamps which he had devised to simplify gastro-enterostomies, and Will Mayo had since made it a classic technique of stomach surgery at the Clinic.

'He was one of the great surgeons of this century,' Will Mayo once said of him. 'He was without superior in craftsmanship, and he was also a speaker whose poise, polish and urbanity put us country bumpkins in despair.'

Moynihan returned the compliment. To a young Canadian doctor who came to him for advice he said:

'If I were your age, my boy, I would try to attach myself to the Mayo Clinic, because there in my opinion is the most outstanding centre for surgical and medical advance in the world today.'

Shortly after he had watched the McIndoe demonstration in Chicago, Lord Moynihan arrived on a visit to the Mayo Clinic and the red carpet went down for him. Doctor Charlie and Doctor Will took him on a tour of the theatres, and he came first to one in which Doctor Alfred Adson, a brilliant young thirty-year-old, was just making ready to operate on a case he had diagnosed as a spinal tumour. The arrival of the great man discomposed him. A spinal tumour is difficult to diagnose. What if he found he was wrong? The thought of Moynihan's eyes upon him gave him an attack of nerves which Doctor Will quickly noticed; he suggested that the party move on. But Moynihan had drawn up a chair with the words: 'I want to see this.' And he sat down close to the table while the unfortunate Adson cut into his patient. The tumour was there and quickly removed.

In the next theatre, Archie McIndoe was in the middle of a stomach operation. He was not normally averse to an audience, but perhaps because of some friction at home he was in a liverish mood on this occasion. When the visitor and his hosts came through the door, he loudly remarked: 'This place is getting rather like the Roxy on talent night.' Moynihan stayed only a few moments and then removed himself, but not before McIndoe heard him say:

'By God, first I see a high school boy doing a spinal tumour and then I get ordered out by an infant!'

But at luncheon, when Archie came across to apologize, he was graciousness itself. 'You have hands like a ploughboy, my boy,' he said, 'but they behave like an artist's. Sit down and tell me about yourself.'

What happened after this is a story which has become confused and no amount of checking clarifies it. Archie McIndoe always believed that Moynihan, having learned that he was a New Zealander, said:

'But my dear boy, why do you stay here? The Mayo has taught you all you can learn here. London's the place for you. I am building a new hospital and you are just the man I want. Sell up and come across the Atlantic. England needs young fellows like you.'

Now Moynihan must have known that his 'new hospital' was years from being built, a plan on a drawing-board, a project for the future. But he was in an expansive mood and obviously never dreamed that his invitation would be taken seriously. It was, in fact, several months before Archie McIndoe made up his mind, and during that time he did not write to Moynihan or even make inquiries in Britain about the hospital.

'When I put my foot in it,' he once said, 'by God I really go into it right up to my neck.'

One is, however, driven to the conclusion that he did not write to Moynihan because *he did not want to hear* that the job did not exist. The departure for England was the excuse he needed to get away from Rochester. His domestic relations were, for one reason or another, unhappy and he felt the need of a change. He found the solid security of the Mayo Clinic, with its predictable, step-by-step advancement, irksome and he longed for an opportunity to branch out on his own. He could not very well do that in America for he still had a student's visa and his application for citizenship was clogged in some bureaucratic pipe in Washington. He told Adonia of Moynihan's offer and convinced her that it was solid and certain. Even so, she fought bitterly against leaving Rochester, for she liked its cosy life and had built up a scunner against damp, remote and unfriendly England. It took him several months to convince her that he was determined on it.

'Archie,' she said (she had found a way of pronouncing his name in an abrasive accent which infuriated him), 'your mother once called you a fool, and now I know what she meant.'

He went ahead and announced a sale of his furniture. He told the Mayo brothers of his imminent departure, and they did their best to dissuade him. But Balfour encouraged him. He had grown very fond of this volatile, quick-tempered, talented New Zealander and he realized as the others did not that the Mayo Clinic's urbane and cultivated acres were not the fields in which he could grow; he needed less predictable soil.

'You have two faults, Archie,' he wrote to him later. 'You turn your masters into pupils far too quickly, and they resent it. You also part your hair in the middle of your head, and this drives your friends to distraction! No man should look the same on both sides of his face.'

The furniture was sold and the debts were paid off. Donald Balfour advanced £400 to pay for the passages of Archie and his family to England, and made it clear that it was a long-term loan. The Mayo brothers shook his hand, a little piqued at his departure, and hinted that if things went wrong they were ready to take him back.

Ten days before the departure, he received a letter from Washington extending the President's good wishes and telling him that he had been given American citizenship. He sat on the papers for twenty-four hours and then replied to the State Department that he was leaving the country and had therefore reluctantly decided not to change his allegiance to Britain.

He did not tell Adonia about it until their arrival in Liverpool in the winter of 1931.

CHAPTER THREE

'THE NOSE IS IN THE MIDDLE OF THE FACE'

'DEAR DONALD,' WROTE Archie McIndoe to Doctor Balfour at the beginning of December, 1931, 'this is to wish both of you a merry Christmas and a prosperous and happy 1932. We have settled down in our new home and though we miss our refrigerator and that wonderful American plumbing—the closet is always getting bunged up here!—we are getting along fine. I have had to change my plans because it seems that Moynihan, the old bastard, was being a little premature when he promised me a job in his new hospital. There is no new hospital! But I am studying for my Fellowship and I have several irons in the fire . . . Adonia is enjoying London and has discovered a passion for shrimps! I hope the child won't turn out to be a crayfish!'

It was hardly an accurate account of their state or their state of mind at the time. Far from enjoying London, Adonia was hating it. Her pregnancy was not going well, and her surroundings were not exactly helping her peace of mind. It was their first experience of an English winter, and this one was particularly cold and damp; the spirits of the British had rarely been lower, for unemployment was spread over the land like a blight; and the only lodging they could find to meet their budget was a furnished basement flat near Maida Vale where the grease was thick on the walls and the lavatory smelled. For a couple of weeks or so, the McIndoes could comfort themselves with the thought that it was all very temporary: the weather would get better since it could not conceivably get worse, and as soon as Lord Moynihan opened the doors of medical London for Archie they would have money to move to better quarters.

Moynihan in Rochester proved, however, to be much more

accessible than he was in London. Archie McIndoe telephoned for an appointment and was told to write; he wrote and was given a date far ahead. When he penetrated at long last into his consulting rooms in Harley Street, the great man appeared to have suffered a lapse of memory. According to Archie, the interview went in this way:

'McIndoe . . . McIndoe . . . let me see, didn't we meet in the States?'

'We did,' replied Archie. 'In Chicago and at the Mayo Clinic, remember?'

'Ah yes, splendid place. Well, what's brought you over here? Holidaying?'

'No, sir,' said Archie. 'I'm here in response to that invitation you gave me. You said you had a post for me in your new hospital. I'm here to take it.'

Moynihan looked incredulous. 'Bless my soul, the hospital isn't even built yet. Can hardly give you a job in a place that doesn't exist, can I?'

'But I resigned from the Mayo especially to come here,' said Archie.

The great man slapped him on the shoulder. 'Bit rash that, you know. You young chaps—what a reckless lot you are. Still, I don't suppose you need to worry. Always places in England for the right man, even in these times.' He paused and then said: 'Have you got your FRCS?'

Archie explained that he had got his American fellowship but not an English one.

'Hm, that's unfortunate,' said Moynihan. 'American fellowships are all right, you know. I've got one myself. Won't get you far in this country, though. No, young fellow, until you've got your fellowship from the Royal College of Surgeons of England, I doubt if you'll do any good over here. That's your next step. Go and get your FRCS. That's my advice to you.'

He opened the door with one hand and held out the other to be shaken. 'If I can be of any help,' he said, 'don't fail to come and see me. Just ring up my secretary for an appointment.'

Archie McIndoe waited until he got out into the street and then he said: 'You old bastard!' It was to be his favourite description of Lord Moynihan for the rest of his life.

For the next few hours, he walked the damp streets and wondered what to do next, and how to tell Adonia. He could of course always write or cable to the Mayo and ask to be taken back; they would take him back, and that would please Adonia. But it would mean a confession of defeat, and in his present mood defeat was the last thing he was prepared to accept. He was blazingly angry, and certainly in no state of mind to go home and cope with a wife whose pregnancy was increasingly uncomfortable. 'Adonia wouldn't have been too pleased even if I had got the job,' he wrote to his brother. 'I knew it would shatter her to have to tell her that we were nearly broke, I was out of work and we couldn't move out of the dingy dump where we were living.'

He wandered across Regent's Park and eventually went into the Zoo and found himself in the monkey house, envying the animals their warmth and security on the other side of the cages. 'I thought the animals should be paying to see me,' he wrote. 'There wasn't an animal in the whole zoo that was a bigger freak than me!'

And then from his pocket he pulled a letter which his mother had written to him shortly after his arrival in London. With her passion for family background, she had discovered that Archie's paternal grandmother was a certain Elizabeth Gillies who had married James McIndoe of Rothesay and emigrated with him to New Zealand in 1859. Other members of the Gillies family had also left Scotland for New Zealand and one of their descendants had come back to establish himself in England as a famous surgeon. She asked Archie to look him up. His name was Sir Harold Gillies.

That afternoon, after a sandwich lunch in a pub, he came back to the Harley Street area and found the London Clinic where Sir Harold Delf Gillies had his consulting rooms. He asked to see the surgeon, and was received by Mr Robert Seymour, his secretary, who raised his eyebrows in barely concealed scepticism when McIndoe introduced himself as a distant cousin. He was told to write a note and leave it, and to telephone the following day.

There was nothing more he could do. He caught a bus back to Maida Vale, prepared now to tell Adonia. He had made up his mind once and for all. No matter what happened, he was going to stay on and make a success in England.

A month passed and though Archie fretted he did not waste his time. He had started at once to work on his fellowship and all day, except when he went out to do the shopping or collect Adonia junior from school, he hunched over his books in the gloomy basement. Adonia senior had tired of shrimps by this time but fortunately learned to like sardines and tinned salmon. For both of them it was as near to hell as they had ever experienced thus far in their lives. The gloom was all-pervading and the damp soaked into their bones; it was no place to bring up a young daughter, or nurture another still in the womb, or write a thesis on abdominal surgery.

One day a note arrived from Sir Harold Gillies. Archie was invited to lunch. There was a difference of twenty years in the age of the two men and a gulf even wider between the worlds in which they were living. The butler, Peel, opened the door of the house in Queen Anne Street and led him in to the warm study, the dry sherry, the leather armchairs, the books on the shelves and the pictures on the walls.

'It was such a sudden transformation from Maida Vale that I felt like a country bumpkin,' he said afterwards. 'My hands felt like hams.'

But his host proved not only a good dispenser of hospitality—the claret was light and the lunch was impeccable—but a sympathetic listener too. He encouraged Archie to tell his story and burst into a shout of laughter when he heard of the denouement with Moynihan.

'Why, the old——'

'—bastard!' ended Archie.

But in the month which had preceded their meeting both men had been finding out something of the other. McIndoe now knew that Gillies was a great plastic surgeon and one of the most remarkable 'characters' in the history of medicine. Sir Harold was well aware that this was no indigent relative who had come in search of a handout; not the ordinary kind of handout, anyway. 'I already knew,' he said later, 'that McIndoe's abdominal surgery was of a very high order. With a little encouragement, it seemed to me he could become one of the greatest technicians in the country.' He discovered from that lunchtime conversation that he not only possessed experience but a strong and likeable personality too.

'I rather took to my country cousin,' he said. And he decided to help him. He took him first to Bart's Hospital, where he introduced him to the Dean, Girling Ball, and then to Professor Woollard in the anatomy department.

'I don't know what Woollard expected, but he got a bit of a shock when he started to question Archie,' Sir Harold said. 'He found the fellow was a walking encyclopaedia so far as the human body was concerned. Everyone was very impressed. I was pleased at this. He had got his foot in.'

He began to introduce him to other surgeons, particularly Doctor (later Professor) Pomfret Kilner and Philip Manson-Bahr, both of whom succumbed to his strong personality. He was able to work at Bart's and all of them passed jobs over to him. Each night, however, it was back to his books, sucking in the knowledge he would need if he was to get the all-important fellowship. It was a period in which he worked more intensively than at any time in his life except during the war, and the conditions under which he did so were miserable indeed. Miserable for Adonia as well as for himself. Adonia had discovered that she was expected to have her baby not in the bright clean private room of a hospital such as the one in Rochester where Adonia junior had been born but in the dingy back bedroom of the basement flat, and she found the prospect (as well as the child) almost too much to bear. First the coming child was delayed and there were agonizing hours while she suffered and worried and Archie tried to soothe her with one side of his mind and concentrate on his books with the other. There were protracted labour pains followed by an extremely difficult birth. It was a second daughter and she was splendidly healthy and they decided to call her Vanora. But in giving birth to her, Adonia had exhausted herself, mentally and physically.

It would have been a remarkable achievement for Archie McIndoe to get his fellowship at all in the circumstances. That he got it in nine months is an amazing feat.

His friend and patron, Sir Harold Gillies (now known to him as 'Giles'), had not been idle during the hours of painful labour at Maida Vale. He discovered that there was a job going as a lecturer in general surgery at the Hospital for Tropical Diseases and suggested that Archie should apply for it.

'Leave your referees to me,' he said. 'I'll fix them.'

He attached recommendations from Pomfret Kilner, Manson-

Bahr and himself to the application form, and did a little quiet lobbying on the side. Archie McIndoe was officially informed, just before his fellowship came through, that the job was his.

The McIndoe family raised their weary bones and shook the dust and the damp of Maida Vale from themselves. Archie had found a house in Hampstead with some fresh air and a garden.

He was a long, long way from success yet, but at least he did not need to fear failure any more.

The lecturing job at the Hospital for Tropical Diseases was, however, dull and it was not Archie McIndoe's *métier*. Increasingly he relied upon the work which Gillies and Manson-Bahr put in his way. It is a remarkable fact that here was, in Gillies' words, 'possibly one of the greatest abdominal surgeons in England' at the time, but no one encouraged him to work at his speciality and no hospital recognized him at his true worth. It lends truth to Archie McIndoe's bitter comment a few years later: 'Skill is fine and genius is splendid, but the right contacts are more valuable than either.' So he helped out Sir Harold with his plastic surgical operations. He found them increasingly intriguing.

Life in England was improving, for Archie at least if not for Adonia. He had a facility for making friends and while Adonia stayed at home to nurse Vanora and look after Adonia junior, he found relaxation with some of his more affluent colleagues, particularly Manson-Bahr, weekending in the country. His trigger-finger had not lost its sensitivity, and he was in demand at shoots in Kent and Essex. Working with Sir Harold Gillies at that time were Pomfret Kilner and a stolid, serious surgeon named Rainsford Mowlem, who was also a New Zealander. Mowlem had finished his surgical studies in England in 1930 and had packed his bags and booked his passage back to Auckland, but the house surgeon at Hammersmith hospital had a coronary and died; Mowlem was asked to fill in while a replacement was found.

Gillies had a number of beds for plastic surgery at Hammersmith at the time and Mowlem did not like it. He was out of sympathy with the processes and the need for cosmetic surgery. He arranged for the number of beds to be reduced to two and assigned a junior to look after them. But one day he came into the ward and saw a flap over the face of a patient who had lost his nose through syphilis, and he followed the case all through the process of rebuilding and reconstruction. By the time the patient walked out of the hospital with his nasal organ completely restored, Mowlem was won over. He joined Gillies as his assistant (though he never did become resigned to plastic surgery purely for cosmetic and beautifying purposes).

In 1931 Kilner branched off on his own. Gillies and Mowlem were finding that they had more cases than they could deal with between them, particularly since Gillies was becoming increasingly occupied with his favourite hobbies, golf, fishing and painting.

At the end of a session of surgery at Bart's one day, at which Archie had helped, Gillies said to him:

'Why don't you come in and assist me? There is a partnership for you if it works out.'

McIndoe was excited at the prospect. For some time he had been attracted by the possibilities of plastic surgery, and it would be untrue not to stress the fact that the monetary awards in it were a considerable inducement. He was still living in reduced circumstances compared with his life at the Mayo Clinic, and he missed his comforts. Recognition of his talent as an abdominal surgeon still seemed a long way away. Moreover, the subtleties, the delicacies and the challenges of plastic surgery appealed to him. He knew that he was a fine stomach surgeon even if his colleagues and the world had not yet recognized it, and he was sufficiently egotistic to be satisfied (professionally, at least) with self-recognition. But this new—or new to him—form of surgical reconstruction appealed to him because each time he watched one of Gillies' operations his mind fretted and churned over whether he could have done it so well, or whether he even might have done it better.

He looked down at his stubby strong fingers and wondered whether they could do the lacework, the fretwork, the close-stitching, the delicate skinning for which this branch of surgery called. He did not have to worry about whether there was a future in plastic surgery, for he had seen the well-dressed patients coming into Sir Harold Gillies' consulting rooms at the London Clinic and he had heard from the secretaries what fees they were prepared to pay. He realized (for he had taken the measure of his cousin) that at first he would get all the cleft palates and the fractured jaws, the hare-lips and the industrial burns, while the great man chipped at the noses of society beauties and lifted the faces of ageing dowagers and replenished his cellars, his art-collection and his fishing bag. But . . . well, it was probably wise to see what Adonia would say.

He went back to Hampstead to talk to her about it and found himself mixing it in one of the bitterest domestic quarrels of his married life. Adonia was adamant. To her plastic surgery meant nose-bobbing and breast-reduction and face-lifting. She had heard enough about it from other doctors to be able to call it 'skin-deep surgery' with the necessary scornful inflection.

'Here was a man,' she said later, 'who could open up a stomach and put right what was wrong inside it more speedily and expertly than any man I had ever seen. I know what I am talking about. I watched the others and I watched Archie. He had no equal.'

The idea that he was going to sacrifice this skill to become what she called 'a Bond Street quack, a male beauty specialist' filled her with fury and dismay.

She tore round to see Sir Harold Gillies and said:

'I could have been a great pianist. I gave it up for Archie. I am not going to have seven years of my life thrown away in order to see him become a face-lifter.'

Sir Harold took her into his theatre and let her watch an operation on a young child with a cleft palate. He showed her pictures of some of his burned and mutilated patients, before and after. She was appeased but not convinced.

One can perhaps trace the rift between Archie and Adonia from that moment, and the beginning of his cynicism about women. 'I feel I have something to give to plastic surgery,' he said.

'Yes,' she replied, 'all your charm to all those women.'

In the end, she agreed that her husband had taken the right decision, but it was long after he had taken it himself. He wrote a formal letter to Giles accepting his offer. He did a last operation on a liver at the Hospital for Tropical Diseases. But after that, he said goodbye to abdominal surgery for ever and entered a world that was new and difficult and challenging.

It is time, I think, to say a word about the remote cousin whose timely help changed the face of Archie McIndoe's prospects in

England. Sir Harold Delf Gillies had begun professional life as a medical student at Cambridge, went on to study at Bart's, and got involved—almost literally, at times—with the problems of plastic and reconstructive surgery during the 1914–18 war. Before that he was assistant to Sir Milsom Rees, surgeon to King George V. Sir Milsom was also the friend and doctor of the singers at Covent Garden and it was Gillies' job, in the absence of Rees, to hover behind the scenes and ease the throats of the divas in cases of hoarseness.

'I recall the night of *Aïda*,' he said, 'when I was summoned from the audience to see the leading ballerina. She was a very charming French lady with very little on, and I scarcely knew what to say, especially as she understood no English. By her repeated demonstrations I surmised this lovely damsel had sat on a pair of scissors and wounded a tender spot. She was carefully dressed and patted, and I returned to my seat, the only problem then being to explain to my wife the details of this "throat" case which had detained me so long.'

From ballerinas' buttocks and singers' temperamental larynxes ('He cares more for his golf than for my nose!' Melba complained once, when he was late for an appointment), he was pitchforked into the war in 1915 as a Red Cross surgeon. At Boulogne he met a man with a mission. He was a portly giant with red hair and purple face who drove around behind the front with a dental chair and his drills in the back of a Rolls-Royce. This remarkable man, sparkling in tight breeches, burnished boots and gleaming spurs, was Sir Charles Valadier; and whenever he got a general into his chair and started to fill his cavities with gold, he would propagate his favourite subject—the need for a plastic surgical unit behind the lines. He was smooth and persuasive (and a good dentist) and he got what he wanted. In the summer of 1915 he set up the first British jaw and plastic unit at Wimereux and he took Gillies along as his assistant.

After a few months with Valadier, Harold Gillies came back to England to start a plastic unit at the Cambridge Hospital at Aldershot, and he was now as enthusiastic about the work as his master. When the War Office refused to print labels assigning jaw casualties to Aldershot, he bought them himself and shipped them out. His knowledge of plastic surgery was still rudimentary.

'This was a strange new art,' he wrote later, 'and unlike the student today, who is weaned on small scar excisions and gradually graduated to a single hare-lip, we were suddenly asked to produce half a face.'

But he learned both from his own mistakes and from his books. He rooted back into the origins of reconstructive surgery, back to pre-Christian India where cuckolded husbands revenged themselves by hacking off the noses of their unfaithful wives. As in other commodites, the law of supply and demand worked in this case too, and a caste of Hindu potters learned the art of restoring the noses of the mutilated matrons of the harems by cheek and forehead flaps. The art was closely guarded and passed only from father to son, but by the fifteenth century wandering Indian fakirs had brought the secret to Italy, and less than a hundred years later Gasparo Tagliacozzi wrote his classic book on flap rhinoplasty; but it was another two centuries before ridicule and opposition were overcome and more books on the technique were written.

Gillies found them confused and amateurish. The Germans were enthusiastic plastic surgeons but for only one reason—to get mutilated men back to the front. They paid no attention to how they looked. The French, to his surprise, were not interested in the 'art' side of reconstructive surgery either, and in the early years of the first world war the cynical remark to be heard around French plastic hospitals was that 'the patient looks horrible when he comes in and ridiculous when he goes out'.

On the other hand, as Archie McIndoe was to recall later, the British attitude was hardly better. 'By 1914,' he wrote, 'reconstructive surgery had not one single exponent throughout the length and breadth of the country.' The design and manipulation of pedicled skin flaps, the A B C of the plastic surgeon, was a closed book . . . It is said that in this period a certain leading British surgeon was asked whether he did not think that a plastic surgeon would some day be a necessary adjunct to every big hospital. The surgeon, who had just finished a long day's operating and whose claim to fame was that he could operate faster and more bloodily than any of his contemporaries, surveyed with grim satisfaction his exhausted staff and blood-soaked theatre and remarked: 'If there is any plastic surgery to be done around this theatre, it will be done by me.' This may represent an extreme view, but it mirrors fairly well the attitude of the general surgeon of those days to the field of repair. The truth was that he failed to comprehend what was meant by plastic surgery. He looked with disfavour upon any promising young student who saw anything of virtue in this field. The time was not ripe for the addition of the creative to the destructive ideal in surgery . . . Auden remarks that the creative artist has a desire to make something, a wish to perceive something either in the external world of sense or the internal world of feeling, and an urge to communicate that feeling to others. Tagliacozzi, the first creative surgical artist, was endowed by nature with gifts of manual dexterity and technical ingenuity . . . but in this period there was no surgeon in Britain of sufficient Tagliacozzian stature and outlook to recognize and integrate the principles of repair which had, in fact, been separately formulated and expressed by many individual surgeons over three hundred years.'

Gillies decided to change all that. He not only studied the techniques but the aesthetics of reconstructive surgery. He was a considerable draughtsman and artist and he always drew a picture of his patient as he would like to see him 'after' before he went to work on him. His expenditure on the labels paid him dividends for after the Battle of the Somme two thousand cases of jaw and facial mutilation arrived for him at Aldershot, and he endeavoured to give each one of them his individual attention.

He learned the subtleties of the art in the hardest of schools, from experience in the wards. There is one form of mutilation which happens frequently in infantry encounters, when a bullet tears its way through the nose and gives a man what is called 'a bird-beak deformity'. Gillies discovered that the bullet usually took away one of the man's eyes as well.

'It is important to remember when remaking the nose for a one-eyed lad,' he wrote later, 'not to build the bridge so high that he cannot see the motor bus coming from the blind side. In fact, this straight new bridge may be dangerously high. There was the one-eyed Duke of Montifeltre who had a portion of his nasal bridge removed to increase his field of vision. Thus his one good eye peaking through the notch in his nose discouraged friends sitting on his blind side from trying to poison him.'

Gillies' work on the bashed, blasted and burned faces and bodies of the mutilated men and women of the first world war was largely pioneer work. To a lay reader it will probably mean little if I add that he devised the tube pedicle graft, the onlay eyelid graft, the palate push-back, as well as innumerable new methods of restoring skin and tissue and shape to those places on the human anatomy where the works of man or the inadequacies of nature have destroyed them; though I hope their significance will become clearer later in this story.

He was an innovator of genius. He was also, though a New Zealander, a 'card' in the real Cockney sense of the word. To get the flavour of the man I cannot do better than quote two of his own stories.

'Near the end of the first world war,' he wrote in his famous treatise, *The Principles and Art of Plastic Surgery*, 'I began to wonder whether there would be a living in civilian plastic surgery. Already at Sidcup I had taken on a few private patients and can remember one in particular, the wife of a prominent journalist. She had allowed a beauty shop to inject some paraffin into her face and offered to pay me to remove it. It was my first experience of paraffin and I was unaware of the difficulties of its removal. The job went reasonably well, but the patient did not look one hundred per cent immediately after the operation. I was trying to explain that it takes time for these cases to settle down nicely when the husband, not disposed to wait, whipped out a revolver and started for me. I have since been informed by my more experienced colleagues that a well-tailored bullet-proofed vest can be worn with comfort.'

In 1924 an accident happened aboard the Danish cruiser *Geyser* which killed several, blinded two and wounded sixty. It was Gillies' work on the injured men which brought him international fame and the gratitude of the Danish people was, as will be seen, long-lasting. Sir Harold's description of how his assignment came about is typical of his language:

'One day in 1923,' he said, 'while operating, I must have let my eyes drop to the floor in a moment of relaxation. There I spied a pair of extremely long feet belonging to no-one I had ever seen before. Several hours later I met the owner, an extremely tall Dane who remained with us that day. It was some time later that an invitation arrived for me to go to Denmark to treat a group of

Danish naval burns. This was surprising because I had been my usual rude self to this precursor of the frogmen and had, mind you, commented to him on the enormous length of his feet . . . Seventeen to twenty officers and men were severely burned. In the initial blast many pieces of phosphorus had been blown into the faces of the men, penetrating sometimes quite deeply. It was a common thing, while wandering the wards late and aided by the luminosity, to pick out glowing bits of remaining phosphorus from their necks and faces. So, during a fortnight early in 1924 in Copenhagen, thirteen operations were performed, most of which were merely skin grafts to ectropic eyelids and graft coverage to raw areas.'

It was arranged that the patients should come to England for further treatment.

'Before departure,' recalled Gillies, 'I was summoned to the Palace and ushered with a naval attaché into the royal chamber in the presence of His Majesty the King of Denmark. He was most charming and every bit of seven feet, and only by craning my neck far back could I see the top of him. The medal of the Commander of the Dannebrog, with its red and white ribbon, was brought in on a velvet cushion. As the king reached down to hang it on to me I went up co-operatively on my tiptoes. He then thanked me for my grafts to his navy and we shook hands.'

He was an inveterate practical joker and liked to go down to the wig-makers, fit himself out in a false beard, and then come back to scare his butler or fool his friends. He once mouthed a lecture on facial surgery to an assembly of doctors in Hitlerite Germany while a gramophone behind him spoke the German words, and the exploit pleased him not simply because his hosts did not guess that he spoke not a word of German, but also because the record of his lecture had been translated and recorded by a close friend who was a German, a refugee and a Jew. He was a good fly fisherman, an expert golfer and a competent painter, and he much preferred his three hobbies to the more boring phases of his surgical work. He could be dilatory for appointments, he was lazy, he bullied his associates and hated to think anyone was a better man at his profession than he was. He was proud, haughty, and he loved power and money.

But had it not been for the pioneer work of this rumbling,

rambunctious, temperamental and mischievous old leprechaun, reconstructive surgery would have become moribund in England between the wars and the world would have had to wait—perhaps for decades—for the spectacular breakthroughs which he invented.

In this field of surgery at least, he may also be said to have invented Archie McIndoe; and though they had their differences later on, he was as proud of that achievement as he was of his tubular pedicles.

Plastic surgery is a meticulous craft and a difficult art, and from the first day Gillies hammered home the principles of it to Archie McIndoe. 'You can be a great surgeon on the bowels or the head or the lungs,' he said, 'but you will be a hopeless duffer if you do not bear in mind that this kind of surgery is not just opening up, taking out, and sewing up again. A great percentage of our practice is beauty surgery, and here perfection is necessary. Reconstructive surgery is an attempt to bring a mutilated face or body or limb back to normal; cosmetic surgery is an attempt to surpass the normal. You will never be able to call yourself a plastic surgeon until you are adept at both. You will be a menace until you do. Anyone can cut off a bit of nose, but the art and skill is how you shape it afterwards.'

Giles was a hard taskmaster. He overworked his assistants. He was brusque with them in public and liked scoring off them.

He illustrated on a blackboard the art of taking a graft to a bevy of visiting doctors, and then turned to say:

'And now my assistant, Mr McIndoe, will show you how to take a perfect graft.'

He would stand over him, grinning diabolically, while Archie bent over the patient and cut the square of skin. And he was not spared if he made a mistake.

'He must have cut enough skin to cover a cricket pitch before I had finished with him,' Giles said. 'You couldn't have played a league match over some of the stuff he did at first. But he learned. Soon he was skinning as smoothly as a groundsman at Lord's.'

Six weeks after he had joined Sir Harold, Archie received a letter addressed to 'Mrs Archibald McIndoe' telling him he had been recommended for a position as a charlady at the Royal School of Needlework and would he come for an interview. (Giles had forged it.) His stitching at first was bad. The meticulous work needed to sew together two pieces of skin and leave no mark was maddeningly difficult, and at first he could not master it.

One day he was told that he would be expected to assist the great man at an operation which was particularly tricky. A small child had been born and grown up with a considerable amount of long hair attached in a tuft to her skin. But when Archie arrived at Bart's he found that Sir Harold had gone off to keep a golfing engagement. He left behind a note:

'Dear Archie,—Do you know the fairy-story about Hairy Rouchy? There were once three sisters, the two elder ones being fair and smooth but the youngest, though an angel in temperament, was unfortunately covered all over with long hair, just like a bear. They were taken to see the King of Spain who took to little Hairy Rouchy and told her that if she could beard the local giant and bring back the apples of perpetual happiness which he guarded, he, the King, would give his three sons to the three sisters in marriage . . . Hairy Rouchy outsmarted the giant and brought back the apples because she was smart and lively and when he was in the hollow she was on the hill and when he was on the hill she was in the hollow—a plastic principle you should learn . . . On the wedding day each bride was accompanied in her coach by her prince. Alone of the princes the one assigned to Hairy Rouchy looked pensive. The procession passed an old witch on the road who begged to be admitted to each coach but was refused until Hairy Rouchy stopped her carriage and gave her a lift. Upon arrival at the church each prince bounded from his white horse and took his bride, all except Hairy Rouchy's prince, who climbed off slowly and looked the other way as he took her hand. But suddenly the crowd began to cheer, and he turned to see his bride. She was no longer covered with hair but was a beautiful princess. The old woman had been a fairy and had broken the spell.'

Attached to this legend was a postscript. 'Archie, I have appended some notes on this operation. Now out you go and be a *plastic* fairy!'

Said Archie later: 'Giles was full of tricks like this. He never told you in simple language how to do something. He was a sort of latter-day Aesop, embroidering every lesson with a fable. He would say: "I've been trying to catch a wonderful wily old trout for some months now, but whenever I get near him he never rises. So one day I looked over the situation carefully and realized that there was a water-hen's nest nearby and every time I came near the fluttering of the mother warned my fish I was approaching. So that night I had water-hen's eggs for hors d'œuvres and trout for my main dish. So remember, next time a trout comes into your consulting room, diagnose the situation before you commence fishing. Diagnose, diagnose, diagnose!" '

Archie's stubby fingers had become adept at the close-knit work of the plastic surgeon, and he could now have shown the craftswomen at the Royal School of Needlework a thing or two which even their nimble hands could not have equalled. And once the techniques were learned, the job became absorbing and exciting. Like his master, he was engrossed in the aesthetics of his new work and he would go to infinite trouble to make each case an achievement of artistic reconstruction rather than a patching up. But he diagnosed quickly whereas Sir Harold Gillies took days and sometimes weeks to work out a problem. He cut clean and he probed and pared and stitched with quite remarkable speed.

'I have never seen another surgeon, except for my husband, who cut so beautifully as Archie did,' said Lady Gillies, Sir Harold's widow. 'In those days I was Giles' nurse and because plastic surgery was still frowned upon in general hospitals in those days he and Archie would sometimes have to operate in the same theatre. Archie and his nurse and anaesthetist would break off at lunch, having done three and sometimes four cases. Giles would still be at work on his first.'

For those first few years it was Sir Harold who did all the well-paying plums of the partnership. The nose-bobbings, the face-lifts, the cleft-palate and hare-lip cases with rich parents came to him, and McIndoe and Mowlem were left to do the rest. 'These two slaved away, cutting grafts, sewing up pedicles and taking on all the hard-luck cases,' Sir Harold wrote later, 'while I went fishing or golfing. Perhaps, looking back and assessing their positions today, they don't resent those years too much.'

At first Archie McIndoe did not. He had come to an arrangement with Sir Harold to buy his partnership in instalments of £500 a year, and it was a struggle to find the money and keep his wife and growing family; but it was worth it if by taking on all the difficult cases he learned every facet of his craft. In those early days he became adept at three types of operation which tax the skill of the reconstructive surgeon to the utmost, and, in at least two cases, are a far cry from the 'skin-deep' surgery usually scoffed at by ordinary surgeons.

One of them he perfected in association with Giles and this was mammaplasty or breast reduction. Was this cosmetic surgery? 'That sort of question does not worry me,' he wrote in a letter to New Zealand. 'But if I had to justify mammaplasty, I would say this: when an adolescent woman comes into my office and she is slim and normal except for long flabby pendulous breasts, I feel it is good for her health and important for her state of mind if I reduce them. You can go into hospital waiting-rooms and see women holding their breasts in their hands because they are so heavy and painful. It is ridiculous not to help them. Women get large breasts as a result of pregnancy or obesity or glandular deficiencies. Some of them have one giant and one small. They get back-ache from it, bad posture, weariness. They get into a mental state. They can't dance or swim or ride. If their health is good and I think their state of mind will be improved, I operate.'

Between them, Giles and Archie perfected a technique for mammaplasty which has since been adopted throughout the surgical world, and the need for justifying themselves has long since passed. In 1938 they produced their first joint paper on the technique, and they ended with these words:

'From the psychological point of view the patient finds herself able to go among her friends with a new-found equanimity. Those girls who feared married life with a sensitiveness amounting almost to melancholia regain their self-confidence . . . there would appear to be no question as to the satisfactory end-results of the operation provided that all the precautions enumerated are carried out.'

In less serious words, Archie would sometimes emerge from his operating theatre and say to Rainsford Mowlem:

'D'you remember that girl who came in here carrying a pair of railway buffers? You should see her now. I've just given her a couple of beauts!'

In the meantime, he was experimenting on his own, and two operations which emerged from his researches disprove the charge that even in those early days he was a technician rather than an

(*Above*) Ken, Archie and John McIndoe
(*Below*) Archie and Adonia McIndoe with Adonia junior and Vanora, at Christmas, 1938

Four of England's greatest plastic Surgeons: (*left to right*)
Rainsford Mowlem, T. P. Kilner, Sir Harold Gillies
and Sir Archibald McIndoe

innovator. One was a reconstructive operation on women and the other on men.

'A woman wrote to me some time ago,' he noted in his day-book, 'to say that her daughter was planning to marry in a few months' time and was very nervous about it, and not for the usual reasons. When I examined her I discovered she was quite right to be worried. She was completely without what the female sex usually have in this region.'

He made inquiries and discovered that the deficiency was not uncommon and that some attempts to restore it had been made by the use of free grafts, almost always with painfully unsuccessful results. He began to experiment with a device of his own, involving the use of a hollow vulcanite mould by which the graft was carried and held in place. His paper on the subject, *An Operation for the Cure of Congenital Absence of the Vagina*, first published in 1938, is still read and followed by surgeons today.

A year before he had written a paper on *An Operation for the Cure of Adult Hypospadias* which did much to alleviate a tragic deficiency in men.

Nor did he neglect the general run of plastic surgery and reconstructive work while conducting these researches. Thanks to the growing reputation of the partnership, more and more patients were arriving at the Clinic. This is not surprising in view of the fact that, in England at the time, there were only four men specializing in plastic surgery: Giles, Archie, Rainsford Mowlem and Kilner. But Archie's papers had drawn attention to him. Appointments began to be offered him, and he could number among them Chief Assistant in Plastic Surgery at Bart's, Assistant Plastic Surgeon, St Andrew's and St James's Hospital, and Consulting Plastic Surgeon, North Staffordshire Royal Infirmary. He had had some spectacular successes in facial surgery, including a society girl who had lost half a face in a burning accident, a hunter who had been mauled by a tiger in India, and some badly injured victims of the earthquake at Quetta. When they came to the Clinic now, patients did not automatically ask for Giles. Doctors had begun to recommend Archie for the work.

It is true that he got some of the jobs because he was cheaper. An indication of how some of them came his way is given in this letter which was sent to the writer:

'My daughter was a singer on the stage in the early 1930s when she found herself "resting". She had an idea that it would be an advantage to her looks if she had a more attractive nose. She had a good voice and I was afraid the operation might interfere with her breathing. However, I saw a picture of a famous actress in an evening paper. In fact there were two pictures with captions "before" and "after". It seemed that her nose had been altered but of course the name of the surgeon was not mentioned. I received a charming letter in which she said that Mr Harold Gillies as he then was had performed the operation and I telephoned and made an appointment. In those days a consultation was three guineas and although I was not well off we managed that sum. Mr Gillies was a wonderful man. He actually drew the new nose he envisaged on the old one. When it came to the question of the cost of this operation it was a sum I could not afford and I told him so. It was then that he mentioned his colleague, Mr McIndoe, and said: "He makes a speciality of altering noses. His fees are much less than mine." He went on: "You can see him now. He's in the same building." I was very impressed with Mr McIndoe and it occurs to me now that he was very young. My daughter told him about her singing. Then he asked us how much we could afford. While I was thinking what to say she said: "I am on the dole at the moment." '

Seeing the mother's embarrassment, McIndoe suggested a sum. 'It was a quarter of what Mr Gillies had said and only a trifle more than I was thinking of . . . He changed my daughter's looks so much no one recognized her and when he saw her afterwards he said one side was better than the other and he would like to do it again. But she said she was satisfied. It was a lovely nose. It was amazing the difference it made to her looks and I was thrilled.'

Later on, Giles did not take so kindly to Archie's fee-cutting. 'They'll only despise you if you charge them too little,' he said. 'Get the money in advance if you can, too. It's better for them to sue you if they aren't satisfied than for you to sue them because you haven't been paid.'

Archie agreed to put up his prices. In truth, he was getting a number of nose cases, and not simply because Giles passed them on. The *McIndoe Nose* was beginning to be talked about, and the fees from it made a difference to the life of the McIndoe family.

They moved from Hampstead into a comfortable flat in Harley Street, close to the Clinic. (It was a little too close, perhaps. In later years, Archie used to tell students: 'Never keep a wife too near to your work. It can be annoying if she keeps bursting into your consulting room—especially if you're in the middle of examining a beautiful patient.') Adonia junior had been packed off to a good school and there was no need to worry about the fees. There was a family car—it would soon be a Rolls-Royce—and holidays in the South of France.

The picture of Archie McIndoe that his friends retain of him from those years is of a stocky, well-built young man in a well-cut grey pin-striped suit, a cigarette always between his lips, for he had become a chain-smoker, a grin on his face even though he now started work at nine in the morning and rarely finished before eight at night. He made a handsome figure despite the fact that his hair was still plastered down flat and parted exactly in the middle. With his material circumstances eased, he had become relaxed and confident; and though he could be brusque to the point of rudeness when something went wrong in the theatre, though he found it hard to forgive mistakes, and though he had a terrible temper when roused, his charm was devastating and he was always (or almost always) forgiven by those he had rated.

By 1938 he was doing the lion's share of the work in the partnership, and so long as he did not demand the lion's share of the profits Giles was unruffled, if sometimes a little rueful. About this time, an unknown colleague produced an elaborate illustrated book of doggerel verse called *The Plastic Surgeon; Its Habits, Diet and Behaviour. A Study in Unnatural History* which is a gay spoof not without its kernel of cynical criticism. Of their habit when theatre work was at its peak of taking refreshment beside the operating table, the unknown wrote:

> The surgeon has no time to eat.
> He carves the patient or his meat
> With one hand or the other,
> Murmuring as he sips his Oxo
> 'Now just lie still and do not rock so,
> Dear sister (or dear brother)'.
> It gives a meal a charm, no doubt,
> To take your steak and drop of stout

While gouging someone's liver out,
Or tacking on a chin.
But sometimes little things occur
Which makes one feel they *should* prefer
To pasture in an inn.
For plastic surgeons ought to be
Particularly careful,
Yet sausages (designed for tea)
Are sometime inadvertently
Stitched where the pedicle should be,
And the result is fearful.

One section of the poem deals with Archie in these lines:

The kindest man I ever knew
Was Mr A. H. McIndoe
His eye was mild, his heart was tender,
Of damaged faces he was mender.
Alas, his quite peculiar charm
Became a source of some alarm.
For patients far from getting bored
Refused to own that they were cured,
And when he told them to get up
Would promptly ask him out to sup,
Or murmur in his burning ear
'Okay, we'll go together, dear!'
Till strained relations vowed to stew
Th'insinuating McIndoe.
Weeping to see them mope and suffer
He thought 'I really must be gruffer.'
And so he sought to steel his mind
In theatres of a different kind;
When he had done the operation
Left them to find their own salvation;
Gave bottle parties to his friends,
Took long and numerous weekends,
And just abandoned them to fate,
Till they began to suppurate.
Now, answering Nurse's wild appeals,
He waits until it's time for meals,
Then wanders in between the courses,
Mixing the saline with the sauces.
No more he holds the fevered hand,

But pokes them in the belly-band;
Tears off the dressings and their skins
And parks his forceps on their shins.
You'd fancy this would make them sore?
They only worship him the more,
And Harley Street is one long queue
Of Fans in wait for McIndoe.

The story of Archie McIndoe's apotheosis in pre-war Harley Street would not be complete without a mention of the two assistants who made up his team and deserve considerable credit for his success. A quatrain in the doggerel verses reads as follow:

Hush, little patient, and do not perspire,
Here's the anaesthetist come to inquire.
Smile at him nicely, and if you are quick
You'll be able to thank him before you are sick!

It is a satiric reference to John Hunter, who was, in fact, so great an anaesthetist that he rarely made his patients vomit. Later, when he worked with Archie at East Grinstead on the burned and mutilated RAF casualties, he had a standing wager with them. If they even so much as felt nausea from his ministrations, he guaranteed to set them up a pint of beer; if not, they bought one for him. 'One had only to meet John to see who came out ahead,' recalled Giles.

John Hunter was the Mr Pickwick of the medical profession: an amiable, jam-roll of a man with a kind heart, a gregarious nature, a ready wit as redolent as old port, and a love of life that extended to almost everyone he met, with the possible exception of other anaesthetists. He loved company and he loved beer and he did not stint himself of either, even though he was a lifelong sufferer from diabetes. 'No one really knows what a hangover is like,' Archie once said, 'until he's seen old John the morning after.'

Archie had met John Hunter in his early days at the Hospital for Tropical Diseases and they had formed a school of mutual admiration. For a time they shared fees, because it was John Hunter who found the jobs and he who made the financial advances when Archie lacked the money to pay his bills. But it was for his great medical skill that Archie chose him as his associate on all his plastic operations from 1936 onwards. Giles had the strong right arm of Doctor (later Sir Ivan) Magill behind him and he leaned on it heavily. It was Magill who had invented the tube named after him for passing gas and oxygen through the nose directly into the trachea, by which a patient mutilated about the mouth and jaw could be put to sleep. It was he who had pioneered many other of the anaesthetic techniques whereby plastic surgical cases were saved from almost certain death.

'Some of the cases,' he reported, when he first began his experiments, 'if placed flat on their backs would get immediate respiratory obstruction [which meant that they choked to death]. In the crushed jaw cases the tongue, having lost its anterior support, would flop back and along with the flood of blood and mucus would block the airway [which meant that they died]. If it was difficult to maintain an airway with the patient conscious, imagine the hazards of an anaesthetic!'

He found the way to do it, and his technique became the accepted one for anaesthetists.

John Hunter, if never an innovator, like Magill, was nonetheless a 'doper' or 'stuffer', as Giles called them, of surpassing skill and he had a way with him which put patients into a contented coma long before he gave them drugs or injections. In the art of plastic and reconstructive surgery the anaesthetist plays a much more important part than he does in other branches of medicine. Reconstructive surgery is often a long and patient procedure in which a patient may need as many as a dozen separate operations. A passage in the doggerel verses runs:

I do not like surgeons,
They are a brutal race.
They came and sliced my tummy up
And parked it on my face.
I do not like surgeons
For they are not refined.
Who wants to have a forehead made
Of slabs from her behind?

Each graft cut necessitates an operation. Each flap skinned and attached for growth to an injured face needs another. The plastic surgeon skins his flap, wraps it up in a Gillies tubular pedicle, stitches it to the end of the smashed face or burned cheek, and then waits for at least six weeks until it has grown—after which he snips it off the stomach or arm or buttock from which it came. The good plastic surgeon does not hurry. He does each phase of his work, and then waits. 'Never do today what you can reasonably put off till tomorrow,' is his motto. This means that his patient has time to think—only too much time to think—about each operation. If the anaesthetist has made him ill, his revulsion against each succeeding ordeal under gas will grow until it becomes an obsession.

John Hunter could claim that he had few patients who refused to go on with the operations (as some did) because they could not put up with the dreadful nausea. He was working in the beginning with methods which may seem crude today, but he possessed an anaesthetic which seemed more powerful than his gases and drugs, an almost hypnotically powerful personality—a deep and benign influence for soothing and comforting—which lulled his patients into a state of confident and painless trust.

I would add that John Hunter was not only a humane person but also a loyal one. He not only loved working with Archie McIndoe but he also loved the man.

The third member of the McIndoe team was his theatre sister, Jill Mullins.

Say the verses:

> The Nurse is sweet,
> Or strong and neat and capable or cursed.
> The patient likes the second kind,
> The surgeons like the first.

Not even her best friends would ever have described Jill Mullins as sweet. She was a tall, slim redhead with blue eyes and a brisk manner whom Archie first met when she 'scrubbed' for him in the operating theatre at Bart's. She and another staff sister, Margerie Clayton, often used to work with the plastic surgeons, and they were both young women of phenomenal efficiency. The good theatre sister is born with a silver scalpel in her hand; she must know what instruments to hand over before she is asked; she must know the methods and idiosyncrasies of her surgeon; she must be cool in an emergency; and she must be chemically compatible with her master. All this, of course, in addition to knowing her medicine and her craft.

Jill had these formidable accomplishments to a remarkable degree, and Ireland, that fertile womb of good nurses, has rarely produced a better.

The curious thing is that Giles recognized her worth before Archie McIndoe did. When his own nurse left him for new ventures, both he and Ivan Magill agreed that Mullins was the sister they must have as her replacement. Whether she had her ambitions fixed even at this time is uncertain, but what is certain is that instead of accepting the offer herself she recommended Margerie Clayton. Giles could not have been better suited. They worked together with mutual respect and admiration, and after the death of Giles' wife their relationship ripened into marriage.

Jill Mullins went back to her wards at Bart's and waited. She joined McIndoe in 1935, and the team of McIndoe, Hunter and Mullins was formed; there has rarely been a more skilled and successful one in the history of Harley Street. They worked in instinctive harmony in the theatre and they became close companions in their off-hours, though by no means so intimate as the propinquity of East Grinstead stimulated in the years to come. John Hunter had joined McIndoe because he admired his skill, warmed to the man, and found working with him challenging and exciting. It is probably true to say that Jill Mullins left Bart's to become a member of the team because she was resourceful and ambitious and she had taken the measure of McIndoe; she knew he was destined for great things and she wished to rise with him. Once the triumvirate was formed, however, the human elements in the association gradually replaced the calculating ambitions; it was, in any case, difficult not to warm to Archie McIndoe, for he had a chemistry which drew all women and nearly all men to him, and in addition he had an attitude towards his work which made it seem like fun when things were going well and adventurous when a crisis had arisen.

Even in those days Archie eschewed the formal parlance usual between doctor and nurse in British hospitals.

'For God's sake don't go on calling me Mr McIndoe,' he said to his new sister. 'My name's Archie and this is John, and we shall call you Jill.' He added: 'It won't stop me blasting your ears off if anything goes wrong.'

In fact, there were occasions later when he grew angry with her, and then he very stiffly addressed her as 'Miss Mullins' or even 'Sister'. But that did not happen very often. To watch the team at work was a study in perfect co-ordination. Hunter's head would be close to the patient's face, his kindly bloodshot eyes watchful, his ear cocked for the sound of even breathing. Mullins, her red hair peeping beneath her cap, would preside over the table of instruments like a major-domo at a banquet, never needing to be told what to pass and when to pass it. And Archie would cut, peel, pare and chisel with not even a gesture needed to indicate when one instrument should be changed for another. They moved fast and they worked in silence; and it was one body operating with six supple and experienced hands.

Sometimes, however, Archie would be in a talkative mood, especially when there were visiting doctors.

'There is one thing to be remembered when doing a nasal reduction,' he said during one such operation, 'and that is to remember that the nose is in the middle of the face. Though if you will study Sister Mullins when she removes her mask, you will notice that a slight variation from this norm can sometimes even enhance a woman's attraction.'

And on another occasion, when doing a mammaplasty: 'An esteemed colleague of my anaesthetist once suggested that it would save time and trouble in levelling the lie of a lady's breasts by building up the sole of her left shoe. We do not believe in such stratagems, gentlemen. An even balance in everything.'

Amid the growing number of applications for cosmetic surgery he still spent most of his time on the infinitely more difficult and painstaking reconstructive cases. For his skill at the *McIndoe Nose* he began to receive publicity in the newspapers, usually from the grateful actresses and models on whom he had operated, and sometimes his name was mentioned. This brought him—as it did his colleagues in similar circumstances—into immediate conflict with the British Medical Association and the professional embarrassment more than counterbalanced any benefits he might receive from the attention brought to his work.

'If I could stop this use of my name,' he wrote later, 'I would do so, but it would mean getting up in public and saying that I neither reduce noses nor do face-lifts. I do both, and I think they are, in the right cases, justifiable operations. But I do other things which the public prints are not in the least interested in. So there is a slight dilemma here and I am sure the answer to it is eventually a programme of education.'

He could have added that for each nose-reduction he performed there were at least half a dozen hare-lips and cleft palates, a steady stream of burns and facial fractures, and not infrequently the restoration of a face or body ravaged by cancer and mutilated by the ordinary surgeon's knife.

'We had a case in here some time ago,' Jill Mullins wrote to a friend, 'of a young woman who had undergone several dental operations and been subjected to an overdose of X-rays. She developed a severe carcinoma of the face, and when the cancer men had finished hacking at her she came to us. Her complete lower jaw had disappeared. The boss began chipping away at her bones to build up a new lower jaw. In seven months he had provided a place upon which she could rest her tongue. He calculates it will be three years before he has restored her face to something approaching normality. Meanwhile, he keeps her amazingly cheerful and full of hope. When he went away for the weekend once she slipped out of bed and tried to do herself in with a knife, but fortunately the tube pedicle from her right arm to her mouth severely restricted her stabbing power, and we got her in time. The boss broke his weekend to come back to see her. "For God's sake don't start any of this suicide stuff," he said, "until that pedicle is all right. It needs at least another month. When I've snipped it off your arm you have my full permission to do yourself any harm you like—only please don't ruin my lovely flap." She started to laugh and cry at the same time and she has been as good as gold ever since.'

In 1938 Mabel McIndoe and her eldest son, John, arrived in England on a visit and they stayed with Archie and Adonia in Hampstead (it was just before they moved to Harley Street). Mabel McIndoe was delighted with her two granddaughters. 'Adonia junior is pretty but perhaps a little too solemn and serious,' she wrote home to New Zealand. 'I sometimes catch her looking at her mother with a cool, appraising stare which I find rather disconcerting when she turns it upon me. As for Vanora, she is bright, mischievous and thoroughly charming, and she knows it, the little minx!'

Kenneth McIndoe, Archie's other brother, happened to be in England on his honeymoon with his new American wife (he had become a geneticist with a rubber firm) and it was obviously the occasion for a family reunion, the first for fourteen years. So Mabel Elizabeth, the kid sister, was summoned from Edinburgh, where she was now living. It was an opportunity for Archie to display his material progress to his family and he did not miss it.

'For the first night of our arrival,' John recalls, 'he had arranged a dinner party at Kettner's. Archie entertained us with princely hospitality. Speeches were made and toasts were honoured. It was a memorable occasion, and the last one when we were all together. For the remainder of my stay he was equally generous. He took me everywhere and introduced me to his friends, and it was evident that he knew everyone and was popular with everyone.'

For a weekend outing, Archie and Adonia took John to the old Brooklands race-track to see the motor races.

'We narrowly missed being killed,' said John, 'when a racing car on fire crashed through the fence near the pits and mowed down the spectators in its path. Several were killed or injured. I watched Archie pull his jacket over his head and dive towards the blazing inferno which had been a car. From under it he dragged a woman. She was dead. He looked round and saw that both Adonia and I were unhurt. Then, with the cars still racing round the circuit, he gave his attention to the wounded. When he came back, all he said was: "But for the grace of God . . . Come on, let's go and have a whisky." '

That Easter Archie took out the Rolls and drove his brother John to Broadway, in Worcestershire, where they parked the car, donned rucksacks and set off on a tramp through the Cotswolds. The weather was perfect and the two brothers, always comfortable in each other's company, rediscovered the intimacy which had made their boyhood together so idyllic. There was no jealousy and no rivalry between these two: John, solid, secure, content to be the linchpin of the family, happy in his routine job at the printing works, rejoiced at but did not envy his younger brother's success.

For both of them it was the opportunity to unburden. John fretted a little about the apron-strings which his mother still attached to the business in Dunedin. He ran the works, brought in the business, looked after the profits, but Mabel McIndoe still retained control and insisted on being consulted on every decision. Archie talked about the problems of his domestic life and made it plain that though life in Harley Street was rich and rewarding in every sense of the word, the same could not be said about his life at home.

Uppermost in both their minds, however, was the possibility of war. It was the Easter before Munich and in the Sudetenland of Czechoslovakia pro-Nazi goons were wrecking and sabotaging, provoked and encouraged by the rantings of Adolf Hitler. The future would bring what—war or peace?

At one point, Archie said:

'John, last week I paid off the final instalment of the purchase price of my partnership with Giles. I have paid all my debts. All I possess is my Rolls, the household goods and'—holding out his stubby hands, palms upwards—'these ten fingers. If it is peace, in ten years I shall be able to retire. If it is war, I'll be put in uniform and pushed around by Jacks-in-office.' He paused, and then added: 'I've gambled on peace.'

CHAPTER FOUR

THE BATTLE OF BRITAIN

HE WAS THIRTY-EIGHT years old, and, as may have been guessed from this story so far, neither a very subtle nor a very sensitive man. Not yet. It was not that he was hard or cynical; so far as his work on the operating table was concerned, Archie McIndoe was always aware of the human problems involved in his cases. He knew what difference could be made to a child's future if he mended its hare-lip so that it did not show. He recorded one of his greatest triumphs in his day-book in these words:

'Three years ago I had a girl who was a cleft palate and instead of an obturator [which is gripped to the roof of the mouth by teeth and suction, and is painful] I grafted in a tube. I met her again last month in a flight from Paris and the weather was very rough. I was a proud man when I saw her being sick. In other circumstances, she would never have been able to be sick like ordinary people.'

But medicine is a closed world and it absorbs its specialists in almost day-to-day engrossment in their job. The day is spent in diagnosing, operating, sometimes improving on nature, sometimes rectifying nature's mistakes, sometimes prolonging life and not infrequently saving it. The leisure hours, at least for a young surgeon, are spent in the social battle for improvement. In the medical world, as in most other professions, it is not by skill alone that a man moves upwards, and the gifted hand in the hospital will not necessarily lift a surgeon so swiftly as the gifted tongue at the cocktail parties.

Archie McIndoe was well aware of this. And content with the situation. Since he possessed skill and talent to an extraordinary degree so far as medicine was concerned and also had what is known as 'a way with him', he did not grumble about the need to use his free time in making contacts.

In 1938 and 1939 it would be fair to say that his main concern, outside the operating theatre, was to improve his material condition. If you had asked him how his feelings were about Germany, he would probably have said: 'From my experience with them, the present lot are a pretty rotten crew.' But if you had also asked him whether he was in favour of doing something about it, he would have undoubtedly said: 'Good God, no!' His career was going well and he did not want it disturbed.

He had gambled on peace, as he said to his brother John.

His plan was to break away from the partnership with Giles, who was, in his opinion, taking too much of the share of the profits and doing too little work in return. (They were, in fact, dividing eighty-five per cent of the profits. Mowlem got the rest.) His income was now somewhere in the region of £7,500 a year, and he had set himself a target. For the next ten years he would do all the operations and accept all the work which came to him; and save his money. After this, he would adopt Giles' policy, though not necessarily Giles' way of life. He would take his savings and buy himself a villa in the South of France, and he would work only half of the year: on noses, faces and scars to bring in a steady income, on hare-lips and cleft palates in young children because he liked them and he was proud of the skill his stubby fingers had developed inside their undeveloped mouths.

He badly missed the sunshine of New Zealand and had never become reconciled to the bone-aching rigours of the British climate. And, too, perhaps a sweeping change would restore some of the balance to his married life.

In the meantime, with no real realization of how the political situation was shaping, he yearned and hoped for peace. He had everything to lose if war came.

Not that he entirely neglected his insurance in the event of its coming. For several months he had been substituting for Giles on the occasions when the Royal Air Force requested expert plastic surgical work or advice. Sir Harold Gillies had for long been principal consultant in plastic surgery to the RAF, but he was apt to find a golfing engagement in Wiltshire, a landscape in Essex, or a lucrative face-lift in Harley Street more tempting than a facial fracture at Halton. Archie suggested that his frequent substitutions might well be put on a more permanent basis.

Giles was not unwilling. He had his own plans if war came. For some months he and the great dental surgeon, Kelsey (now Sir Kelsey) Fry, had been members of a consultative committee working out how and where the London hospitals would be evacuated in the event of war, and Giles had already decided where he would be and what he would do.

On June 11, 1938, Archie received a letter from Air Commodore A. V. J. Richardson, of the RAF Medical Service, which said: 'Sir Harold Gillies has indicated to me that you might be agreeable to be the Royal Air Force Representative Consultant in Plastic Surgery vice Sir Harold himself for whom you have deputized on so many occasions. If you will confirm this and also concur in the attached draft form of contract and fee, I shall be very pleased to arrange for your name to be included in our lists of Consultants.'

He replied:

'It was with very great pleasure that I received your intimation that my name is to be included in the list of Consultants to the Air Ministry, and you may rest assured that my services will be at your disposal whenever you may need them.'

To Archie McIndoe it was a way of making sure that he would, at least, have his foot in the military door if war came. He had no idea at the time that it would lead him to East Grinstead and into some battles royal with the military machine.

With the advent of war in 1939, Britain possessed four fully-experienced plastic surgeons—the aforementioned Gillies, McIndoe, Mowlem and Kilner—and another six at the registrar level of training. It was not many but, for the moment, it was enough.

'With this small but efficient nucleus,' wrote Archie McIndoe later, 'there was this time no fumbling uncertainty about what should be done. Four primary centres were established, at Basingstoke, Hill End, Roehampton and East Grinstead. [Later Roehampton moved to Stoke Mandeville.] In these centres intensive training of younger men enabled subsidiary centres to be established throughout Britain.'

Kilner had decided that he would like to be with the Ministry of Pensions at Roehampton, so that the other hospitals were at the disposal of the partners. But Giles, of course, had the first choice, and he chose Rooksdown House at Basingstoke and placed a deputy there until he could wind up his practice in London and take up residence. Mowlem went to St Albans. Archie had meanwhile done a reconnaissance to East Grinstead and was pleased with what he found there. The Queen Victoria Hospital had only been opened for three and a half years—a replacement for the old cottage hospital—and it was clean, modern, surrounded by well-tended lawns and flower beds. There were two twelve-bed wards, one for women and one for men, a six-bed ward for children, a number of private rooms and (for Britain in 1939) up-to-date equipment.

'It is a nice little hospital on the outskirts of a nice little town,' Archie wrote to his mother, 'and I think something can be made of it.'

Under the emergency medical scheme the Queen Victoria had been pencilled-in by the planners as a centre for burns and facial injuries. Since it was midway between London and the coast, it would be convenient as a reception centre for the air-raid injuries expected when London was bombed and for service casualties in France. But by an agreement between the three of them, the partners arranged that Giles would concentrate on naval casualties, Mowlem would deal with the Army and Archie would tend the wounds of the RAF.

Archie went down early in September to set up his unit, and with him came John Hunter, Jill Mullins, and a young assistant plastic surgeon named Percy Jayes. Kelsey Fry was already there, establishing a dental unit for the jaw injuries they were expecting. It would be pleasant to be able to say that the hospital board and the town welcomed the newcomers with open arms, but life doesn't work that way and at first they were viewed with grumbling suspicion, especially when the children's ward was evacuated and turned into a double operating theatre, and an ugly long single-storied hut was thrown up behind the main building. It was called Ward Three, but at that time it didn't mean a thing to anyone except that it was an eyesore.

Those who recall Archie McIndoe in those first few weeks of

war remember him as a dapper little man in a pin-striped double-breasted suit, a carnation in his lapel, and a worried look in the grey eyes behind the round horn-rimmed spectacles (he had taken to glasses a few years before). People remembered that he was brisk to the point of curtness with the staff, pushed them around, rated them for dilatoriness, treated them like country cousins, and rarely smiled. For Archie an unsmiling face was unusual, but he was, in fact, a man with problems on his shoulders, and not all of them professional.

From a financial point of view, the war for him was something of a tragedy. In times of national crisis, people continue to have diseased appendixes, tumours continue to grow and livers go wrong; the work of the ordinary surgeon goes on. But the vanities and complexes which bring patients in for nose and breast reductions or face-lifts disappear, at least for the time being. Except for those cases which were still being treated, cosmetic surgery in Harley Street came to a halt.

Despite the fact that his income had been rising steadily, Archie McIndoe's assets were few. The money for the partnership and the payment of old debts, plus the increase in his standard of living, had sapped his bank account. He was forced to contemplate the future on an income of not much more than the £980 a year he would receive as RAF Consultant. Reluctantly, he mounted his beloved Rolls on blocks and took to a smaller car. He removed Adonia junior and Vanora from their expensive school.

'Dear Mr McIndoe,' wrote a friend, F. E. Maitland, on September 23, 1939, 'we are very sorry indeed to learn from Miss Joslin that being called away from your practice is making it impossible for you to send your daughters back to the Francis Holland School here [at Oxford]. In different ways we have been landed with two German Jewish refugees, probably for the duration of the war at least. This rather handicaps us for doing other things, but it would give me much greater satisfaction if I could do something to help an English Christian. My wife has already told Miss Joslin that we shall be glad to take your daughter Vanora without payment. I don't know whether the school has been able to offer you any reduction of fees, but if you were willing to accept any temporary help from me to enable you to send your daughter back to school I should be very glad indeed. I am too old to do much in the way of war work and this way I should feel that I was doing *something* to help . . . If you preferred you could regard it as a loan to be repaid when you return to regular practice . . .'

But Archie had other plans in mind and he was working on them. Almost as soon as war began he had received letters from his old friends at the Mayo Clinic, Donald Balfour and Virgil Counseller, to tell him that there would be a home in Rochester for his wife and children whenever he decided to send them. So far the bombing had not been heavy, but he was worried for the safety of his children. But he was not willing to send them alone, and Adonia was reluctant to leave his side. There were emotional scenes in the household and his temper was not improved by his wife's adamant determination to stay; but at last she was persuaded. They departed for the United States early in 1940, and shortly afterwards he was writing to them:

'I am missing you all terribly but at the same time feel better than I have for months. The nagging weight of anxiety for your safety was beginning to make itself felt, but that is now gone . . .'

The evacuation of his family was a relief in more ways than one. For the first time for years he felt free of the domestic encumbrances and crises which had been trying his temper, and for the first time he could get down to the business of settling his future without the constant (and often resented) advice of his wife. He decided to keep on the flat in Harley Street and took a furnished cottage near East Grinstead, but for the moment the cases were not coming in and most of his work was concerned with administration; he spent much of the week travelling around various hospitals in the Home Counties, arranging for burns cases to be sent to him as and when they came in.

His main concern was his status. The RAF had offered him a commission as a Wing Commander, but he rightly considered that this comparatively junior rank would restrict his powers.

'The early part of the week,' he wrote, 'I spent in a round of RAF hospitals inspecting arrangements for burns and I have just completed a big report on the matter. The question of my status is still *sub judice*. I am beginning to feel that my civilian status gives me more scope and power than if I were in uniform. It certainly gives me more freedom, a commodity not particularly easy to obtain in these hard times.'

Slowly the Queen Victoria Hospital was taking the shape that Archie McIndoe wanted, at least so far as his part of it was concerned. He had found volunteer workmen to chip away the dun-brown and baby's-yellow government paint from the walls of Ward Three and substituted light greens and other colours more calculated to cheer a patient's eyes. Down each side of the ward were twenty beds, packed close to each other but divided by a locker for each patient, a table in the middle with a radio on it, and a piano at the end. It was simple but it was light and pleasant and airy, and soon it would be more of a home for many than the ones they had previously known. At the opposite end of Ward Three, separated by a curtain which could be drawn across to screen it, was an ordinary bath-tub. It rested on the floor with the taps still attached to it, though it was filled by bucket. But to Archie McIndoe it was no ordinary tub but his pride and joy, and he told Sister Hall, the sister-in-charge, to instruct her staff always to refer to it as the Saline Bath Unit. He had already recruited a staff of RAF medical orderlies and instructed them in its use.

McIndoe had always believed in the saline treatment of burn cases, and it was no new thing to him that salt water could soothe, cleanse and help to heal. In one of his lectures before the war, he had referred to the case of the swashbuckling Italian surgeon, Fiorovanti, a pioneer of plastic surgery, who witnessed a duel in Africa in 1551 during which one of the contestants lost his nose. The nose fell in the sand.

'The quarrel ended and the poor gentleman remained without a nose,' Fiorovanti recorded. 'And I, who had it in my hand, all covered with sand, urinated on it and having washed it in urine, I attached it to him and sewed it on very firmly and I medicated it with balsam and bandaged it. And I had him thus for eight days believing it was going to rot. However, when I untied it I found it was well attached once again and I medicated it and he was healthy.'

As if to reinforce this ancient lesson, some of the first cases which began to reach the hospitals after the outbreak of war were those of serving men who had been immersed in the sea after suffering burns—sailors from sunken warships, soldiers picked up during the evacuation from Dunkirk, airmen shot down over the Channel —and it was noticed that their skin and flesh were much more amenable to treatment than the dried or suppurating flesh of land casualties. Even so, there were only three saline bath units in British hospitals in 1940 and it took some time for the lesson to sink home, especially since it was not part of official medical routine for burns.

'I remember the first time we dipped a character in the swill,' recalled Taffy, one of the RAF medical orderlies. 'He had been badly burned somewhere abroad and he was a real mess. The Maestro* had already sewn a flap on him and told us to dip him to cool him off. He must have thought the water was boiling hot, or something. Anyway, he jerked the moment he touched the water and you could positively hear the stitches being ripped out. Funny, some of them never could get used to it at first. We had one badly burned child who used to scream every time we carried her to the water, though she just loved it once she was in.'

The character of the war was changing. Dunkirk had come and gone, but most of the casualties had been sent to Mowlem at St Albans and Giles at Rooksdown. But from the air raids over the Home Counties and London—which were being stepped up at the beginning of September 1940—East Grinstead began to receive an increasing number of casualties.

'I worked on a child here today with a smashed face and broken leg,' he wrote to Adonia. 'She is the only survivor of a family of nine—four younger, four older, all killed last night. Splendid military targets . . . Yesterday I had four shot-down Nazi pilots and they were a lousy lot. Two of them died and the other two, with minor injuries, I sent to a hospital in the East End where they can see what they are doing.'

But he still had time for other things in this period, and so far as he was concerned the fight had not yet begun. He sent Adonia a diary of his days in a letter dated September 8, 1940, and it reads:

'Monday, Sept. 2. Went up to town with Maisie [the maid who, for a time, worked for him both in London and East Grinstead]. No practice. Wrote all day on RAF reports. Visited two hospitals. Dinner at home alone.

'Tuesday. Worked at 149 [Harley Street] in am. Went down to

* Nicknames for McIndoe varied, but usually he was known as Archie to his colleagues and friends (though some called him Mac), the Boss to his staff, and the Maestro to his service patients.

E. G. pm spending 1½ hours in air raid shelter at Reigate on the way. Croydon is now closed. Spent pm at hospital, and the night here [his furnished cottage] for the first time and I can tell you I slept with a good deal greater feeling of security with the excellent air raid shelter so handy.

'Wednesday. Breakfast in bed as usual. Operated during the morning. Giles came down and did a job, then we left at 2 pm for Whitehall where we attended a presentation of an American Dental Ambulance from the US dental profession to the Maxillo Facial Unit. I took Maisie up with me. I left her at the flat but when I returned at 5.30 she was gone leaving a note to say that she was too scared to stay any longer and had gone home (to E. G.). There was nothing really to worry about though of course there had been a fair amount of racket (from anti-aircraft guns and bombs).

'Thursday. At 149. No practice. Wrote reports.

'Friday. I set to work and cleaned the flat myself in the absence of Maisie. She was a useful girl but, my God, she had the same bad habits as the rest of them. E. G. cupboards a mess, icebox like a sink and food going bad in every corner. With my customary zeal I went through the kitchen like a tornado and after four hours had everything bright and shiny like a new pin. The flat on the whole is in very good order and all is well except for the parts she thought I didn't see. That too is now all right. Friday night. Dinner at the Bolivar.

'Saturday. I came down here and went to see Mrs West [Maisie's mother]. The trouble with Maisie was under three heads: (*a*) The 17/6 I pay her still rankled. She thinks she ought to get 22/6. (*b*) Mother (and the neighbours) think that although I am a gentleman (!!!) it is not right for Maisie to be running up and down with me. They have told everyone I keep a housekeeper (I nearly died at this one but managed to keep a straight face). (*c*) She finds my trips up and down too trying for her nerves. So there you are. It will be best to retain Maisie here and get someone in London to vet the flat. Blast these women!!

'Last night was the big air raid on London docks and East End. The devils did plenty of damage and we had them going over all night but nothing happened here. No doubt there will be an influx of casualties today and tomorrow so I might have to stay down here for a few days and cope with the trouble. That is the sum total of my week's activities and you can see that there is nothing exciting in it.'

It was the last letter he was to write in that vein. A few days later, he closed up the flat in London and brought his beloved Rolls down to East Grinstead for safety, but not of course for use. By the end of September he was writing that he was 'immersed in work,' adding: 'Yesterday I caught up with hospital arrears—now 150 cases in the wards and more to come—and then in the evening prepared a big presentation for tomorrow at the Royal Society of Medicine on the depressing subject of burns. Today I was in London and attended a meeting of the War Wound Committee on the same depressing subject. These things take up the most appalling amount of time and as it is necessary to leave London now by four o'clock in order to get down here by six (blackout time) there does not seem to be much time to do anything.'

He resolved to cut his time in London to a minimum and concentrate on East Grinstead. On September 27, he wrote:

'As you know, the blitzkrieg has got more and more intense and I was so busy coping with the casualties that I have scarcely been in bed and like everyone else did not get my clothes off.'

The great air battles which he and John Hunter had been watching over East Grinstead had been taking their toll of RAF pilots as well as Germans. In scores of cases the pilot who got shot down also got himself badly burned on his way out of his plane or when he crashed on the ground. He took some time to reach East Grinstead. First he was taken to a dressing station for first-aid treatment, and then to a general hospital in London, East Anglia or Scotland for the attention that would keep him alive.

As Giles had done during the first world war, Archie had made arrangements with the authorities to have all burns cases sent through to him at East Grinstead. But they took time in coming. Several times a month, he would take out his car and go on a tour of his 'burn units', looking at patients and deciding when they were fit enough to come to him.

Now the flow began. And Archie was horrified when he saw the condition of the patients with whom he would have to deal. It was not so much what the Germans or even the flames from their planes had done to them, but how they had been treated once they reached the ground.

He began the first of his bitter battles with authority. In his minute-book he called this one 'Down with Tannic Acid!'

The case of Geoffrey Page, since it was typical, will perhaps serve to show why Archie McIndoe became so blisteringly angry—and 'blisteringly' is a not inappropriate word—with the medical authorities during this period of the war.

Page was a Pilot Officer* flying a Hurricane over the Thames Estuary and the Channel during the heydays of the Battle of Britain. His plane was hit by a Messerschmidt 109 during a dog-fight, and he baled out into the Channel, but before he could get free of the cockpit a petrol tank blazed and engulfed him in flame. He had taken off his goggles, the better to see the enemy planes, and his gloves, to give him closer control of his plane and its guns. On the way down to the sea he was conscious of one thing only, the smell of burned flesh. By the time he had struggled clear of his parachute shrouds in the water and watched skin and torn flesh floating away from him as he did so, he slowly realized that he was smelling himself.

A motor-boat picked him up and carried him to the shore and he was given first-aid at the dressing station in Margate. He was by this time in considerable pain and the doctor and nurses followed the routine laid down for such cases. They coated his raw and blackened face, his back and his dreadfully burned hands with thick layers of tannic acid. This was intended to coagulate the blood oozing from the raw flesh and thus provide a protective covering which would ease the pain and prevent him from dying from shock.

In his armadillo encasement—for tannic acid gradually hardens on the skin until it forms a thick and unyielding hide—he was driven to the Royal Masonic Hospital in London and there, most of the time under morphia, he remained for some weeks. His first conscious memory is of a nurse and a pretty VAD bending over him as they removed his dressings.

The VAD was staring down at him as if hypnotized. 'Following

* He lived to fight again and became a Wing Commander.

her stare,' he recalls, 'I looked down with watery eyes at my arms. From the elbows to the wrists the bare forearms were one seething mass of pus-filled boils. Then for the first time I noticed my hands themselves: from the wrist joints to the finger-tips they were blacker than any Negro's hands, but smaller in size than I ever remember them to be. I shared the VAD's horror until the sister said: "That black's stuff's only tannic acid. It's not the colour of your skin." '

He elbowed himself out of bed a few days later, after having been refused a mirror by the nurse, tottered over to a mirror on the wall, squeezed the pus and water out of his injured eyes, and looked at himself. His face had swollen to three times its normal size and it too was black.

It was a few days later that Archie McIndoe came to see him.

'The visitor,' Page recalls, 'had dark hair parted in the middle and flat to the head, horn-rimmed spectacles, broad shoulders and a friendly, mischievous grin. His whole appearance was not unlike that of Harold Lloyd, the film comedian. Grasping a leather briefcase firmly inside a hand that would have done credit to a professional boxer, he advanced round to the left hand side of my bed and seated himself on an upright chair. Extracting a sheet of paper and pencil, he viewed me from over the top of his glasses. The words came out crisply.

' "Hurricane or Spitfire?"

' "Hurricane."

' "Header-tank?"

'I laughed. "Yes. The wing tanks in my machine were self-sealing but some bright type forgot to treat the tank in front of the pilot."

'His eyes twinkled. "Just can't trust anyone, can you?"

'He didn't stay long and during his short visit the conversation was light-hearted and dealt with seemingly inconsequential details; was I wearing goggles and gloves, how long had I been in the water, and how soon afterwards was the tannic acid treatment given? The visitor rose and took a cheery farewell of me. He waved a large ham-fisted hand. "Goodbye, young fellow, see you again." Little did I realize how often this was to be.'

In fact, Archie McIndoe left seething with rage. He had seen one more example of the damage that tannic acid could do to a man badly burned about the hands and face. He knew exactly what was going to happen to Geoffrey Page's hands, and the knowledge of the torture which awaited this nineteen year-old boy in the days to come was hard to bear.

Under his instructions, the Polish Wing Commander in charge of the burns unit henceforth spent each day picking away the armour plating which the acid had formed on Page's hands, covering the raw places with saline dressings. But it was too late.

'Day by day my strength increased,' Page said, 'and with it the condition of my hands deteriorated. Fraction by fraction the tendons contracted, bending the fingers downwards until finally the tips were in contact with the palms. Added to this, the delicate skin toughened by degrees until it had the texture of rhinoceros hide, at the same time webbing my fingers together until they were indistinguishable as separate units. The Polish surgeon watched impotently as the contractions continued. Then one morning he said: "If your hands continue to form this thick scar tissue I'm afraid it will mean a series of skin-grafting operations. Are you prepared to try and prevent this?"

' "What's the alternative?"

' "We may be able to keep the skin soft by the use of hot molten baths, followed by massage."

'The hot wax bath treatment commenced the same afternoon.'

The baths were a nightmare and the electric treatment was worse. And still the fingers curled inwards. It went on until the Polish surgeon confessed that it was no use.

'Your hands will have to be grafted,' he said, 'I will arrange for you to be sent to East Grinstead. To see Mr McIndoe.'

In the meantime, Archie McIndoe was writing in his minute-book. 'God damn and blast this tannic acid. It shouldn't be used. We've got to stop them using it.'

Already he had in the wards at East Grinstead a Flying Officer named Richard Hillary who had been shot down on the same day at almost the same place as Geoffrey Page, and his face and hands had been covered with hideous, skin-tightening acid. There too was Squadron Leader Tom Gleave, his face black with it, his eyelids withering away with it, his left leg—peeled of skin from thigh to ankle after his 'row', as he called it, with the Germans—smeared and caked. And there were plenty of others.

Giles had come down to East Grinstead for a visit and stayed the night with Archie at Millfield Cottage, and Archie did not lose the opportunity of inveighing against the use of coagulating fluids on airmen's injuries.

'You'll never stop it,' said Giles. 'It's laid down as standard medical procedure. Cut the chap's clothes off and then cover him with tannic. They've got the stuff in every home, dressing station and hospital in the land, and they'll use it. Stops the chap from whimpering. Makes him think something's being done. Regulations, Archie. Don't tell me you're trying to change regulations?'

Archie said: 'That's just what I am going to do. I'm writing a paper. I want your backing.'

The older man looked at him with a twinkle in his eye and then said:

'What d'you want me to do?'

'Spread the word among all your pals,' he said. 'Tell 'em we're on the warpath. And then call a meeting of the Royal Society of Medicine.'

Giles said: 'If you'll do the big spiel, I'm with you.'

Archie said, 'If you'll support me, I'll talk my head off.'

On November 11, 1940, Archie wrote to Adonia:

'Somehow, between all this, I have to produce a paper on burns for the Royal Society for immediate publication. This follows the show on Wednesday which happened to be the biggest meeting ever held in the RSM on any subject. We won the day hands down and have brought in far-reaching changes in the treatment of burn casualties.'

But it was not won as easily as that. Before the meeting he bombarded the Air Ministry with letters damning tannic acid and other coagulants on the faces and hands of burned airmen. He was very practical about it.

'Eighty per cent of RAF burns involve the hands to a greater or lesser degree,' he wrote. 'This is due to the peculiar risks which the airman's calling involves, and to his regrettable but understandable failure to wear gloves . . . It is no exaggeration to say that the local treatment of burns in the RAF is dominated by the problem of the burned hand. Therefore any burn occurring on the hands of a man whose technical ability and training make his value to the country of supreme importance must be regarded seriously and treated with the utmost care. Together with the burn of the face in the helmet area, the Airman's Burn, it is a burn which no other can equal as a therapeutic problem or cause of subsequent disability. *In the treatment of it, there must be total prohibition of coagulation of the hands and face.*'

The medical sections at the Air Ministry at first treated his strictures coolly and obviously settled down to a long correspondence. But he was not having that. He picked up the telephone. When he could not get any sense out of Air Commodores, he started bombarding the Air Vice Marshals. For the first time he began to realize how wise he had been in keeping out of uniform. He did not have to go through channels. He could rant and bully to his heart's content. They could only sack him.

It says much for his determination—a determination reinforced every time a new casualty arrived at East Grinstead—that he got his way, and it says much for the enlightenment of the Air Ministry that they let him have it. The meeting of the Royal Society of Medicine heard him give a quietly impassioned and reasoned paper well supported with examples, and voted at the end of it—against a powerful minority of diehards—to have him expand his theories into a document to be circulated to all emergency medical branches throughout the country.

The RAF medical chiefs, on the other hand, listened and were converted. They sent out an order banning tannic acid on third degree burns of the hand and face immediately. It was several months before the other branches of the service got around to it.

In the meantime, Archie went back to Ward Three to work on the burned airmen to whom the damage had already been done. He found problems there in addition to those caused by tannic, subtler problems, more difficult problems because they were problems of morale.

For the moment he did not quite know how to deal with them, and he spent a lot of his time alone, brooding about them.

'How much I am missing you all,' he wrote to Adonia about this time. 'It is worst of all at nights when I am alone, as I have been for the last fifteen months wondering how you are and living on the memories of past years. It is strange how one can live under these depressing circumstances, with only the hope of future reunion to keep one going. Life has altered radically and completely and I think we shall find more satisfaction and peace of mind than we knew before when all this is over. My outlet is a complete immersion in my work which may possibly be its own reward.'

He added: 'Actually, the hospital is making something of a noise for itself, though again probably more than it deserves. As a relaxation I find that the piano which is always open and to hand gives me most pleasure. I have improved my technique considerably and there are fewer of the discords which used to gripe your soul.'

Meanwhile, at East Grinstead, the Welfare Committee of the Queen Victoria Hospital was growing restive. Strange rumours were beginning to float around. A nurse complained that a patient had abused her in Ward Three and asked to be removed. There were stories of drunken parties and wild goings-on. The Committee decided to call a meeting to discuss it, and requested the urgent attendance of Mr A. H. McIndoe.

CHAPTER FIVE

WARD THREE

ACCORDING TO ITS LIGHTS, the Welfare Committee certainly had a point. Strange and disturbing things were happening to the Queen Victoria Hospital, and they were neither young enough nor mentally pliable enough to accept them easily. The hospital had been built to care for the sick and the accident cases of a small, quiet, solid English country town, and suddenly, it seemed to them, it had been invaded by young madmen. Routines had been upset. The stiff, formal relationships between doctors, nurses and staff had gone by the board. Pretty VAD auxiliaries swarmed about the wards, chatting and flirting with the men. When committee members came to pay their duty visits to the wards they expected to be greeted by the quiet, long-suffering smiles of patients bravely bearing their cross and instead were often hailed with ribald comments from mouths which smelt distinctly of alcohol. It was the idea that drink was actually consumed in the wards which shocked them most, and they were determined to put a stop to it.

It so happened that the meeting of the Welfare Committee, which took place some time in November 1940, came at a time when Archie McIndoe was harassed, overworked and worried. It is not considered to be a good thing for a doctor to be too deeply troubled by the sufferings of his patients, and in his sixteen years of surgery he had seen enough tragedy and pain to have built a coral reef around himself to protect him from the onrush of sympathy and concern which otherwise might have been too much to bear. But though few of his colleagues suspected it, Archie was at this period aware of a breach in his defences. He had always considered himself to be a tough professional technician for whom surgery was 'just a good plumbing job', and the humanities of the case had rarely bothered him until now. One of his staff, when trying in later years to analyse the secret of his success said:

'I think one of the reasons was his complete lack of sympathy. He was, I think, a completely unsympathetic man. I once asked him what I should do about my wife, who had been concussed in a motor accident, and he said: "Get her to a good doctor," and though we had worked closely for years, he never even asked how it happened or expressed any sorrow. It was this lack of feeling, I believe, which made him such a success with the RAF boys. He could look at their terrible injuries quite dispassionately, with no pity and no feeling; and it helped them because it stopped them from feeling sorry for themselves and gave them confidence in his judgment, because they knew he wouldn't bother to encourage them just to cheer them up. They were just cases to him.'

This seems to me to be a complete misreading of the man. Into his care from this time onwards came an inflow of young men who may well be described as the flower of the youth of England. RAF standards, at least for the first half of the war, were high indeed so far as pilots and aircrew were concerned. They needed to be superbly healthy in body and quick and agile of brain. Few of them were much more than twenty years of age and they were quick with life and exuberant in spirits. But in one minute's ordeal by inferno and flame, they had been destroyed, their faces burned away, their hands frizzled, their bodies scorched.

Archie McIndoe wrote a note about them which had this to say of his charges:

'The impact of disfiguring injuries upon the young adult mentality is usually severe. The majority have been strong and healthy, and have given no consideration to illness or injury, nor to its possible future effects. They are usually unprepared mentally for the blow, so that for a period they may be psychically lost, depressed, morose, pessimistic, and thoroughly out of tune with their surroundings. It is difficult to gain their confidence or to convince them that they can be of use to the world. They believe that their former social status and facility of performance are at an end, that they are no longer marriageable, and must remain objects for well-meant but misguided pity.'

This was part of a memorandum for officialdom, but to a man

who was soon to be one of his closest friends, Edward Blacksell, he put it more bluntly this way:

'Imagine how they feel, Blackie. On Friday night they are dancing in a nightclub with a beautiful girl and by Saturday afternoon they are a burned cinder. A fighter pilot can't help being vain because the girls all swarm round him like a honeypot. He can take his pick. Think what it must be like for that young man to go back into the same circle with his face burned to bits. One minute has changed him from a Don Juan into an object of pity—and it's too much to bear.'

He found himself increasingly concerned not only with the surgical side of his work but in the rehabilitation of his cases. His manner was crisp with his patients and his attitude was always cheerful and optimistic, but beneath the surface he was wrestling with new ideas for therapy and, at first in a fumbling way, he was trying to do something about them. He realized that Ward Three was a problem ward, but they were problems for which he had a steadily increasing sympathy.

On one thing he was determined. No outside influence was going to be allowed to make his problem children unhappier than they need be. And so, at the meeting of the Welfare Committee, he was in no mood to take criticism and he sat through the complaints of these good but safe and solid dowagers with scarcely concealed impatience. They complained of the 'free and easy' atmosphere, they complained of the men's language, they complained most of all about drink. When they were through, he rose.

'I have several things to say, some of which you are not going to like,' he said. 'The war has been going on for over a year now, yet you as a group obviously wish things to continue as they did in peacetime. You had better realize this. The Queen Victoria Hospital no longer simply serves the local community. Primarily this hospital is to be used for the physical and mental rebuilding of airmen injured in the course of their duty. I had hoped for some time that you would realize that from now on this hospital will become less and less a civilian organization as the Services send in their casualties. You have disappointed me.'

His jaw jutted at them. 'Whether you like it or not, from now on this hospital will cater for the injured airman and his particular problems. Some of you object to pilots and aircrew having alcohol in their wards. Normally I might perhaps agree with you, but in this matter you overlook two points. Firstly, these men are not sick or badly injured. Their bodies may be broken temporarily but their youthful spirits are still with them. Secondly, normal hospital discipline is all very well for a patient who is admitted for a few days or a few weeks, but it has to be relaxed when a man is to be treated for several years. Half my battle is to see that their morale does not suffer through boredom.'

There was a silence after he was finished, although Archie confessed afterwards that he could 'hear their prejudices churning over', and then the elderly lady whose objections had been most vehement rose to her feet.

'I expect we deserved that rebuke,' she said. 'Perhaps we did not think it out too well. But if only Mr McIndoe would take us into his confidence about what he plans to do, it may be in our power to help rather than hinder.'

'Thank you,' said Archie. 'Now may I suggest that the next time you go visiting in the wards, forget that these are cases. Think of these boys as human beings—think how you would treat them if they were your own sons—and remember that you're not doing them a favour by visiting them. They're doing a favour by speaking to you.'

The chairs began to scrape as the chastened committee got up to go, but he stopped them with a gesture of his hand.

'There is just one more point. You will probably have noticed that I am allowing certain of my patients who are fit to move around to go into East Grinstead. Some of them are not very pretty to look at. A man with a flap hanging down from his face may look like a monster. A man who has lost his nose and is in process of getting a new one may not exactly resemble Clark Gable—though I seem to recall that he once looked like a pterodactyl until a plastic surgeon altered the shape of his ears. I want you ladies to spread the word around the town that these men must not be made to feel uncomfortable. I don't want people going around and feeling sorry for them. I don't want sympathy. I want everyone—shopkeepers, publicans, customers at the four-ale bar—to be normal with them and casual and not gape at them as if they've come out of a freak museum.'

He paused. And then: 'This is where you ladies can use your

Among the first patients at East Grinstead were Geoffrey Page—a fighter pilot, like so many others (*above*) —and Richard Hillary (*right*)

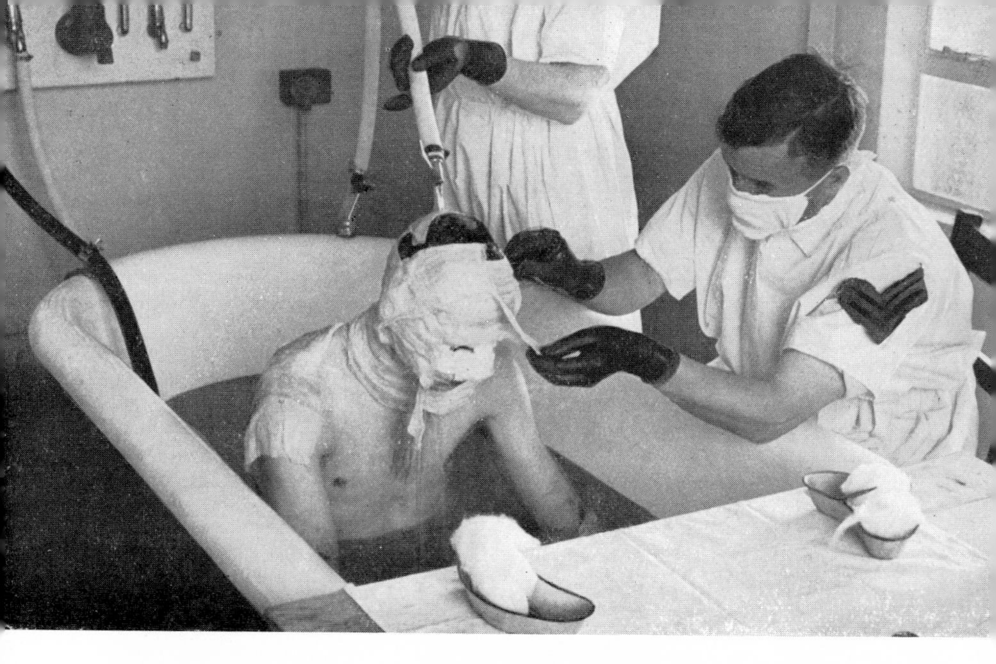

In the famous Saline Bath at East Grinstead dressings were removed under a stream of saline (*above*). Then, all dressings removed (*below*), pus and sloughs were washed away with cotton-wool swabs and eyes, ears, nose and mouth were cleansed

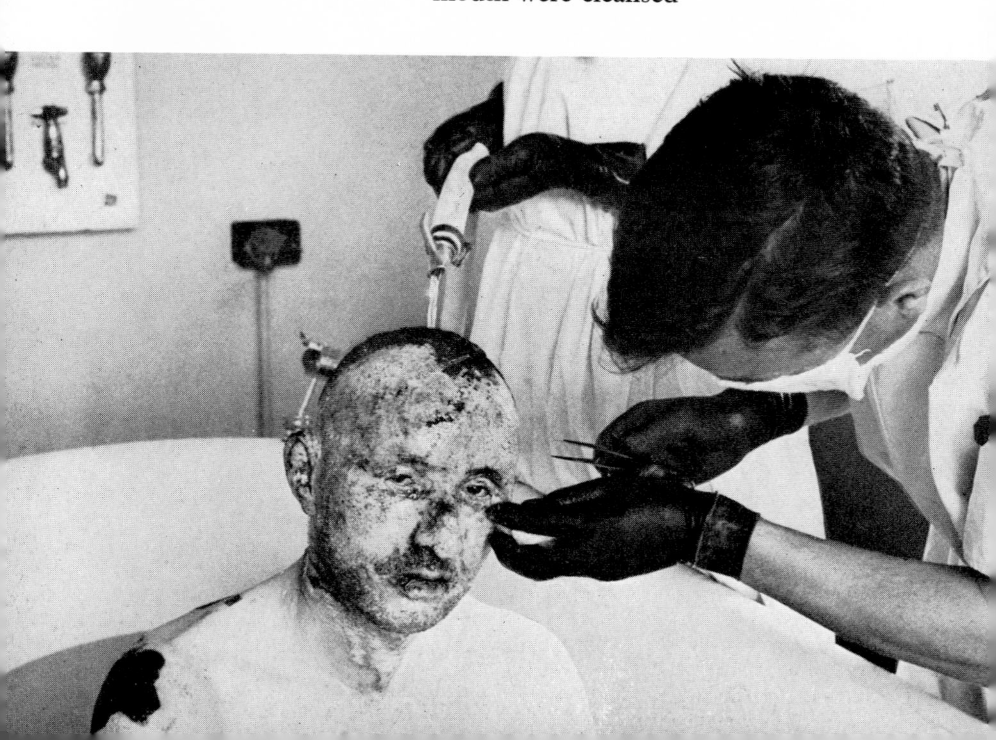

influence. Tell everyone you know that these are normal young men who happen to be in temporary difficulty. Buy them drinks. Invite them into your homes. And please, for God's sake, don't pity them' He added, half under his breath: 'I'm sure, when they discover what sort of lads they are under those flaps, that your daughters certainly won't!'

In truth, Ward Three was a fearsome place, and sometimes more for the visitor than for the inmate. Someone bitterly suggested that a notice should be put up outside the door saying: 'Beware of the wounded animals'. It was a brave nurse who survived the first few days or nights of duty in this ward, because the men in the beds could make life hell for her.

Mary Rea (who is now a theatre sister at East Grinstead) remembers the first night she went on duty in Ward Three. She had come down from a training course at Bart's in London and she was stiff with the starch of nursing protocol. Her predecessor had asked to be replaced because she could not stand the rawness and rowdiness of the ward, but Mary Rea was sure that she could cope. She was determined that there would be no nonsense with her.

As she made her rounds, the fact that she was Irish gradually impressed itself upon the men in the beds.

'God almighty,' she heard someone saying, 'another worm's crawled here out of the Old Sod.'

From the end of the ward there came sounds of argument, and then a voice said:

'You stupid bastard, Richard.' And then, as she drew nearer: 'Ooops, sorry, nurse.'

The shape in the bed beside the voice said sarcastically:

'Don't worry about nurse. They're used to bastards in Ireland.'

An hour later, there was a disturbance at the entrance to the hut and presently two figures staggered through. One wore air force uniform, the other the tartan trews of a Scottish regiment. The two figures staggered about in the darkness, obviously looking for the toilet in a cubicle near the door. But the officer in the trews had missed his way. He blundered through the green curtain leading to the saline bath unit, tripped and sat down in a bucket, and from that moment on a stream of fluent curses in an unmistakable Irish accent filled the ward.

It was the voice of Lieutenant Patrick O'Connor of the Highland Light Infantry. He was a patient in Ward Three for the repair of a jaw which he had smashed in the blackout in Glasgow; but it was not his jaw he was worrying about at the moment. He had sat in a bucket of cleaning lysol. Mary Rea introduced herself to him by divesting him of his trews, turning him on his stomach, and treating him for a first degree burn on his buttock. He was very drunk. His trews were never the same again; nor, in a way, was Mary Rea. In one night she had had the starch knocked out of her.

In the next few days she learned what the staff had to cope with, and it was no place for a delicate ear or a delicate stomach. In every bed lay a shape which had once been a young man: some with bandaged eyes, some with grafts hanging down from their cheeks, some curled up into queer shapes to keep long tubular flaps attached to their faces and chests. There was one with a nose hanging down in front of his ravaged face like an elephant's trunk, another staring through watering, lidless eyes. There were the jawless and the noseless and the ones with holes in their heads through which the bones obtruded. The ward smelt of a queer mixture of scent from the flowers on every table, the odour of burned flesh, and the tang of salt water.

By day the radio jangled all the time. But above it and through came the sound of voices, shouting, laughing, arguing; there was never any silence. For a nurse to see such sights is no great ordeal if she is trained for her job; but what was upsetting was the tremendous vitality, the seething tumult of these men. They may have been wounded but they were certainly not sick, and they made Ward Three throb with life. It looked like Walpurgis Night. When you came through the door, it was as if you were entering a ballroom on Hallowe'en with all the young guests decked in the most fantastic masks they could find.

Archie McIndoe had insisted from the start that he needed special nurses for these special men, and no sister stayed for long in his wards unless she was cheerful and human as well as efficient. He gathered the staff together and lectured them not only on his surgical techniques but also on their attitude and demeanour.

'Of no less importance than the standard of physical comfort here,' he told them, 'is the atmosphere which pervades the wards. I want flowers on every table, and I want them changed every day.

I am having these regulation hospital beds thrown out and replaced with the box-spring jobs these boys would get if they stayed the night at the Regent Palace. I want cheerful music and, above all, I want a cheerful staff. The qualities I am looking for must radiate from you—by your enthusiasm for your work, by your efficiency, by your anxiety for the patients' welfare above all else, and by your devotion to duty tempered by optimism, tact, understanding and good humour.'

Gradually, and not without agony of spirit in the case of some, they learned to unstarch themselves. It would not be true to say that things always went smoothly. Matron Hall clashed with Archie on several occasions, and she could be formidably strict with the men when she felt that her discipline was being threatened —as Richard Hillary found to his cost.

But then Hillary, despite his great heroism, and for all the courage he displayed while his grotesquely mutilated face and hands were being mended, was far from being an amenable patient. His experiences had embittered him and he quenched the mental and physical pain by taunting the nurses and his fellow patients with a rapier-like sarcasm that knew just where to penetrate. He was not greatly loved by anyone.

Geoffrey Page, shot down in the same battle, burned in the same way, was one of the few who perhaps understood the way he was feeling, but even his first encounter with Hillary was not calculated to induce affection.

'Standing at the foot of my bed,' he recalls, 'was one of the queerest apparitions I have ever seen. The tall figure was clad in a long loose-fitting dressing-gown that trailed to the floor. The head was thrown right back so that the owner appeared to be looking along the line of his nose. Where normally two eyes would be were two large bloody red circles of raw skin. Horizontal slits showed that behind still lay the eyes. A pair of hands wrapped in large lint covers lay folded across his chest. Cigarette smoke curled up from the long holder clenched in the ghoul's teeth. There was evidently a voice behind the mask and the tone was condescending. "Ah, another bloody cripple!" he said. "Welcome to the home of the aged and infirm." He laughed and walked out of the ward. Roy Lane, in the bed next to mine, said: "Don't let him get you down. He's a conceited young man with a sharp tongue and a large inferiority complex. For years he's been told by his mother what a wonderful boy he is, but in the Service he's had his backside kicked and he's a bit mixed up." '

Hillary's clash with Sister Hall (not to be confused with Matron Hall, her sister) came shortly after new eyelids had been grafted on him. This meant five days bandaged and in bed, fed by the nurses.

'But we could (thank God),' he wrote in *The Last Enemy*, 'get up and walk to the lavatory, escorted by a nurse. Were there no nurses about, the others would sing out instructions to the needy one until he arrived safely at his destination. Being unable to see had, I discovered, some distinct disadvantages. As I could not read, I talked; and as everyone knows, there are few more pleasant pastimes when one is indisposed than grousing and swearing. After a few unfortunate incidents I always asked Tony [another burned fighter pilot, Tony Tollemach] if any of the nurses were about before opening my mouth, but Tony was unreliable, getting a hideous pleasure out of watching the consequences.'

The third day of his confinement, a nurse in the ward dropped a bed-pan.

Hillary rose in his bed. 'Jesus Christ,' he said, 'what a hospital! It stinks like a sewer, it's about as quiet as a zoo, and instead of nurses we've got a bunch of moronic Irish amazons!'

Unfortunately for him, Sister Hall was standing beside his bed.

'Not another dressing do you get until you apologize,' she said. He had a clear picture in his mind of the grey-haired Miss Hall, her lips tight and her eyes unsmiling, and he opened his mouth to say the appropriate words. Instead, he started to roar with laughter.

When he had finished, there was a long silence, and then the sound of shuffling. He felt his bed beginning to move. He was being banished from the ward. He hopped out of bed and refused to budge. At which a doctor was summoned. Despite Hillary's pleas, Sister Hall was upheld and he was wheeled into exile.

'You bloody bitch!' he said as she slammed the door on him. But he learned to be more tractable after that.

In the alcove near the entrance to Ward Three lay Squadron

Leader (later Group Captain) Tom Gleave, probably the only patient who never gave his nurses or doctors any trouble. In a way he could be called the Father of Ward Three because he was at least ten years older than his bedmates.

(It should be mentioned here that, in other hospitals, an officer of his rank would probably have had his own private room. But one of Archie McIndoe's innovations had been to abolish rank. At first he had lumped his squadron leaders and airgunners and flight-sergeants together for reasons of space, but he continued it for reasons of therapy. In their private cubicles the officers were inclined to fret, and their progress was slower. Mixed in with the others, they almost immediately improved.*)

Tom Gleave had been shot down over the Thames Estuary and was badly roasted in his burning plane before he was able to free himself from the cockpit and parachute to the ground.

When he picked himself up, he found that his slacks had disappeared except for portions that had been covered by the parachute harness. 'The skin on my right leg, from the top of the thigh to just above the ankle,' he remembers, 'had lifted and draped my leg like outsize plus-fours. My left leg was in a similar condition except that the left thigh was only scorched, thanks to the flames having been directed to my right side. Above each ankle I had a bracelet of unburnt skin: my socks, which were always wrinkled, had refused to burn properly and must have just smouldered. That my slacks should have burned so easily is not surprising; oil mist percolates one's clothing, and I probably had enough on my person to lubricate a battleship. My service gloves were almost burnt off, and the skin from my wrists and hands hung down like paper bags. The under side of my right arm and elbow were burnt and so was my face and neck. I could see all right, although it felt like looking through slits in a mass of swollen skin, and I came to the conclusion that the services of a doctor were necessary.'

For the next few weeks he lived in a moiling torment, encased in dry tannic acid, in dreadful pain because his burns had turned septic. His greatest torture came on the journey to East Grinstead,

* Though one distinguished naval captain with a Victoria Cross never did get used to being called 'Sailor!' by the erks on either side of him and subsequently departed from the hospital damning the place for its 'terrible mateyness and outright indiscipline'.

because—as, for some reason, they always did—the orderlies had dressed him in his uniform for the journey, and the painful rubbing of the cloth on his exposed and suppurating flesh was exquisite.

This suffering, twitching mass of blackened flesh was gently carried into Ward Three. That evening, with his three-day old dressings still clinging to him—for attempts to tear them off at the other hospital had already done him considerable damage—he was immersed in the saline bath. For the first time for weeks he experienced relief from pain and it is one of the ecstatic memories of his life. While he lay there the bath-unit staff examined his burns and made notes about them. He saw the hated bandages float free. He lay there, in blissful contentment, for half an hour, and even managed to laugh when one of the RAF bath-boys said: 'It's a good job you kept your hand on it when it happened, Squadron Leader. Your marital prospects are perfect.'

His burns were dressed with Archie's own invention, a network of large mesh soaked in Vaseline and antiseptics to prevent it from adhering to the flesh, and he was put back to bed. And every two hours during the night a nurse would come, pull back the bedclothes, and water his poor parched flesh with a rain of salt water from a watering-can with a rose on the end. Wonderful, wonderful!

'One day the Maestro,' as he called Archie at the time, 'toured the ward and I met him for the first time. He stood over me looking at me through those horn-rimmed spectacles with a clear candid gaze I have never seen in the eyes of any other man. It gave one immediate strength. You had an instinctive feeling that this man was not going to fool you. He weighed up my face, and then said that the first facial grafts I needed were eyelids, top and bottom. My burns were healing rapidly. I could see new skin every time I was put in the bath—or "the Spa" as we named it. But the Maestro thought the process could be speeded up. "We will pinch-graft the two large patches on your leg," he said, "and give you two top eyelids first. Your eyes will be covered for a week." He paused and his eyes twinkled. "You won't like it, but it's worth it." '

Gleave added: 'It was just the way he said it. I believed it. I felt like a shipwrecked man who has been floating around in the sea for hours when a lifebelt suddenly comes by.'

Geoffrey Page had the same experience. 'Archie bent over my crippled hands, turning them over slowly to examine the damage,' he recalls. 'Without raising his head he looked over his glasses. "Long job, I'm afraid." I asked him whether he would have to operate. This time the head went back and his dark eyes looked firmly into mine. "Yes," he said, "many times, I'm afraid. But you'll be all right in the end." Somehow I believed him.'

Great pain and prolonged suffering do not necessarily bring out the best even in the young, and the inmates of Ward Three were not always improved in their minds or their manners by the ordeals which they were forced to undergo. In the circumstances, however, it is amazing how bravely they reacted even when the experiences through which they went were more than they could bear.

In one of the beds was a faceless young man named Paul Hart. He had set fire to a training plane and his features from chin to hair had been almost literally burned away. There was no question of a repair job with Hart. Archie McIndoe examined him and told him frankly that it would mean starting all over again: new bone for his chin, new skin and flesh for his cheeks, a flap from his shaved head pulled down and filled with cartilage to form a new nose. It would be a long job—two to three years—and it would be far from painless.

Archie McIndoe told him, after one operation, that it would not be unseemly if he allowed himself the odd groan when the pain was particularly sharp. The blue eyes beneath the new lids peered back with a cynical glint in them.

'That would never do,' Hart said. 'You've got to keep a stiff upper lip in this ward even if you haven't got one.'

He took care never to show his weariness or impatience with the long road back, and his courage was the more admirable because, unlike many of the others in the ward, he could not even comfort himself by the thought that at least he had been shot down in action.

'I'll have to live the rest of my life with half my stomach on my face,' he said. 'And when people say: "Look what the Huns did to that poor wounded hero," I'll have to tell them that it wasn't a Hun but a bloody fool Pilot Prune in a training crate.'

The humour was vulgar, often obscene, and sometimes unkind

in Ward Three. There was a tendency for the others to laugh when a graft went wrong or a nose turned out to be the wrong shape. A young Jewish pork butcher who had been injured in the blitz brought out all the latent anti-Semitism in some of the Service patients and he was goaded about everything from his lack of foreskin to his lack of uniform. It was not all comradely sympathy and brothers in distress.

'I'd punch you in the nose,' said Paul Hart to a squadron leader who taunted him, 'if I didn't think it was going to fall off anyway.'

'And I'd clout you back,' the squadron leader retorted, 'if you had a face to hit and I had a hand to hit you with.'

It was the wild and woolly Irishman from the Scots regiment, Lieutenant Patrick O'Connor (he who had sat in the bucket of lysol), who could, however, usually be relied upon to clear the air when things were not going smoothly. O'Connor, as one of his comrades remarked, was pleasantly round the bend and the abnormal was to him normal. As a result of his collision with a truck, his lower jaw was broken and his right antrum fractured. The dental unit had clamped his lower jaw to the upper with a brace; Archie McIndoe had reset the fractured antrum but, in order to keep his broken cheekbone in position, had wrapped a plaster cast around O'Connor's head into which he inserted a three-inch bar. It protruded horizontally, like a weird metal moustache above the damaged areas, with fine platinum wires tied to it and stretched down into holes in the antrum.

In this weird facial cage, topped by a glengarry, with a uniform underneath of khaki jacket, tartan trews and white spats, he looked like a fearsome Scottish headhunter, but he never allowed his trapped jaw to curb his voice or his drinking capacity, and he could always be relied upon to render the bawdiest versions of 'The Ball at Kirriemuir' when one of his comrades, nursing a pain in the watches of the night, seemed in need of distracting entertainment.

The patients were allowed out into the town so long as they could walk, and Patrick O'Connor was one of the favourite customers of the nearby Whitehall Restaurant where the landlord and the clients seemed never to notice whether a man had a face on him or not.

On the night before his sixth operation, even O'Connor's exuberant spirits seemed in need of a little encouragement, and he disappeared down to the Whitehall as soon as it was open. When he came back he was so drunk that he staggered to his bed and lay there all night, and not even two VADs could get him out of his clothes. The following morning he was wheeled into the theatre for surgery. But it was not to be. At the first incision of Archie McIndoe's scalpel a jet of blood burst forth under terrific pressure.

'By God,' said Archie, 'the bugger's drunk!'

He sent him back to the ward for a stomach wash and a pause until his blood pressure returned to normal.

That day Lieutenant O'Connor lost his beloved trews for a second time. Archie confiscated them and locked them in his office until the operation was over.

It was hard, however, to be cheerful when you were having your burned and twisted hands grafted, for the series of operations which this injury necessitated left a legacy of pain which was agonizing in the extreme. Richard Hillary, who had already gone through the experience and would never forget it, looked down through the great red horse-blinkers which McIndoe had given him (they would be trimmed down later into more human-looking eyelids) at Geoffrey Page writhing after his first operation and said cynically:

'Bloody fool. You should have worn gloves.'

It was a gibe directed at himself as well as Page, for he had not worn gloves either.

Archie's chief assistant, Percy Jayes, a remarkably capable and gentle man, was making a particular study of the hands about this time and he used to carry a skeleton of one in his pocket, telling the myriad fine bones like beads as he made his rounds. When he pulled them out of his pocket, it was rather like looking at the trunk and branches of a leafless tree.

'It was as if many nails were being hammered inexpertly into the fingers,' Geoffrey Page remembers of the aftermath of his first operation. 'Then pincers would wrench the nails out, after which the hammering would start again.'

He could not prevent himself from moaning and rolling his head with pain, and only repeated injections of morphia gave him respite. At the end of the fifth day—*or was it the fifth year?* Page asked himself—Archie McIndoe came to see him, and though his greeting was as usual cheerful his eyes were perturbed.

'How goes it?' he asked, and then noticed that his patient was in tears. He called for the dressing trolley. He lifted the heavily bandaged arm from its pillow rest and removed the safety-pin from the elastic crêpe bandage. Removing several reels of crêpe he bent and sniffed at the discoloured material now being revealed. He looked grim.

As each layer of bandage was removed, Page could feel the monstrous pressure on his hand being released and life flowing back into it. But with the sensation came the smell—the acrid-sweet smell, like vomit, of putrefied flesh.

McIndoe turned to Sister Hall. 'Saline arm bath immediately.'

The smell grew stronger and the attendants behind Archie adjusted their masks. Page remembers staring in a kind of panic as he watched McIndoe remove a flat wad of blood-soaked yellow cotton-wool from the back of his hand, to reveal something beneath which did not look like a hand at all. Was this what he had been suffering for? He stared at the surgeon. The surgeon stared back, but this time he was grinning.

From the beginning he had followed the policy of telling his patients exactly what he was doing to them. In fact he did more than that. He invited them into the operating theatre to watch what he was doing to their comrades. Now he said:

'You want to know what has been happening to you? As you know, your hand was completely covered in keloids—thick scaly scar tissue. Well, I stripped all that off from the knuckles almost to the wrist. In its place I put a paper-thin layer of skin taken from the inside of your thigh. We call that a theirsch graft. I sewed this skin graft into position—and in your case it took about sixty-five stitches and left long threads from some of them hanging out. After that I cut a dry sponge the exact shape of the grafted area, tied the hanging threads over it and knotted them.'

Page was interested enough now to be able to ask why.

'Well,' said Archie, 'you see the sponge was then moistened. This makes it swell. But the threads restrain it, so that it can only exert pressure against the hand, forcing the new skin against the raw surface. That way the two surfaces join together.'

He smiled sympathetically. 'It's the pressure that causes most of the pain, I'm afraid, and the elastic bandage only adds to your misery. Hurts like hell, doesn't it?'

Page nodded.

The work on his hand had been suspended while Archie was talking, but now he said:

'Ready for some more? Right. Stitch scissors, Sister!' He snipped through the last threads. 'Tweezers!'

Slowly the bloody sponge was eased up from his hand and lifted clear.

'I remember looking at what was underneath,' says Page, 'and I went cold. All those days and nights of fiendish torture couldn't result in this—this stinking pulp of rotten flesh and oozing pus! It wasn't fair.'

Then he looked up in his despair at Archie McIndoe. There was a self-satisfied expression on the broad face.

'Luckier than I thought,' he said. 'That's about a fifty per cent take, I think,' To the sister: 'Get the hand into the bath. Let it soak for half an hour, then the usual dressings—plenty of sulphanilamid powder. The stitches can come out tomorrow.'

The infectious grin came across his lips and he patted Page on the shoulder. 'That's fine,' he said. 'Now we've got to get you fit enough for the next lot.'

There was still another graft to go on his hand. His face needed patching. And then they would get around to giving him new eyelids—the eyelids that would enable him to close his eyes when he went to sleep, that would end the terrible grating of the corneas as he rolled the pupils away from the tatters of the old eyelids, that would keep him from always bursting into tears.

Ward Three was jammed now, and more cases were coming in every day. There were Czechs and Poles and Free French; there were pilots and air-crew; there were badly burned victims of the blitz, and, behind a curtain, a once pretty factory worker who had been burned over face, back and arms by red-hot sugar. In only one way did Archie McIndoe get any relief, and that was the result of an RAF ruling that all burns and facial fractures should be sent to him at East Grinstead. He no longer had to spend some five hundred miles a week on tours of other hospitals.

So far as his surgical work was concerned, this was his greatest moment. He worked practically every day until he dropped and he grumbled about it; but his skill and speed were unimpaired.

He cut clean and stitched each face 'as if', in the words of one of his assistants, 'it were a Bayeux tapestry.' The team of McIndoe-Hunter-Mullins worked through the long day like an inspired machine, and the patients adored them. The portly John Hunter had, in fact, become almost as much of a favourite in Ward Three as Patrick O'Connor himself, for he not only rarely made his patients sick when he injected them but also made them laugh.

'The rotund figure in its white theatre gown looked more like a pork butcher to me than an anaesthetist,' one of his patients said. 'Above the paunch was a friendly face consisting of chubby cheeks, double chin, rimless glasses, a small moustache and a few wisps of hair which failed to hide his baldness. "I'm John Hunter, better known as The Gasworks," he said. "Which reminds me, have you heard the story of the girl called Virginia——" And he launched into a ribald story. As the rabelaisian details rolled out he continued his preparations. He massaged my arm in the direction of my elbow and then he said: "Just a little prick, if you'll pardon the expression." '

Those words: 'Just a little prick, if you'll pardon the expression,' were to become a wild rallying cry in Ward Three.

On January 13, 1941, Archie wrote to Adonia:

'I have had a very heavy week with nothing but work. Monday. All day at E. G. with a large operating list. There does not seem to be much to record about it except that I began at 9.30 and finished at 6 pm. In the evening I worked on case notes for a lecture at the Royal Society on fractures of the facial bones (as cured at E. G.!). This is a "do" before the Dental Society and is to be a review of all the jaw fractures we have had since war began. We have had no less than 115 of these so you can see we have not been wasting our time since you left. Tuesday. Up to London first thing in the morning but very little work to do except for typing my paper and correspondence. Giles and Mowley were there too but were equally devoid of jobs. I had a committee meeting in the afternoon which dragged on till so late that I had to crawl down in the blackout—a most unpleasant business these days. Wednesday. Big day in the theatre. In fact all three theatres were going full blast all day. The hospital is now so full with new cases and the old ones returning for their repair that we shall have to ask for further extensions. It is an awful job getting cases out so that new ones can fill the beds. More writing in the evening after lectures to the Staff. Thursday. Almost a repetition of Wednesday only more so. Friday. To town. Saturday. Another day in the theatre. This is getting a bit monotonous. It is weeks since I have had a weekend off and I am beginning to think that the only way to get a rest is to get clear away from the damned place. Sunday. Round the hospital in the morning and after lunch to meet specialists from Halton.'

It was in the midst of this whirlpool of work that disaster struck. The legacy of tannic acid and other coagulants was still plaguing the burns unit at East Grinstead. Men were still coming in from the first-aid stations with greasy preparations or coagulants plastered over their seared flesh, and, as Archie McIndoe had repeatedly pointed out, this was a prime cause of infection. The preparations were often, to save the victim from pain, coated over dirty skin and infected hair. Sterilized lint bags to cover burns were as yet only in limited use. Aseptic routines were not being followed. Cross-infection was, as a result, inevitable.

As the nurses and VADs moved through Ward Three during the second week in January 1941, they were troubled by a smell much more unpleasant than those to which they had already become accustomed. They began their daily round of dressings, and they were appalled. Flaps which had seemed to be taking well fell away. Grafts were not taking. In his bed at the entrance to the ward, Squadron Leader Tom Gleave felt a sense of relief. Archie McIndoe had taken a flap from his shaven head and turned it into a new nose, but the hairs growing out of it had been pricking him in the eye. They were no longer doing so. When the bandages were lifted it was apparent why. The flap was suppurating and had come away.

It did not take Archie long to diagnose that streptococcal infection was rife in the ward. He surmised that the beds were infected, the clothes, the towels, all the paraphernalia in the ward, and he made his decision. He announced that Ward Three was to be evacuated at once.

'But where are you going to put them?' asked Matron Hall.

Archie said: 'In the Dewar Ward.'

The Dewar Ward had been endowed by John and Kathleen

Dewar (of the whisky firm) who had built their home in the district, and it was reserved for local women patients.

'But you can't put them in there,' said Matron Hall. 'It's full of patients.'

'Any of them serious?' asked Archie.

She admitted that there was none.

'Then get them out. I want my boys washed down with antiseptic soap, dusted with M and B, and put across there before the night is out.' When Matron Hall hesitated, he said: 'And get on with it, woman.'

Matron Hall went instead to the resident doctors. The resident doctors came in a body to argue with McIndoe. He blistered them, then waved an authorization from the hospital committee, and said:

'If any more men lose their faces because of this delay, I'm bloody well going to report the lot of you to the BMA.'

The evacuation order was given. Ward Three was moved over. They carried the smell of their infected flesh with them, and Richard Hillary ostentatiously doused himself with eau-de-cologne 'to keep out the odour of the barnyard.' But even this stratagem failed to keep his own smell from himself, and by February 15 he was not only down with streptococcus but also with a mastoid in his ear. The ear took the germs and nurtured them.

'It was during my second night,' he wrote in *The Last Enemy*, 'that a 2,500 lb bomb landed a hundred yards away but did not explode. I heard it coming down with a curious whirring sound, and as I heard it I prayed, prayed that it would be near and bring with it peace, that it would explode and take with it me, the extension, the ward, the huts, everything. For a moment I thought I had it, so great was the force of the impact, but as I realized slowly that it had not exploded I found that the tears were pouring down my face: I was sobbing with mingled pain, rage, and frustration. Sister immediately gave me another morphia injection.'

Archie McIndoe decided that this was too dangerous. The Dewars had already put the main part of their home near East Grinstead, Dutton Homestall, at the disposal of the servicemen at the Queen Victoria Hospital as a convalescent home. He ordered the bulk of his patients to be taken there at once. Those too ill to be moved would be sent back to Ward Three, furthest away from the ticking bomb.

'I imagined that I would go along with the others,' wrote Richard Hillary, 'but after taking a look at me McIndoe decided that it would be too dangerous to move me. Sister Hall offered to send a special nurse with me, but they thought even so the risk was too great. Sister looked at me. "I'm afraid that means the huts" (Ward Three), she said. At that something exploded inside me. McIndoe's chief assistant came into the ward to arrange for me to be moved and I let fly. I had not spoken since my operation and I saw the surprise on his face as I hauled myself up in bed and opened my mouth. Wild horses, I said, would not drag me back to that garbage can of human refuse. If anyone laid a finger on my bed I would get up and start to walk to London. I preferred to die in the open rather than return to that stinking kitchen of fried flesh. I had come into the hospital with two scars on my upper lip: now I had a lip that was pox-ridden and an ear with enough infection in it to kill a regiment. There was only one thing to be said for the British medical profession: it started where the Luftwaffe left off.'

The assistant surgeon was, in fact, Percy Jayes. With typical calmness, he said, mildly. 'You're not making this very easy.'

But he arranged for one of the consulting rooms to be turned into a temporary private ward and had sandbags heaped in a wall all around Hillary's bed.

'That night,' wrote Hillary, 'McIndoe came to see me. He was still wearing his operating robes and sat down on the end of the bed. He talked to me for some time—of the difficulties of running a unit such as this, of the inevitable trials and setbacks which must somehow be met. He knew, he said, that I had had a tough break, but I must try not to let it get me down. I noticed that he looked tired, dead tired, and remembered that he had been operating all day. I felt a little ashamed.'

It was this heaping of emergency and temperament upon the backbreaking routine and day-after-day surgery which may well explain the tone of the letters which he wrote to Adonia about this time.

On February 14, 1941, in the midst of the streptococcal emergency, he sent her an eight-page letter which detailed what he had done with the stores of emergency food she had left when she sailed for America, where he kept her jewellery and the children's bank books, how he spent his days, and ended:

'Like you I am no more anxious to prolong this separation further than necessary and it will cease at the earliest possible moment. Please therefore desist from your constant nagging on this subject—it will do no good and only tends to make the children miserable. What you *can't* alter had better not be hammered at on every opportunity. We can take it as understood. Concentrate on the effort you are undoubtedly making for your children (and mine) and for your country and leave the rest to old father time.'

But on February 20, 1941, in the midst of the worst of the crisis, the strain begins to show.

'Your letter,' he wrote, 'was full of a desire to know what was to happen to you if I am bumped off. Well here is the story. Really you know it all already but I suppose it is necessary to hash it all over again. You had better preserve this information so that I don't have to contemplate my demise once more. From what you say it would appear that my death would leave you and the children in such a bad way that you would have to go out charring! Well, well! Far from it, my love, as things go these days and a damn sight better off than if I live.'

The position, he wrote, was as follows: 'My insurance amounting to something over £9,500 including one which pays you an income £450 per year for twenty years (now sixteen for I have had it four years) would immediately be payable to you whether I was killed by a bomb or cut my own throat or died of chicken-pox. The income derived from this sum together with the above-mentioned £450 per year would fetch in a nice income when invested (as it must be) in certain securities specified by *law* and my will and directed by my executors, Sir Harold Gillies and C. Naunton Morgan. In addition to this little nest-egg there are certain securities to the value of £4,000 lying at Barclay's Bank against an overdraft of £3,000 (my only liability apart from taxes). In the partnership of Gillies, McIndoe and Mowlem I own leasehold (my rooms) to the value of about £1,600 or alternatively my rooms can be let at a *profit* of £150 per year for sixteen years. My capital in the partnership amounts to several hundreds and my *equity* owed by Mowlem to £4,000—now outstanding at four and a half per cent per annum. So that from this source alone you have further expectations of from £4–5,000 plus leasehold producing £150 per year for sixteen years.'

He pointed out that all his obligations to Giles were now paid off in full and went on:

'Quite apart from all this there is the matter of personal furniture and belongings, cars, etc., which at a conservative estimate are worth £1,500. If you total this up you find that on my sudden demise you come into a tidy sum of close on £20,000 with liability of £3,000 to the bank leaving £17,000 to struggle along with and an assured income from the insurance. Bankers: Barclays; Solicitors: Moon, Gillies and Moon; Trustees: Gillies and Morgan; Cigarettes: by Abdullah; Furniture: by Maples.'

In this letter there is the first hint that perhaps their marriage, which had experienced its trials before the war, was reaching a phase when they were both rethinking their future.

'Now as to living,' he wrote. 'My dear, I have no dead hands reaching from the grave to dictate when or how you should live. That is entirely your own affair. Perhaps you might want to stay in the USA, perhaps you might like to come back here (I think the children would but perhaps I am wrong) or New Zealand might attract you though I doubt that now. You are not sufficiently adaptable for that. This then is the financial position. . . . On the other hand, should I live through this performance you will be a mighty poor woman—too bad, ain't it? I will have plenty of work to do to pay for all your doings in the States but please remember this, that I am happy to keep you there till this show is over, that I do not regret sending you and that your sponsors need not fear that you will be on their hands for very long.'

He ended: 'Please don't ask me to go over all this again. It is too morbid!'

It took several weeks for the streptococcal invasion to be driven from the Queen Victoria Hospital, and it was to attack again in the future. 'Those lousy, evil-smelling bugs!' Archie called them. He was particularly cast down when his work on Squadron Leader Tom Gleave—stitching a graft to an exposed nerve in the temple which was giving him appalling pain—went for nothing. And he was bad-tempered for days after an emergency operation on the face of a badly-burned pilot—conducted by night during a particularly intensive air raid—was nullified by the virus. He went around the wards, taking off the stinking flaps and flinging them into the slop-pan, and his language brought a wry remark from Richard Hillary: 'Welcome to the school, Archie!'

But the infection did bring him one consolation. The virus specialists came round to see his patients and then put their heads together.

'I am to have a pathological department of my own,' he wrote, 'so it is an ill wind that blows nobody any good. If this goes on I shall make this quite a hospital.'

CHAPTER SIX

THE DEATH OF HILLARY

EAST GRINSTEAD HAD CHANGED profoundly since the days of the phoney war, not least in the attitude of its people towards the mutilated and the faceless ones of the Queen Victoria Hospital. The latent hostility towards the Service 'intruders' into their proud little local hospital had given way to a communal desire to help these men, and they did it in various ways. To some extent the little town had become a place where it was permanently Hogmanay, and a burned airman knew he could knock at any door at any time of day or night and be asked inside for a cup of tea or a drink if one was going. No one shrank any longer at the sight of a man with a flap where a nose should be or a pair of horse-blinkers for eyelids. Sometimes the patients were allowed to make the journey to London and, after the easy tolerance of the town, they were apt to get a shock. 'People shouldn't be allowed out looking like that,' said a woman in a Soho pub to Richard Hillary. Geoffrey Page, at the conclusion of a long series of operations on his face, was shaken when a bus conductor took one look at him and said, with every evidence of sympathy:

'Coo, you don't arf look a mess! You ought to see one of them plastic surgeons, mate. It's amazing what they can do for you.'

They were glad to get back to the womb of East Grinstead.

The local landowners, for this was a prosperous part of Sussex, rallied round too with hospitality and gifts. John and Kathleen Dewar had turned over most of their home, Dutton Homestall, as a convalescent home for Service patients and it could hardly have been a more salubrious spot for recuperation. The original part of the house had once been John o'Gaunt's shooting lodge in Ashdown Forest to which Kathleen Dewar had moved a large Tudor mansion from Cheshire brick by brick and married it with the original. There were horses in the stables for those who could ride. There was plenty of liquid refreshment—for who if not Dewar could procure whisky in wartime—and butter and eggs from the farm. The staff consisted of pretty VADs—refugees, no doubt, from the factory call-up, but who cared about that?—who babied the boys.

'Blanket baths take on a new significance in my mind!' said Patrick O'Connor as a ravishing blonde came in to do the morning ablutions.

Not far away, the lovely home of Elaine Laski* was always open to them.

It is true that, at first, many of the men were reluctant to accept the repeated invitations from the locals to come out for drives or for tea. Archie McIndoe could not understand why they held back. It was his welfare officer, Edward Blacksell, who spotted the reason soon after his arrival.

'What happens after they've had a couple of cups of tea or a few beers?' he said. 'They want to get rid of it, and they're shy. With their injured hands they can't do it themselves, and they can hardly say to some respectable dowager: "Please, Missus, will you come into the lavatory with me and undo my flies?" What we need is something easier to undo than those damned buttons.'

It was Blacksell who picked up an American magazine and saw an advertisement for these new-fangled zip-fasteners, and he rushed around to Archie.

'We've got to get some of these,' he said. 'They'll make all the difference.'

Archie sat down to write letters to all his friends in America, and soon enough zip fasteners were arriving to fit all the trousers in East Grinstead.

The arrival of Edward Blacksell was a godsend to Archie McIndoe. He was a young Barnstaple schoolmaster of extraordinary wisdom and great personal charm who had volunteered for flying duties early on in the war. For some reason which he was never able to fathom he found himself instead on a course as a PT instructor after which he was posted to a unit in Plymouth as a PT corporal drilling the reluctant erks.

* Later, with her husband, Neville Blond, to become one of the Queen Victoria's greatest benefactors.

In 1941 he was transferred to the Queen Victoria Hospital at East Grinstead with only a vague idea of his duties.

'I suspected that someone in the Air Ministry had decided that the burned patients in Ward Three must be getting jelly-muscled,' he said, 'and I was expected to put them through the hoop and over the vaulting horse. I took one look at my future charges and realized that both they and I had greater obstacles to jump than anything they ever thought up in physical training.'

He met Archie McIndoe for the first time and they went back to Millfield Cottage for a long talk, and though neither of them had any idea what precisely Edward Blacksell's duties would be both of them cemented a relationship which clung for the rest of their lives. Shortly afterwards, 'Blackie', as he was inevitably called, moved into the convalescent ward at East Grinstead to live with the burned airmen; and, in a sense, he has been living with them ever since.

In the early spring of 1941, after several weeks in which he had been doing between nine and eleven operations a day, Archie took seven days' holiday rough-shooting from a cottage which he had been lent near Rye. He came back to a spate of letters from Adonia demanding that she and the children should be repatriated. She had become extremely unhappy in America. She had also begun to receive hints—and they became more than that later—that her husband had been seen in the company of other women, the kind of gossip, even when well-meant, which was calculated to arouse her into a frenzy of jealousy.

'A thorough rest,' he wrote in March, 'has done me a lot of good and I am much more able to cope with the day's work than before. The weather was sunny and full of the foretaste of spring and with nothing much to worry me I recovered rapidly. Sunday and Monday were quiet enough but last night and tonight the most terrific blitz on the south country and London has again broken out and the noise is beyond belief. My dear good wife, for the love of Mike let me hear no more of your wanting to come back here just yet. It is enough to scare the pants off the most equable minded person let alone you three. Tonight for the first time for a long time I was really frightened and as you will admit I don't scare easily. Three times already I have been flat on my face on the cottage floor and the mere thought of this sort of thing happening to you makes my blood creep. No, my dear, under no circumstances whatsoever would I agree to your returning to England until this show is a good deal safer. You speak in your last letter about my having made the wrong decision about taking the kids out of here. Fathead that you are, it was the most far-thinking thing I have ever done and by the same token I would like to hear a whole lot less about your miseries and uncomfortable surroundings. Do please remember that happiness lies mainly in mental adjustment to your surroundings whatever they may be and God knows they are infinitely better than what you would have over here just now. Quite apart from the question of life, I would point out to you that the food situation is very far from fun especially for growing children and on this score alone you are now in a position to ensure them plenty of good plain food. If this decision had to be made again it would be absolutely the same—only it might have been New Zealand!'

He went on to exhort her to do some good works on her side: 'Now about the hospital. We have been full to overflowing for the last six months and at last the committee and the good people of East Grinstead are beginning to appreciate some of the work done here. Anyway, two months ago a local resident stumped up £400 and after a considerable search we found what we wanted (an X-ray machine) and disposed of that. The next thing was enlarging the hospital and putting in massage departments, etc., etc. Well, a committee has been formed and money is being raised to do all I want. In addition I have at long last secured the Dewars' equipment (the beds and other facilities at Dutton Homestall) and this goes into service next week. I have re-equipped two operating theatres and two wards . . . Now, it seems, if we can pay for things ourselves we can get almost anything we want and with the public inclined to help I think we can pull it off. Therefore if any of your friends would donate *money* it will do one of two things: (*a*) avoid the necessity for using valuable shipping space, or (*b*) enable us to get quickly what we really want and so prevent overlapping. With £10,000(!!) I can do a hell of a lot. Frankly, dollars are more useful than anything else just now.'

It was his birthday on May 4 and he wrote: 'Apart from your cable my only other worthwhile greeting came from one of the wards. I walked in and all the men sat up and sang "Happy Birthday". This from the famous Ward Three now containing little else but seriously burned officers and men from all over the country. I felt somewhat of an idiot but also rather proud of it.'

At last, in mid-June, he got the real break from the struggle for which he had been waiting. He did not tell Adonia that he was suffering badly from stomach trouble and suspected that he had an ulcer. Nor did he mention that he was finding it harder and harder to write in longhand. He had taken to the typewriter for most of his personal letters as well as the increasing amount of paper work which the various ministries demanded; but when Adonia rebuked him for sending her 'printed communications' he reverted to ordinary handwriting again to her, but did not say that he had to rest a good deal between paragraphs because his strong right surgeon's hand, whose thumb and forefinger cut so swiftly and so cleanly, often suffered from what he put down to 'writer's cramp'.

He went to the Port Sonachan Hotel on Loch Awe in Argyll and, contrary to Adonia's suspicions, he went alone. 'I have set about making every minute count in the matter of getting fit again,' he wrote, 'in the shortest possible space.'

He fished and he walked and he enjoyed eating the 'ten nice trout' he and the gillie caught in a mountain loch, and he added: 'One of the most enjoyable things to me was the complete absence of human kind and the beautiful clarity of the little lochs, absolutely unspoiled by beer bottles, orange peel and other evidence of human habitation. Round the edges were nests of seagulls with eggs galore. I gathered some and boiled them in a tin and boy, were they good. Eventually we were fishing stripped to the waist and I collected a satisfactory dose of sunburn . . . After a couple of weeks I shall be a very different bloke to the washed-out individual who arrived fairly like death warmed up.'

For the moment, what he called his 'tummy-ache' had gone and strict attention to the typewriter rather than the pen had given him some relief in his right hand. He was inclined to suggest to Adonia—and from the tone of her letters it was easy to understand why he did so—that he was living a hermit's life, though this was not entirely true.

He spent an increasing amount of time with the men in Ward

Three and liked nothing better than to sit down at the piano in the ward and lead a sing-song. He saw a lot of Elaine Laski, who was becoming a close confidante and friend, in the most comradely sense of the word. He also took to going on outings to the Whitehall Restaurant with the patients. To all of them now he was 'the Maestro' and they worshipped him. He sang and played with them. He was always close when they faced a sudden pain or emergency. He seemed to match drink for drink with them, though in truth his stomach was now so delicate that he made a special pact with Landlord Bill Gardiner to serve him nothing more than a soupçon of gin drowned in plenty of water.

He had begun to give a few parties at Millfield Cottage, where Jill Mullins acted as his hostess—'she has to run three theatres full blast, with consequent increase in her staff, and is getting a bit thin,' he wrote to Adonia—and the guests were Edward Blacksell, with whom he was becoming increasingly close, and a crowd of burned airmen who almost always included Richard Hillary and Geoffrey Page. Hillary fascinated him.

'He is obsessed with death and keeps asking me whether I know when it's coming to a patient,' he wrote. 'I tell him I know but they don't. This doesn't seem to comfort him. He is a strange bloke. The boys in the ward don't like him. He has a sharp tongue and an intellectual approach which gets them on the raw. He mixed them up so much recently that they bombarded him with their precious egg ration and this quietened him down for a time. But like all of his type, he bobbed up again.'

He had warmed to Geoffrey Page almost as if to a son of his own. Page was quiet-spoken, gentle, and yet there was an iron will behind his softness which quickened Archie's interest.

'The bloody fool wants to fly again,' he wrote in his minute-book. 'He'll never be able to do it, of course. But fancy thinking of it, after all he's been through!'

His great disappointment came at Christmas 1941, for he had planned a celebration for all his friends and believed that among the stock which Adonia had collected during the phoney war was a consignment of liquor.

'I was looking over the stock of eats and drinks which you left,' he wrote, 'and decided to open the case which had resided in the wine cellar for so long and which I have always believed contained twelve bottles of red wine. I took the wires off the case and opened it to find it full of sultanas. Hell! Well, every cloud has some sort of lining for telling someone of this nasty mishap I was told that I should keep the sultanas quiet as they have disappeared entirely from the market and are now worth almost anything. The idea then struck me that I should make them up into small parcels and give them away for Xmas presents. Inexpensive and very welcome, for the lack of fruits of this sort will make the old plum puddings pretty few and far between.'

He had his Christmas dinner with John Hunter and his wife who were, by this time, looking after his rations. 'John has made a great study of cooking in the past 18 months and turns out a dashed good meal. He gets a diabetic triple ration in most things that matter and is thus able to go in for a good deal of fancy cooking denied to the rest of us.'

By the beginning of 1942, more than two hundred and fifty burned airmen had passed through Queen Victoria Hospital and most of them had come under the care of Archie McIndoe. Many of them were still there. It seemed sometimes as if many of them would never be anywhere else.

Paul Hart's face was now draped with large pieces of skin from his stomach. 'If this lot gets the dog-rot,' he said, cheerfully, 'they're going to put the next grafts on with rivets.' Yorky Law, a bombardier who had been badly burned when his plane was shot down after a raid, had for months been nothing but a pair of eyes staring out of a no-face, but now Archie had meticulously sewn small grafts which he called 'bacon strips' on to the places where the cheeks had been. The grafts had come from his legs, small postage stamp squares cut in various sizes and stitched together with mathematical exactitude. 'I'm just a bloody human jig-saw puzzle,' Yorky Law said. 'When I get home I'm going to pull them off for Christmas and give a quid to the first kid who can fit them back again.' There was the erk with a picture of a Union Jack tattooed on his chest to whom Archie said: 'I'm tempted to take the red part for your lips and the blue for your eyelids. Then you'll never need to use lipstick or eye-shadow for the rest of your life.' There was Edmonds, the pilot who had crashed his bomber on his first training flight and had remained in his blazing plane longer than any of them. For nine months he had been a blackened and suppurating mass, but now the painstaking job had begun of making him whole again.

Ward Three was once more an all-male ward. For some months they had had with them a factory girl who had been burned all over her head, face, arms and chest. She screamed whenever they took her near the saline bath. She lay, bald, frightened and despairing, whimpering in her bed, and she was the only one whose sufferings chastened the exuberant airmen. They gave her a monogrammed silk scarf when she left, but they were glad to see her go.

On behalf of his charges in Ward Three, Archie McIndoe had already ridden roughshod through hospital routine and Service regulations. They had sent him a consignment of convalescent 'blues' for his patients to wear when they went out into the town. 'I'm damned if I'm going to let my boys run around like convicts —no, like invalids, which they're not.' He had the 'blues' consigned to the stores and kept only half a dozen in his office and used them as a threat to any of the men who were rude to the nurses, rowdy in the wards or came in drunk. He also instructed local pub-keepers to refuse service to anyone dressed in 'blues' and this proved the most effective form of punishment. Only one pilot was ever handed the shameful uniform, and he came hang-dog back from the town confessing that he had been treated 'like a bloody pi dog'.*

But there was a much more formidable Service rule which worried him at this time. This was the ninety-day rule. 'By this, from time immemorial,' Archie wrote, 'an injured serviceman was given three months to return to duty. If, at the end of that time, he was still unfit he was invalided as useless and passed to one or other of the various civil or pensions hospitals for further treatment. After this he was pensioned off for as small an amount as

* Two of them were, however, sent back to Depot at Uxbridge, most condign punishment of all, for continual infraction of rules. One was Stewart Jones, who had a wig, and Ron Pretty with a false arm. After a week, Uxbridge sent them back to East Grinstead as 'hopelessly insubordinate'. Every time Stewart Jones saluted his wig came off, and every time Ron Pretty saluted his arm flew through the air. Archie took them back when they promised never to misbehave again. Shortly afterwards they helped to kidnap a local fire engine in which to drive a comrade to London.

could be determined from the schedule of payments authorized for his particular disabilities. If the convalescence was a long one this system absolutely guaranteed that the man would arrive back in civilian life without hope, broken in spirit, bitter and disillusioned. He could also be in debt for, with invaliding, his service pay ceased and the eventual pension would not be settled for a long time. During this period he lived on charity.'

He was determined that this should not happen to his boys. But how could he prevent it? Plastic surgery is a long job. Some of the men would be with him for years before he could repair their faces or mend their hands. But this, he insisted, jaw jutting, did not mean that they were *invalids*. They were healthy young men only temporarily withdrawn from normal activity. But his attempts to make this point at the Air Ministry found him butting his head against the sorbo-rubber ramparts of bureaucracy. 'There are times in life,' he wrote, 'when an approach "through the usual channels" is sufficient to drive a way through rules and regulations. Here it was impossible, for no civil servant would dare to break King's Regulations. These would have to be altered before this problem could really be solved. Creating a precedent with a cast-iron case at a very high level seemed to me to be the best approach.'

He found his 'cast-iron case' in a fiery and belligerent young man named Colin Hodgkinson.

Hodgkinson was a burly six-footer who had joined the Fleet Air Arm just before the war and was one of the most aggressively healthy pilots in the Navy. But early in 1940, while under training his plane was in collision with that of another cadet and there was a crash from which Hodgkinson escaped with his life but minus both his legs. He was fitted up at the limb centre at Roehampton with a pair of tin legs and invalided out with a pension of £3 a week.

It was his good fortune that before he was sent back to civil life he managed to persuade his doctors to give him a spell of convalescence at the expense of the State.

He was dispatched to Dutton Homestall and it was there that Archie McIndoe met him for the first time.

'He was a red-headed thick-set figure,' he recalled, 'precariously balanced on two artificial legs which were planted firmly apart and braced backwards to support his swaying body. His face was badly scarred. His eyes reflected the bitter desperation mixed with wariness which betrayed a constant anxiety to maintain his balance. He kept within reach of a wall or a convenient chair. He was watching me carefully and obviously had something to ask me. We moved into a corner and talked.'

Hodgkinson made no bones about what he wanted. 'They've paid me off,' he said, 'but I'm perfectly fit. I don't think it's fair to throw me out like this. I want you to help me get back in the Navy.'

Archie said: 'Quite a proposition with those pins. How well d'you walk on them?'

'Not too badly,' said Hodgkinson. 'It's coming gradually.'

'Well,' said Archie, 'if you can only stop floundering around there might be something we could do.' He stared at the young man's face. Hodgkinson had already had some reconstructive surgery done on his face by the doctors at Roehampton. They had mended his broken chin but they had been less successful in removing some ugly keloids, or scar tissues, from above his left eye.

Archie said: 'You ought to come over to the hospital sometime. I'd like to fix up that eye for you.'

As he wrote afterwards: 'This was a great healthy bear of a chap and he was ideal for my purpose. With him I might drive a hole through the regulations and force the powers that be to reconstitute them. But first I had to have him under my wing, as one of my patients, so that I could fight for him.'

The operation was a minor one. Under a local anaesthetic the skin was opened, re-crocheted and the scar was gone. But Hodgkinson was on Archie's books. He opened his campaign at once.

He wrote letters to the Admiralty and, when these had no effect, he picked up the telephone. Meanwhile, he encouraged Hodgkinson to perfect his walk and persuaded a friend, Charles Hughesden—husband of Florence Desmond, an old friend of Ward Three—to let him fly his light aircraft. When the young man came and badgered him he said: 'You get on with your walking and leave the admirals to me.'

It took several weeks and by the end of it everyone at Dutton Homestall had decided that Colin Hodgkinson, never a type to keep his own counsel, was definitely the establishment's biggest bore. 'For God's sake get the chap out of here!' they used to cry when Archie came to see him. 'Give him back to the Jerries before he drives us crazy.' But one morning Sir Victor Warrender (now Lord Bruntisfield), secretary to the First Lord of the Admiralty, appeared at Kathleen Dewar's luncheon table and Archie McIndoe was the only other guest. He talked long and persuasively.

A few days later, Hodgkinson received a call to the Admiralty from Sir Victor. He was examined by the doctors. He filled in forms. He came back to Dutton Homestall and fretted, badgered and sulked.

'Give it time, give it time,' said Archie. 'The penny is beginning to drop.'

At the beginning of November 1940, Colin Hodgkinson received an order informing him that he had been called back to active service and had been posted to a naval station in Cornwall. He was the first man ever to return to service drawing a pension for the very injury which had caused him to be invalided out.

But he had done more than that. He had established a precedent which led to a change in the rules. Shortly afterwards all the services agreed to abolish the ninety-day rule. If a man, at the end of his hospitalization, was fit for service he was called back. It was a decision which the walking members of Ward Three celebrated with a glorious beer party at Little Warren Cottage with Archie. To most of them it made all the difference in the world.

For several of them it was not merely a question of getting back into the RAF. They wanted to fly again. After all this pain and torment, the idea of being chained to a desk for the rest of the war was the ultimate torture.

Geoffrey Page had acquired for himself a small rubber ball, and with this in his gnarled hand he slid his arm under the sheets and then the agony began. His fingers were bent and the tendons contracted, but he went on squeezing the rubber ball for hour after hour until he was wet with sweat and the pain exquisite.

He had been down to the dental unit and there he persuaded one of the laboratory assistants to make him four metal splints.

These he made the nurse strap to his fingers each night, and when the bandages were put over them he ordered the girl to strap them tighter, tighter. Slowly, he was forcing the fingers to straighten. The day when he was able to crawl out of bed and tie his own shoelaces was an occasion for celebration, for it brought the cockpit of an aeroplane just that much nearer.

That night in the bar of the Whitehall Restaurant he celebrated a little too well. A riotous evening reached its climax when Lieutenant Patrick O'Connor swung into the bar, surveyed the flapped and pedicled patients and roared:

'What a dreary, unkempt shower you lot are! You know what you types need? A little Army discipline.'

He formed the drunken, roistering group into fours and marched them across the road to the hospital, where they marched through the grounds raucously singing *Deutschland Uber Alles.*

'Squad—right!' roared O'Connor. 'About turn. Come on, pick up your dressing by the right—steady.'

They tramped into Ward Three. 'All right, fall out the officers!' They fell out literally. 'Squad dismiss!'

The superiority of the Army proved, O'Connor climbed into bed and was asleep, his glengarry perched over his eye, before the matron arrived to administer a different sort of discipline.

Richard Hillary had gone off on his disastrous trip to America. It had seemed a good idea at the time. A young RAF hero, ravaged by the war, talking of his experiences, would surely make good propaganda for Britain among the Americans ignorant as yet of the nature of war. But in Washington the know-alls at the British Embassy looked at Hillary's face, swallowed, and decided that he would frighten the mothers of America into pacifism. He skulked back to New York, more bitter and cynical than ever, where a plastic surgeon performed another operation on one of his eyes. Then he came home. He brought with him the manuscript of his book, *The Last Enemy*.

Archie McIndoe had not wanted him to make the journey at all. 'I have still a lot of work to do on him,' he wrote to Adonia. 'I don't think it does justice to our work to show him off at this stage.'

But when he heard of Hillary's humiliation he was lividly angry. He wrote to the Air Ministry and he wrote to Washington and he

Bob Brumble

used words like 'goats' and 'stupid baboons' in his comments. To Hillary, however, all he said was:

'They've made a bloody awful mess of that eye. You'd better come back to the ward and I'll put it right for you.'

Hillary was more morose than ever in the next few weeks. On top of his humiliation in America had come an unhappy love affair. He was still on poor terms with the members of Ward Three to whom he referred as 'baby boys', and he had won the enmity of one of the most powerful of the local hostesses by giving her the sharpest edge of his tongue. He had only one idea left and that was to get into operations again, where you could drown your feelings in a saline bath of bullets and danger. That and the publication of his book.

Geoffrey Page recalls the moment, one night in April 1942, when he confessed to Hillary that he hoped to go back to flying at the conclusion of his next operation.

'So am I,' said Hillary, 'but no more of this bloody day fighter nonsense. Night fighters are the answer for us. If you get in a dog-fight by day, your hands mightn't be able to cope with the speed of the situation. Whereas by night you creep up behind your target, take your time and shoot the bastard down.'

Page didn't agree. He considered night fighters too heavy to be handled by men with semi-crippled hands, but Hillary would not be convinced. They decided to go together to see Archie, and at their first encounter he shattered them.

'You haven't a hope in hell of getting back,' he said.

Page said: 'I don't see why the medical boys should turn me down. I feel fit and I'm certain my hands will cope with an aeroplane.'

Archie said coldly: 'Not only do I not approve of it. The Air Force won't let it happen. How can you expect them to let injured persons like yourselves back into a squadron? It might have a bad effect on the morale of the other pilots.'

'But what about armless and legless types?'

'Not the same thing,' said Archie. 'I'm sorry, it's a cruel thing to say, but I'm pretty certain that's the way the Central Medical Establishment would look at it.'

The two young men slunk away to drown their sorrows.

It happened, however, that Geoffrey Page had formed a close

friendship with Jill Mullins, Archie's assistant. 'Dismally I told her what Archie had said,' Page recalls. 'She looked at me with those large, sympathetic eyes and put a soothing hand on my arm. The real reason, she told me, was that McIndoe felt that both I and Hillary had done our fair share and that now the fighting should be left to someone else. The story of the Central Medical Establishment's reaction was just an excuse to hide the surgeon's true feelings.'

Page rushed round to see Hillary and tell him the news. 'We agreed on our course of action. Although we differed in viewpoint between the merits of day and night fighters, we were of one accord that McIndoe should be badgered until he gave his support to our ambitions.'

It took them several weeks of nagging, but Archie finally threw up his hands in disgust. 'If you're determined to kill yourselves, go ahead. Only don't blame me,' he said, and sat down to write out their medical certificates.

Three weeks later, with notes in their pocket to an old medical friend of Archie's, Air Commodore Stanford Cade, they set off for the dingy London hospital where the medical boards were held. Page was called first. They leafed through his medical history, tested his blood pressure, his urine, his ears, his eyes, and then made him hop around, blindfold, on one leg.

When it was over, the verdict was announced: he could elect to be invalided out or classified for limited duties in the United Kingdom only. It was a blow which Page refused to rock under.

'What I'm after, sir,' he said, 'is a flying category.' And then, as he saw the doctor frowning: 'I managed to do some unofficial flying recently with a friend in one of the squadrons.'

He was lying and the doctor knew it. He leaned forward and said:

'Grip my hands.'

Page recalls how he reached out and took the doctor's hands in his own. 'Every ounce of physical and nervous energy,' he says, 'I concentrated into my two maimed hands and I gripped and gripped and gripped. The months of hard work with the rubber ball had not been wasted, and I saw the Air Commodore's eyebrows shoot up in surprise. "More strength in those than I imagined, Page," he said. He took up his pen. "I am passing you

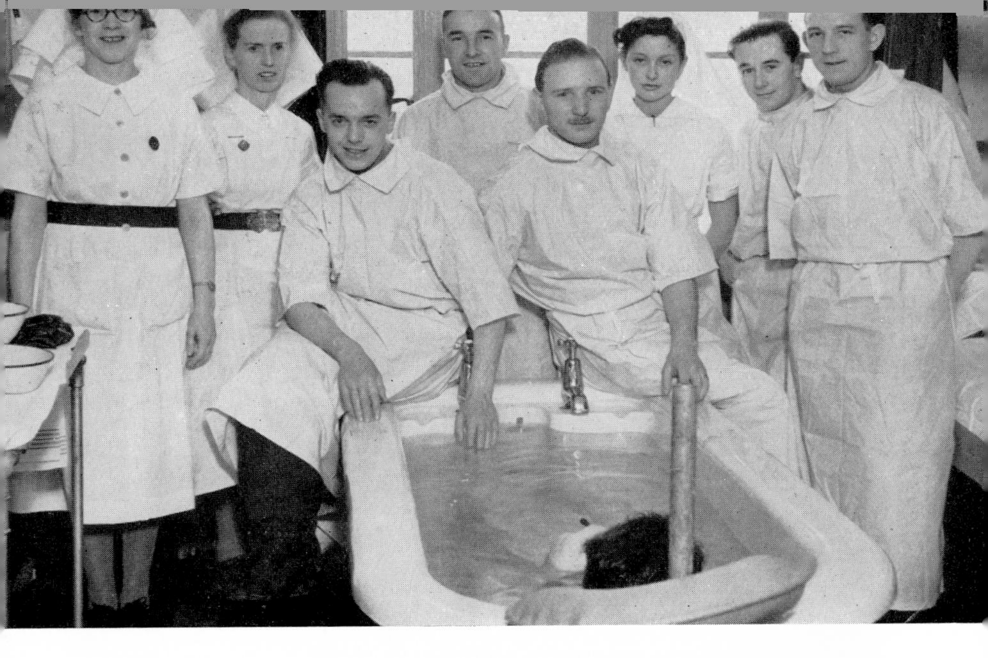

(*Above*) The original salt-bath unit and crew (notice that the patient is enjoying a cigarette during treatment)
(*Below*) The first meeting of the Guinea Pig Club. Tom Gleave is on the left with Russell Davies next to him; Geoffrey Page (in wheelchair) and Peter Weeks are seated; and Michael Coote is second on right, next to the Maestro

McIndoe (back row, right) with airmen, nurses and visitors—including Jill Mullins (seated, left) and Clark Gable (seated, right)—at a luncheon party given in September 1943 by the Commandant of the Fighter Pilot Rest Centre, East Grinstead, Sqdn. Ldr. C. Douglas Stephenson A.F.C.

fit for non-operational single-engined aircraft and if you've coped all right, we'll give you an operational category." '

To Hillary, waiting to hear his news, Page said joyfully:

'I'm back, I'm back! They're letting me fly again!'

'Congratulations,' he replied. 'Let us hope they don't kill you off too soon.'

But for Hillary himself the half-feared hunger for action was not appeased so easily. His eye was still troubling him. His clawlike hands, practically fleshless, had not, unlike those of Page, been passionately squeezing a rubber ball all these months. After his examination, he slipped away and went home to his parents in Rutland Gate.

'They're going to make me an office boy,' he told his mother. 'They refuse to let me fly.'

It was perhaps as well for him that this was the period when his book had been published, although the inmates of Ward Three were not exactly gushing in their praise of it. One of the pilots said to him:

'I think it's beautifully written, Richard. In fact I'm surprised that a supercilious bastard like you could produce something like this. There's only one thing I don't understand. You write of your being an irresponsible and conceited young undergraduate before the war. Then, as a result of your wounds you change, and presto, here you are a different person.' The pilot looked at Hillary and shook his head. 'It's not true. In my opinion, you're still as bloody conceited as ever.'

Hillary gave a cynical shrug and walked away. 'This,' noted Archie about this time, 'is a *very* unhappy young man.'

The publication of *The Last Enemy* produced its uncomfortable moments for Archie McIndoe. The British wartime edition of the book in fact contained no mention of McIndoe's name, but he was, of course, easily identifiable to those who knew East Grinstead. The *Evening Standard* made inquiries and spread itself in an article which named him as the hero of East Grinstead.

'Hillary's book has just burst upon the public here,' he wrote to Adonia, 'and has caused me some amount of embarrassment. I got an American copy from him and read it the other day. No real harm in it but you know what my colleagues are and how they hate public references to anyone else. The difficulty is that the damn thing has received hell's own publicity due to it being a Book Society Choice so that the reviews have been pretty fulsome. Our old friend the Londoner's Diary in the *Evening Standard* spread himself to a bit of a splurge. I shall be grateful when the war breaks out and people have something to talk about.'

He was only too well aware that even in wartime undue attention could cause trouble for him, for the British Medical Association was a salivating watchdog where publicity was concerned. He did not mention his worry to Hillary, but other people did. He wrote to Archie from Rutland Gate on May 17, 1942;

'Dear Mac,—Very many thanks for your letter to Stanford Cade [the medical bigwig at the RAF Medical Board] which was a great help although it did not carry the day. After a long consultation the President was very charming but refused to give me an operational category. I am very glad in a way as now I know finally I can settle down to this Staff job. I am not feeling too fit at the moment and my eyebrow is still mucky but I must be in this job within a month so suppose we must forge ahead with the operating. However, I'll talk to you about that when I see you.

'What I am really writing to you about is the article in the *Evening Standard* giving my book a write-up and in which your name was mentioned. In point of fact I said nothing about you or the hospital but having read the book the columnist obviously knew that you were my surgeon. I would not have given the matter a second thought but for the fact that —— in the course of her praiseworthy efforts to ruin my reputation and blackguard me over London is now telling everyone that you are furious and will have to appear before the Medical Council. This, I may say, is the least of what she is saying and a number of eminent and sane citizens have told me that I must stop her mouth somehow even if it means taking her to court. Needless to say, I don't want to do that but I shall have to say something to her. I do, however, apologize if by some mistake I have caused you some undesirable publicity. Yours ever, Richard.'

He came back to Ward Three for further operations on his eye and then climbed into what he called his 'squalid little job' on the Staff. But Archie was well aware, despite his expressions of contentment in his letters, that he had only one desire left and that was to get into the air and be damned to everybody. Without telling Archie, he asked for, and got, another medical board and this time he was given a flying category. He still believed that he was in no condition to handle Hurricanes or Spitfires in daylight operations, where facility with hands and eyes meant the difference between life and death. He was convinced that night fighters were the answer for him, and in the autumn of 1942 he was posted to a night-fighter unit in Berwickshire.

That December Archie McIndoe ran into him in London and they went off to a club for a drink. Hillary looked tired, worn, doom-laden.

'I have always been certain that he knew what the end would be,' Archie wrote afterwards. 'Three weeks before his time he came to see me and said that unless he could be shifted from night flying he could not last out much longer. But he stipulated that the course on which he was flying should not be interrupted lest someone should say he was afraid to continue. The idea was that he should return to East Grinstead for another operation. Disturbed by his news and impressed by the passive way in which he gave it, I wrote immediately to his station medical officer. Richard was suffering from that common complaint where his body would not tolerate what his mind could contemplate. His nervous system had not brought his physical responses under control.'

Archie was filled with premonitions of disaster. He went back to East Grinstead and from there he wrote a letter to the Medical Officer of the RAF Station at Charterhall, Berwickshire. It was dated December 17, 1942.

'Dear Sir,' he wrote. 'Re Flight Lt Richard Hillary. This officer has, as you know, had a long series of plastic operations for the repair of severe burns of the face and hands. I saw him the other day and was impressed by the fact that his left eye did not appear to be standing up to the strain of night flying, as might be expected, a fact of which Hillary is aware but which I think he is very loath to admit. As you know, he is a very able young writer and I feel very strongly that flying under these conditions can only end in one way. This would be a grave pity. He unfortunately was boarded by the CME before I knew that he was going, and I am afraid he brought great pressure to bear to get back to operative work. I have, in fact, more to do to his face and particularly his left lower eyelid, which will necessitate his attendance at East Grinstead in the future, and I would therefore be glad if you would arrange for his return to me at an early date.

'In the meantime I do feel if you could with discretion restrain him from further flying, it might save him from a very serious accident. After I have dealt with his eye, I can reopen the matter with the CME, and a more satisfactory disposal could be arranged for him.

'Would you be so good as to treat this letter as private and confidential to yourself? The feelings of these young men are very apt to be hurt in relation to this vexed question of operations work following an injury. I feel, however, there is a strong case here for intervention. Yours faithfully, Archibald H. McIndoe, Consultant Plastic Surgeon RAF.'

If ever there was an urgent warning this was it, but the tocsin did not apparently sound as clear in Berwickshire as it did at East Grinstead. There was no reply to Archie's letter for three weeks. The chief medical officer was away on leave and the 'private and confidential' communication lay on his desk unopened. On January 7, 1943, however, he wrote back:

'Dear Mr McIndoe,—Thank you for your letter of the 17th inst. about Flight Lieutenant Hillary. I am sorry to have delayed replying but I have been away from the unit and until I had returned I had not the opportunity of checking up the points you raised.

'I find F/Lt Hillary difficult to deal with, as any indication that his condition was not progressing as it should would result in him immediately withholding his own personal feelings on the matter. Without indicating that I had had a personal letter from you I asked him how things were going. I suggested that his left eye looked a little irritated but he insisted it was better than it was before he came to this unit. This is a point, of course, on which I have no information.

'I may have imagined it but I think there was a certain caution exercised to prevent me from finding out Hillary's real view. I agree with you that intervention is suitable in such a case, but I am also sure that Hillary's self-respect is an enormous obstacle. He is due to go to London about the 19th of the month, and he has promised to call and see you while in London. I did not tell him you had specifically desired it, but said that I considered it was only fair to a surgeon who had devoted so much time and trouble to effect a cure to let him check up from time to time and see how things were going.

'I will remind him when I see him making preparations to go off to London, and I hope that this will meet with your approval. Yours faithfully, ——, Squadron Leader.'

This did not by any means meet with Archie's approval. He wanted Hillary on the ground, and right away. But by the time he received the squadron leader's letter there was nothing more he could do. Richard Hillary was dead. He had taken off with his observer from Charterhall airfield just after 1.37 am on January 8. A Polish pilot had spoken to him in the briefing room just before he left and noticed that he looked tired, strained and 'very red of the eye'. Shortly afterwards he watched Hillary's plane come down the runway, climb and then suddenly plummet to the ground. Both he and his observer were dead by the time the ambulance reached them.

It was a squalid and unnecessary death for both of them, and though by this time Richard Hillary was an unhappy, tormented, disorientated young man, no one knew better than Archie McIndoe that this was not the way he would have chosen to die. His anger was not diminished by a further letter from the squadron leader medical officer which he received on January 11, 1943, which said:

'Dear Mr McIndoe,—No doubt you will be aware of the tragic fulfilment of your fears in connection with F/Lt Hillary. He and his observer were killed in an accident at 0137 hours on 8.1.43 less than 24 hours after I wrote to you. Unfortunately Hillary had been given a very special observer, an old Cambridge Blue, with temperament just calculated to suit Hillary and the prospects were that they would make a good pair.

'The mental conflict in Hillary's mind must have been great, because with his past "incident" the risk of flying must have been so much more real to him. I think he was determined that his will should rule his mind. It shows what strength of character he had, but what an obstacle that is to understanding existing between patient and doctor. It is easy to be wise after the event but with Hillary insisting that there was nothing the matter with him and a Medical Board less than two months before, I could not put him off flying arbitrarily and I had hoped by the 19th of January you would have been able to give me the necessary assistance to do so. He was in London about Xmas but I imagine he did not call and see you.

'This accident has distressed us all here considerably and though Hillary's reputation has caused much public attention, the loss of the observer is one the country cannot well afford either. Yours faithfully,——, Squadron Leader.'

Archie made only one comment on the letter. 'By God,' he said, 'the fellow's passing the buck.'

He did not reply to it but wrote instead to Richard Hillary's parents at Rutland Gate. They were not unnaturally bitterest of all, but the suggestion which was made later that they held Archie responsible for their son's death was as wide of the mark as the rumour that Richard had deliberately wrecked his plane (a rumour which would probably have brought a cynical smile to his lips and the remark, 'I'm not quite as mean as *that*, old man').

In fact, his mother wrote to Archie on January 14, 1943, in these terms:

'Thank you for your letter to us about Richard and your sympathy which we will always value. He had suffered so much in the service of his country that like everyone else I thought and hoped that no more would be asked of him. He of course insisted on returning to the active list—men like him do this whatever they have been through. I feel certain that he met "The Last Enemy" as gallantly as the first and as undefeated in spirit and did not for himself grudge the full cost. For the world I do grudge it, I must not say bitterly, but poignantly. There was so much of good he could and would have done with his brilliant mind. When you have the time to spare we would very much like to see you and to thank you personally for all your many kindnesses to Richard . . . Thine, Edwina N. Hillary.'

Just about the time when Richard Hillary crashed his night fighter, Geoffrey Page was climbing into bed at Lympne RAF station after an evening of celebration. He and his squadron of Mustangs had had a good day. Between them they had shot down five Nazi planes during a sweep over Northern France.

Two days later their victory shared the headlines with the news of Hillary's death. Somewhere in limbo, one could almost see Hillary's bitter smile. By the time the Hillary memorial service was held, Geoffrey Page was a Wing Commander, DFC. A DSO was to come later.

CHAPTER SEVEN

'WE ARE THE GUINEA PIGS'

NO ONE CALLED THEM the Guinea Pigs to begin with. The men in Ward Three had their own names for themselves ranging from the facetious to the obscene, but there was no thought then of forming themselves into a permanent association. In 1941 a number of burned RAF officers, after a meeting in their recreation room at the Queen Victoria Hospital, decided to form a club through which they hoped to maintain contact with each other after they left East Grinstead, but it was to begin with a group confined to pilots only. Tom Gleave and Geoffrey Page were the original organizers, and they were joined by Peter Weeks, Joseph Capka, a Czech pilot, Bill Towers-Perkins and Russell Davies, the anaesthetist.

They drew up a list of rules, settled on a subscription, and wrote a letter to Archie saying: 'Dear Boss, will you be our President?'

It could almost be called a snob club in those days. They met in the officers' quarters. The name chosen was not only rather pompous but also clumsy: they called themselves The Maxillonians, after the Maxillo Facial Unit in which they were being treated. Peter Weeks, who had been badly smashed up as well as severely burned, was made treasurer because he was confined to a wheel-chair and could not run away with the funds.

As a result of Hillary's book and stories in the newspapers, however, people all over the world were becoming conscious of the work being done at the hospital, and they reacted with generosity and sympathy. Letters began to reach Archie containing cheques, money orders and notes, with parcels of gifts, with offers of hospitality and jobs. At first he was embarrassed with them.

'What the bloody hell am I to do with all this?' he asked Edward Blacksell, his RAF welfare sergeant.

Blackie suggested that a trust fund should be started for the men. But how to do that? Some sort of association must be formed first.

It was then that the Maxillonians opened the doors of their club a little wider. It was still the most exclusive club in the world; membership was still confined to flying men of the air force who had been burned and disfigured, and then treated by McIndoe and his men at East Grinstead. The Maxillonians held an extraordinary general meeting at which they were addressed in no uncertain terms by Archie. On January 5, 1942, he was able to write to Adonia:

'On Thursday night I am having quite a bit of excitement here with a reunion dinner for all the RAF boys who have passed through the hospital in the past few years, i.e. flying personnel only. There have been about 250 of them but the dinner will be for about 60 all the others being in various parts of the world. The guest of honour is the Commander-in-Chief (Air Chief Marshal Sir Sholto Douglas) who is coming down specially for it. The boys have founded a club called the Maxillonians of which I am President, designed to look after the interests of the more severely injured men later on when this is over. We have secured enough food for the party and we are looking forward to a good bust.'

It was a good bust indeed. 'Sixty were invited and sixty came,' Archie wrote. 'The C-in-C was guest of honour and we also had an odd Air Vice Marshal or two and various and sundry other blokes. The party was a great success and there were numerous speeches. I am getting an old hand at making speeches off the bat and under the influence of a good dinner threw off quite a nifty line in after-dinner orations.'

But it was not until some months later, when an erk being wheeled in for his sixth operation complained that he was 'just a bloody guinea pig for the Maestro,' that the name was changed. The second dinner was held a year later, this time under the auspices of the Guinea Pig Club. The doctors on Archie's staff—Percy Jayes, Ross Tilley (a Canadian), and John Hunter—were invited to become members, and a section known as the Society for the Prevention of Cruelty to Guinea Pigs was formed to include all those like the Dewars, Elaine Laski, Neville Blond and many another, including a host of friends from show business, who had befriended them.

'All day patients were arriving back at the plastic unit,' wrote Bill Simpson of the dinner in 1943. 'They came from many different RAF stations scattered all over the United Kingdom. The dentists' lecture room in which they congregated and awaited their turn to see McIndoe was filled with an excited hubbub. Everyone present had been operated on at least once. Some had lain as many as twenty and thirty times upon the operating slab. Each one bore some signs on his person to bear witness to his right to membership of the club. It was almost possible to date a patient's stay in hospital by the type of scars he still possessed. One saw new eyebrows and ears; jaws and chins, lips and cheeks, legs that had been restored by graft and hands that had recovered their lost usefulness. Those whom many of us had last seen with faces that were distorted and ribbed with scars, or lying in their beds with hands or head obscured by dressings, were now fit and robust, their grafted hands and faces bronzed and healthy . . . Each one a miracle himself was surrounded by miracles of surgical skill. For McIndoe and his assistants this was indeed a great day.'

Simpson might have mentioned that it was a great day for him also. He had been shot down and badly burned in France in the days when France was collapsing, and his injuries had not only wrecked his face and his body but his marriage as well. By neglect, his hands, which might have been saved, had been allowed to rot away. He had arrived in East Grinstead at the end of 1941 with, as he himself described it, 'my legs still stiff and heavily scarred from below each knee to the groin. My eyelids had been burned off along with the wing of the left nostril of my nose. My mouth, cheeks and forehead were ribbed with keloid scars. But worst of all were my hands. No fingers remained—they had rotted and had then been torn off during dressings. A few short stumps remained on the right, but I had not yet learned to use them, and they were a mass of nervous reactions. The outlook for my future life seemed very black.

'I was entirely dependent on other people. I could not even feed myself. At times it seemed to me that I had lost everything—my health, youth and career. Added to all this came the complete collapse of a marriage that had seemed ideal, and had been very happy before the war.'

By 1943 he was back at work in the Air Ministry. He had a new nose and face. One arm ended in a stump but on the other Archie had saved a part of his first and index fingers, and with these he could do practically anything. He could withdraw coins from his pockets and drop them into his lap for bus fare; he had learned to write with these mannikin fingers, handle a fork and spoon, press-stud his clothes together, hold a comb: and, between the two mutilated arms, grip a tankard of beer or a glass of whisky.

For Peter Weeks it was now possible to decamp with the Guinea Pig funds had he wished, for he was walking again. Weeks was a huge and luxuriant man, as large as an oak, who had come to East Grinstead with his limbs shattered and his hands—because they had been bound in plaster over the burns—webbed together. Archie or his assistants had operated on him thirty-five times, cutting through the 'frozen' hands and grafting new skin on them, mending his legs. He would never fly again, but he would live to work and teach again.

There were the failures, of course. Some of the men in Ward Three had suffered to no avail. Their grafts would not take. Their wounds would not mend. There were those who were reshaped and sent back, only, like Hillary, to be killed. At the reunion in 1943 was a great hulk of a man named Holebrook Mahn, an American who had joined the RAF in the early days through Canada. He came down with his crew in the North Sea after a raid on Norway and floated around for days, his legs hanging outside his dinghy because he was too big to fit it. One by one his comrades died. He kept alive by catching a seagull and drinking its blood. By the time he reached shore, the rot had truly set in.

Archie McIndoe had once confessed to Edward Blacksell during their evenings together at Little Warren Cottage after a day in the theatre:

'There are two things I hate in surgery, Blackie. Two things I cannot do. One is make a spare ear for someone who has had one burned away. I just can't shape the damn things. They look wrong and they always seem to go wrong. Plastic surgery will really have come of age when we can give a man an ear that looks like a real one.'

Blackie asked him what was his other surgical block.

'Amputation,' said Archie. 'Cutting someone's limb off is

something I can't take. I'll do anything to avoid it. It's not surgery. It's butchery.'

By the time Holebrook Mahn reached East Grinstead butchery was really the only thing left to do. The legs were black and gangrenous. But Archie worked on them with a feverish determination to save them. He grafted repeatedly, and waited. When the graft failed to take, he tried again. And waited.

'Doctors are supposed to accept the situation as it's presented to them,' he said, 'but by God, I'll not accept this one. I've got to save Hoke's legs and I'll do it, I'll do it.'

Mahn said to him one day: 'Doc, why don't you just give up and chop 'em away?'

There came a day when he was forced to admit that it was the only thing to do. He delayed, he havered, he went into one of his tempers and made life unbearable for his assistants and his nurses. Then one evening he went to see the young American and told him that amputation was the only way out. That night he cut off one of Mahn's legs.

'We went back to Little Warren that night and I have never seen Archie in such a black mood,' Blackie said. 'I tried to tell him that he had tried—that in any case he had saved the man's life—but he couldn't see it that way. "I hate it," he said again. "I hate being just a bloody butcher." He arranged for someone else to take off the American's other leg.'

A few months later, as if to confound Archie's pessimism, the huge bulk of Holebrook Mahn reappeared at the Queen Victoria from Roehampton, where he had been fitted up with two artificial legs. He was more charming and cheerful than ever. He stayed long enough to propose to a pretty nurse from Ward One and marry her (with Archie as best man) and then the couple departed for Cambridge, where Mahn had won a scholarship.

'Why did I ever worry about that guy?' asked Archie ruefully. 'He doesn't need limbs. He's got it made!'

It was a year later that he heard about Holebrook Mahn again. A telegram arrived to tell him that Mahn had been rushed to hospital for emergency treatment, but had died on the operating table.

He picked up the telephone to ask for details. 'What was it?' he asked. 'What went wrong with his legs?'

But it wasn't the amputated legs which had killed Holebrook

Mahn. He had swallowed a chicken bone, and he had died from a perforation of the intestine.

There was another remarkable American whose stay at the Queen Victoria gave Archie McIndoe every cause to remember him. For reasons which will become apparent, one can only refer to him here by his first name, Mark.

Mark was a young Southerner (from Carolina) who got to Britain aboard a Norwegian freighter in 1941 and volunteered for flying duties with the RAF. He was a small, neat, wire-spring youth with an accent as soft and sweet as molasses and a personality that bowled the girls over. He was posted to a training station near Richmond, Yorkshire, and was soon capturing the hearts of the local female population with the same ease as that with which a certain Northern general once took Richmond, Virginia. With one of the girls he fell in love. Just before he took his final cross-country blind-flying test, she came to tell him that she was going to have a baby.

It could have been bad luck, it could have been inefficiency, or it could have been emotional confusion, but whatever it was, what happened next was tragic. Mark crashed his plane and it burst into flames, from which he was lucky to crawl out alive. He was rushed to a hospital in the Eastern Counties where the doctors took one appalled look at him and decided that there was only one man who could do anything for him. Still encased in his charred uniform, and in writhing pain, he was driven across country to East Grinstead.

I am not trying to be humorous or cynical when I say that there are some men who burn better than others. The same flames, the same exposure to skin- and tissue-destroying heat, will leave one man's face looking still like that of a human being, while it demolishes that of another. Mark was what East Grinstead knew as 'a bad burner'. His face was lean, his hands were slim, and the fire had done its worst. He was little more than a blackened skull with skeleton hands, and only his goggles had saved him from blindness.

Archie took one look at him and ordered him at once to the saline bath unit. He was dropped into the bath, uniform and all, and the slow task began of peeling off the cloth which had been burned into his body. It took hours; but never has the saline bath better proved its quality as an anodyne for a suffering human being. When Edward Blacksell turned up, on the evening of his admission, to see how Mark was going on he found him smoking a cigarette and, for the first time for days, no longer groaning with pain.

Blackie introduced himself, and asked if there was anything he could do. 'Any letters I can write, or telephone calls?'

The blue eyes in the skull-face surveyed him. 'How much power have you got around here, Sergeant?' Mark asked.

Blackie tried his modest best to indicate that if strings needed justifiably to be pulled, he could possibly pull them.

'In that case,' said Mark, 'I'd like you to arrange for me to get married.'

Blackie said: 'But of course, old chap. We've often done things like that. It's all part of the service. In a few months' time, when you're feeling a bit better——'

Mark interrupted. 'Not in a few months' time, Sergeant. I mean now. I want to get married now. I've got a girl up in Yorkshire who needs to be married. She's going to have my son, and no son of mine is going to be born a bastard. I don't know what's going to happen to me after all this mess, but just to make sure, I want to get married—and now, right away. Will you arrange it?'

Blackie said weakly, 'I'll have to talk to the Boss.'

For several days afterwards, it was the same. Each day, the blackened, suppurating body heaved up as Blacksell came by and asked whether arrangements had been made. Mark was so persistent that he interfered with his treatment, waved away the soothing drugs; it was obvious that no progress would be made with his case until something was done to satisfy him. Archie examined him.

'You are in a horrible mess, boy,' he said, 'and it's going to take months before we get you right. But if getting spliced is going to make you happy—and making you happy is what we are here for—we'll get you spliced.' He turned to Blackie. 'You get all the details and fix it. I'll take over after he's made the girl an honest woman.'

It seemed at that point that there would be no great difficulty.

They could telegraph for the girl to come down to East Grinstead. They could make arrangements with the registrar, and the marriage could be performed and Mark popped back into the saline bath.

But they had reckoned without the code of the Southern gentleman. When Mark stated that he wanted marriage, he meant it with all the trimmings.

'I want an engagement ring for my fiancée, and a wedding ring,' he said.

'Okay,' said Blackie, 'I'll pop out and buy them for you.'

The skull-face could not show any expression but the eyes did. 'These are not things,' said Mark, 'that anyone else can do but myself. I must go to London for them.'

Once more Blackie retired to consult the Boss. Once more Archie came along and examined his patient. 'You're doing it the hard way, aren't you?' he said.

'It wouldn't be worthwhile otherwise,' said Mark.

A week later they patched him up and eased him, with Blackie as his guide, into a car which drove them to London. There was no question of any plastic surgery having been done upon him, and he was a frightening—even repulsive—sight. Even those in the hospital swallowed when they looked at him. What would the effect be upon the cocooned people he would meet in London? When Mark asked what was the best shop for rings, Blackie explained that London was full of jewellery stores and that there were some nice small shops in Soho.

Mark said: 'I don't think you understand. These are rings for the girl who is to become my wife. They must be worthy of her. Which is the best shop in London?'

Blackie took him to Mappin and Webb in Regent Street. There a nervous assistant, his eyes carefully avoiding Mark's faceless face, paraded a series of rings which the blue eyes carefully examined. His hands were in his pockets and his fingers, in their condition, could not have picked them up. But as Blackie chose, Mark nodded or shook his head.

'There now,' said the assistant, with considerable relief, feeling that his ordeal was over, 'now we've made our pick, there's only one other thing to be settled.' He gritted his teeth and turned to Mark. 'What is the size of the lady's finger?'

There was a moment's silence. And then Mark said: 'That's easy. It's exactly the same size as my little finger.'

At which he pulled one of his hands from his pocket, and placed it on the counter. The assistant took one look at it and slowly collapsed in a dead faint . . .

Mark, with still half his skin missing, a mass of anointed raw flesh, was married to his love at East Grinstead Hospital a few days later. He spent his honeymoon half in a saline bath and half on the operating table. Archie and Blackie were godfathers to the boy who was born several months later. He is one child who will never know what pain and torment his father went through to make sure he was born a little Southern gentleman.

Someone said of Archie McIndoe about this time:

'It was a funny thing how human he was underneath that crust. I've seen him tear strips off his assistants for clumsiness. I've seen him berate his nurses and his orderlies when they didn't deserve it. He talked tough and he had an evil temper. It always looked so easy when he came in, cut so cleanly, worked so quickly. It was only gradually that you became aware that he worried about his cases, that the gloriously simple and effective surgery he performed was the fruit not of improvisation or even inspiration, but of nights walking around his bedroom, worrying, or hours hung over his desk planning and drawing and measuring.'

The Guinea Pigs appreciated that perhaps more than his staff—who often resented his lashing tongue. There were other fine doctors at the Queen Victoria Hospital. In the dental section, Kelsey Fry and his team were performing miracles with the shattered jaws of the injured airmen. Percy Jayes, Ross Tilley, Jerry Moore—they were all brilliant surgeons. But, as one airman put it, the difference between them and Archie was that 'every time he puts a pedicle on your face he seems to ram a pep pill up your arse at the same time. No matter how bad things are, he always makes them seem better.'

The achievements at East Grinstead were certainly those not of Archie himself but of McIndoe and his team, but it was of him alone that the Guinea Pigs sang when they rose to roar their anthem (written by Edward Blacksell) at their annual dinners:

'WE ARE THE GUINEA PIGS'

'We are McIndoe's Army,
  We are his Guinea Pigs,
With dermatomes and pedicles,
  Glass eyes and teeth and wigs.
And when we get our discharge
  We'll shout with all our might:
"*Per ardua ad astra*,"
  We'd rather drink than fight.

'John Hunter runs the gas works,
  Ross Tilley wields a knife.
And if they are not careful
  They'll have your flaming life.
So Guinea Pigs stand steady
  For all your surgeons' calls;
And if their hands aren't steady
  They'll whip off both your balls.

'We've had some mad Australians,
  Some French, some Czechs, some Poles,
We've even had some Yankees,
  God bless their precious souls.
While as for the Canadians—
  Ah, that's a different thing.
They couldn't stand our accent
  And built a separate Wing.'

But how and why the Canadians got a separate wing is a story that must come later.

If Archie McIndoe was hero-worshipped in the wards, however, his life outside them did not always win him unblemished admiration. It cannot be said, for instance, that he was loved in Whitehall. When he wanted something done, he went over the heads of the bureaucrats, both uniformed and otherwise. An Air Vice Marshal came into his office one morning, puce with fury, and said:

'For heaven's sake let's make that fellow McIndoe take a commission. Make him a group captain or something—and then we can pin him down. D'you know what he's done to *me*? 'Phoned me a fortnight ago and talked to me as if I were a ruddy schoolboy because I hadn't got him the X-ray machine he's been screaming for. I told him there was a war on and he'd have to wait, and he said—to me, mind you: "If you layabouts don't pull your fingers out I'm going to hurt you where it hurts you most. I'm going over your heads." I said that didn't worry me because I enjoyed the fullest confidence of my superiors. So what happens? I've just had a note from the Air Council to say that the Duke of Kent —yes, the Duke of Kent—has been asking where McIndoe's X-ray machine had got to, and what was I doing about it? The fellow's a ruddy menace.'

It was true that Archie would use anyone and any method to get what he wanted for his patients and his work. 'There's only one sin, and that's to be caught,' he once told a group of students. He had inveigled the Duke of Kent into helping him when he came to East Grinstead for a minor operation. Archie had operated on the Duke for a minor Dupuytren's contracture—a contraction of one of his fingers—before the war. In 1941 it was announced that Kent, now a Marshal in the RAF, would pay a visit to the Queen Victoria Hospital to talk to the burned airmen. He did a tour of the wards and then went into the operating theatre to have a surgical adjustment, under local anaesthetic, made to his finger. Archie used the opportunity to tell him all about the dilatoriness of the chairborne officers in Whitehall and extracted a promise of help.

He did the same with Sir Stafford Cripps, then Minister of Aircraft Production, when he visited the hospital shortly afterwards. Unlike most other visitors, Cripps was given the 'full treatment' when he was taken round the wards. 'If he's making the planes,' Archie said, 'he ought to see what can happen to the men who fly them.'

The first man to be introduced to the Minister was Tom Gleave, then in the early and painful stages of his treatment. The smell of burning flesh still hung about him. Bones and nerves stuck out of his skinless temples. He thrust out a mangled arm when Cripps greeted him. Cripps, a sensitive man, swayed and then collapsed slowly to the floor in a semi-faint. Blackie was sent for an emergency tot of brandy to revive him, but he waved it away with the words: 'Thank you, no. I do not drink.' Blackie drank the brandy himself. Cripps was revived with a cup of tea and it was suggested that perhaps he had seen enough. He shook his head.

'If this is the condition to which men can be brought by their war efforts,' he said, 'I think I should see them all.'

He fainted again before the tour was over, but he carried on, flinching but not retreating from handless arms, sightless eyes, and even the frizzled wreck lying smoking in the saline bath. Archie's admiration for his courage increased with every step, and the ordeal, far from alienating the Minister, warmed him to the surgeon at his side. He went back to Archie's office for a talk and subsequently became one of his most useful allies in the fight against the ninety-day rule.

But the civil servants! 'It seems that there is a good deal of unrest abroad at Governmental deficiencies,' Archie wrote to Adonia. 'Somewhere there will have to be radical changes in our system and if it deals the civil servants a good solid smack on the nose no one will be particularly upset. They are a stronghold of smug complacency and need shaking. They seem to resent any form of criticism particularly any directed at their allegedly fool-proof system of procedure. It is certainly proof against decision and action and they regard anyone not a civil servant as so much dirt. The devils always hide behind someone higher up and can't be forced into a Yes when a No is safer from the point of view of their rotten little pensions. As you can guess I have had a few more tilts at them.'

In East Grinstead, too, he had ruffled the fur of quite a few people. It was perhaps natural that some of his surgical colleagues at the Queen Victoria Hospital should be jealous of him. He suffered fools badly. He was inclined to hog all the equipment that was going. When he got into a temper, he would hector in an abrasive voice in front of the staff (though if he was in the wrong, he would always apologize afterwards). The publicity he had received was resented, and some of his colleagues, though loud in his praise in public, sarcastically referred to him in private as The Brahmin.

But it was 'these awful women', as he called them, who caused him the most acute discomfort. Archie McIndoe never had any trouble throughout his life in attracting the female sex. The mixture of charm and ruthlessness which he exuded from every pore drew them to him like mates to a moon moth, and it would be true to say that he 'used' women whenever it was calculated to increase his comfort or his career but never in a conscious or calculating way. He did not exploit his personality but neither did he refuse the help that came his way through the sheer magnetism which he gave out. He took pains to assure his wife on the other side of the Atlantic that he was living a monastic existence, and from his point of view this was not much less than the truth. He was certainly not engaged in any monumental affairs and he was always a person who could put sex on one side while there were other, in his view 'more important things', to deal with. But he was not averse to female admiration or companionship, and the facilities which went with them.

The trouble was that women pressed him too far and wanted too much, and he rounded on them. Those who presumed got the rough edge of his tongue. Those who were repulsed learned to hate him.

In the early months of 1942 Adonia, fretting in America and eager to come home, was galvanized by the arrival of anonymous letters which accused her husband of being a lecher and a womanizer. It was a shrewd move on the part of those who sent them, for nothing was more calculated to disturb Adonia McIndoe. She began to bombard Archie with questions and accusations. He was by nature and breeding a man of most bourgeois standards and he was upset to a degree which, had they known it, would have given his more sophisticated colleagues a quiet laugh.

At first he suspected that the poison pen was wielded by two nurses at East Grinstead who had recently been relieved of their duties for other reasons; though he was definitely wrong in this. He made haste to counter-attack.

'I notice a marked fraying of tempers and outward expressions of irritability,' he wrote to Adonia, 'which must be derived from too little rest and no holidays. This is common to the community at large and is particularly noticeable among the women who do more than their fair share of backbiting and squabbling . . . I am suffering at the moment from a surfeit of the ——'s and the rumpus they are kicking up after their "retirement" from the hospital. Newspaper articles of the more lurid kind describing the "appalling conditions in the hospital" and stuff of that sort. They had a piece in the —— —— which contained more bunk to the square inch than you could shake a stick at. Now they are taking an action for damages against the hospital for wrongful dismissal and I would not be surprised if they joined me in the action. I know they think I sacked 'em. Well, worse guesses have been made. I always thought they were a clever lot but by gosh they certainly take the cake. For pure viciousness they win hands down and I should say that they would do down their own grandmother for fourpence if it would do them any good. They'll go a long way to give me a black eye, that I do know for certain. . . . I am rapidly working up to giving them a good stouching on the nose.'

But it soon became apparent that these were not the culprits. Three weeks later Archie wrote:

'I am cold with fury that you have been made the recipient of anonymous letters and between you and me I am certain where they come from. They originate from the distorted mind of a certain young woman who shall be nameless for the moment. They represent a return present for my somewhat blunt refusal to play her dirty tricks. If I can prove without doubt that she is the author, and if you can send them back, I am going to make a public exposure of the whole affair.'

Adonia's reply to this was: 'I must come home as soon as possible.'

Before he made any further reference to the anonymous letters, Archie quietly moved out of Millfield Cottage and took residence in Luxfords, the East Grinstead house where he and Adonia and the family had resided before the departure of his wife and children to America.

'Like you,' he wrote, 'I have been through a difficult period in which my letter writing to you has got into arrears . . . I have shifted back to the cottage but before doing so I had some extensive alterations made in it which should please you . . . I have now been in residence for one week and so far find it possible to get along quite well. I have given my ration card to John (Hunter) who is an expert buyer of food and manages these things much better than if I had to do it myself. Rations for one person would make a good meal for a mouse. As you can imagine, all this has taken some time and I spent the whole of Easter cleaning, rearranging and making the place possible. The shift from Millfield was a bit of a business as all the stores (still intact, even to the soap, etc.) had to be shifted too. I left Millfield with no regret though I had been very comfortable there. There were no recriminations though I think the womenfolk understood perfectly what it was all about.'

Adonia still wanted to come home.

'And now about your return,' Archie wrote. 'I am as anxious as you to have you back for if you believe half of what you write to me it is time I took a strong hand and taught you differently. But the method of your return does concern me deeply. If it is considered that you must fly, well and good, though that is not the opinion given me over here. It is terribly expensive and expense will have to be taken into account. Secondly I am no longer the millionaire you used to take me for and thirdly most people are returning by sea and in convoy and doing it just as successfully. No one in America can guarantee your passage beyond Lisbon and hundreds of people are stranded there and unable to get away. Therefore *on no account come via Lisbon*. If the North Atlantic route is opened by the summer that is a different matter and you will land in Ireland with some possibility of getting home. But believe me no one on God's footstool will or can help you in Lisbon.'

He then went on to stress the difficulties of life at home. 'Come by ship and bring your trunks with you. Do you realize what life is like here now? A bob's worth of meat a week and everything else rationed. Buy all the clothes you can before you leave. Don't expect to get anything here.' He added: 'You make my blood boil with your slighting references to the Channel action on the [Nazi battleship] *Gneisenau*, etc. You see I had some of the lads who went out on that show and I knew some who did not come back. There were a hell of a lot of them who didn't but the armchair critics thought it should have been quite easy. And of course the Americans no doubt thought it was or ought to have been just pie. Pearl Harbour ! ! !'

These were the kind of letters which made Adonia more anxious than ever to get back. For some time, in spite of the efforts of Archie's friends at the Mayo Clinic, she had not been happy and her malaise had communicated itself to the children. She sailed in convoy from New York in mid-1943 with Adonia Junior and Vanora. There were two ships going, one a fast ocean liner which would make the voyage direct, at full speed, and a slower boat;

she chose the slower boat because it was sailing earlier and had to listen to the lamentations of her children when the faster ship passed them no less than three times, back and forth, while they were still on their way. They landed in Cardiff with not enough money in their pockets to buy their railway tickets to London, a piece of mismanagement for which, in the prevailing circumstances, she was hardly justified in condemning Archie. They borrowed their fare from the stationmaster and Archie met them at Paddington.

'Daddy looked very tired and worn,' Vanora remembers, 'but you could tell—at least my sister and I could tell—how moved he was to see us. I thought he was going to burst into tears when I said: "Hiya, pal." '

Adonia thought his greeting was perfunctory. She considered him a changed man from the husband she had left behind two years before, and from her point of view he had not changed for the better.

It was true, of course; though more sympathetic friends would have said that he had not changed so much as grown in stature. For almost the whole of his professional life until the years of war his wife had been at his side, advising, counselling, trying (though not always succeeding) to influence him; and though he had often been irritated by her interference it was always there, a curb rein round his neck.

Though he had written repeatedly to Adonia to say how much he missed her and the children, there was no doubt that he savoured and learned to like the independence which separation had given him.

'It is a wonderful thing to be able to take a decision without having an argument about it,' he wrote to his mother. 'I won't say that I haven't made mistakes, and they've sometimes got me into hot water. I had to go across and apologize to Kelsey Fry—again!—the other day, and Matron must think I'm an ogre. But I think more clearly and I'm not afraid to take a chance. I don't have to worry about what will be said when I get home. "How could you be such a fool, Archie?" "What's going to happen to us if you've made a mistake?" You know . . .'

The curb rein once slipped could not be put back again, and a less strong personality than Adonia would have been wise enough not to try. But she did try. It was asking to be kicked, and she was kicked.

One sympathizes with her feelings as she contemplated her husband's situation as it had developed in her absence. He had become famous—without any help from her. He moved around with a new authority and there was now no doubt (at least in his mind) whose will and personality were the stronger. He had found new friends, many of them rich and influential, whom she either disliked or distrusted; she would not realize that as a late-starter she must make a special effort to get to know them and she refused to do it. 'I don't like the way they patronize me,' she told Archie. Wartime censorship had prevented him from writing in too much detail about his Guinea Pigs and the mystique surrounding these young men was lost on her; it would be unfair to say that she regarded them merely as examples of her husband's skill with his knife, but she never gave enough of her heart and mind to be accepted by them and admitted to their special circle.

She was late on the scene, through no fault of her own, and she felt outside.

A jealous wife might have blamed another woman for coming in between her and her husband, but in truth there was no other woman in the middle. Not at this time, anyway. His charming and formidably capable assistant, Jill Mullins, was certainly on terms of intimate friendship with him. They had worked together too closely and relaxed together too frequently for it to be otherwise. One of Archie's surgeons came to him one day and complained that Jill had been rude to him. (She could be cutting with young doctors who might be potential rivals of her beloved Boss, though she was always charming to the anaesthetists; they did not compete.) Archie said.

'I'm afraid you'll have to put up with it. Miss Mullins is indispensable to me.'

She was indeed. She worked beside him in the theatre like an extra pair of hands. She helped him with his problems, surgical and domestic. He could confide in her and trust her implicitly. She knew his mind possibly better than anyone. But he was certainly not in love with her; nor, in this period, was she with him. She was having what was to prove an abortive romance with one of the Guinea Pigs.

The person with whom he had spent most time in Adonia's absence was, in fact, Edward Blacksell. With Blackie he found the same sort of companionship, the unspoken communication and understanding, which he had with his brother, John.

'After a frantic day in the theatre and a couple of hours wrestling with Guinea Pig problems,' said Blackie, 'we would go off back to the cottage together for a smoke and a beer. He would be tense and worried, but after an hour's talk—books, theatre, music, anything—you could all but see him loosening up. He would put down his glass, stub out his cigarette, and say: "I'm going to sleep now." And he would go off at once and sleep like a log until next morning.'*

This was a world which Adonia could no longer enter: the enclosed little world of Archie, Jill, Blackie and John Hunter, plus the all-important Guinea Pigs. She was back in East Grinstead but only too well aware that she was not a part of it.

The Queen Victoria Hospital had changed now beyond all recognition, and Archie and Blackie between them were responsible for the bulk of its improvements. Most of the Battle of Britain pilots—except for chronic cases like Paul Hart and Peter Weeks—had gone now, though they came back frequently for treatment. But with the bomber offensive in full swing over Europe, more and more air-crew injuries were flowing into Ward Three.

'How to keep them occupied and happy while we mend them?' wrote Archie about this time. 'That is our main problem here. We've attacked it in different ways, some successful, other less so. The difficulty is to combat boredom in patients whose powers of mental concentration are severely reduced and who at the same time are going through a period of severe mental turmoil. Purely diversionary pursuits are useful here, such as films, concerts, picnics and outings.'

So Archie and Blackie went to London and recruited all the pretty young singers and dancers they could find and brought them back. Many of them stayed on as nurses. They even persuaded Clark Gable, now a flier in the US Air Force, to give the Ward a hilariously successful lecture on how plastic surgery in

* He never had any patience with those who could not sleep. To insomniacs, he would say: 'Try sleeping every other night.'

Hollywood had 'stopped my ears from flapping like wings every time I faced the cameras'.

The houses of the local rich were ransacked for good books, radios, gramophones and records.

'Most hospital libraries are composed of books which no one else wants,' Archie wrote. 'They should be ruthlessly overhauled and ninety per cent sent for salvage. Here now there is an open library both technical and non-technical in each of the recreation and rest rooms which is small, carefully selected and added to regularly by current "books of the month" and other selections. Books of this sort are really used. Daily papers and periodicals are available for those who wish to keep abreast of the times. Music lovers fall naturally into two groups, those who like good music and those who prefer jazz. The usual hospital gramophone is a murderous piece of machinery. Good music is only enjoyable when played on a good instrument, hence efforts were made to secure the best records and a first-class self-changing radiogram, which can be played in a quiet room to an appreciative audience. The result is that more patients prefer Beethoven, Chopin or Brahms to the works of Mr Benny Goodman.'

He added, wistfully: 'It must be recorded, however, that there are many who remain faithful to a steady undercurrent of syncopated noise, whether they are eating, dressing, working or even sleeping.'

There were lectures and 'brains trusts' but not much of the basket-work and weaving that was to be seen in the therapy departments of other hospitals.

'In the generally accepted sense,' he reported, 'occupational therapy means cane-work, leather-work, book-binding, weaving, carpentry. Early in the war this hospital'—he might have added against his advice—'was equipped with a complete department of this description with a trained occupational therapist in charge. After working a year it was found that less than five per cent of the patients who should be working were actually doing so. The reasons were not far to seek. The work has little essential meaning, especially at the present time; it is frequently merely diversional and other interests conflict with it. RAF personnel found it childish and worked only under extreme pressure. Often it was found that having made one bag or cane basket, the patient did not try another.'

Archie took Blackie to see it and asked him what he should do with it.

'Scrap it,' Blackie said.

He had an idea. One of Archie's friends and a frequent visitor to the hospital was George Reid, who manufactured precision instruments for RAF fighters and bombers. He was invited back to the cottage and given a sales-talk by Archie as a result of which he was persuaded to move drills, lathes and presses into an annexe of the hospital.

'We opened up a full-scale workshop for the assembly of aircraft instruments,' wrote Archie, 'with benches for twenty-five workers. The benches were arranged in groups. Constant supplies of parts arrive weekly from the parent factory and are assembled by the working patients under the supervision of a head technician supplied by the factory and four girl workers, one of whom sits at each bench as instructor. Nine separate assembly jobs are handled and each can be learnt in a few hours. The work is clean, interesting and of great remedial value, particularly for crippled hands. The patients feel that it is of national importance.'

The Industrial Therapy Department at the Queen Victoria Hospital quickly ran into trouble, not because of failure, but because of its immediate success.

The patients from Ward Three worked speedily and efficiently, easily mastering the techniques. They continually exceeded the quota asked of them. There were very few rejects. Every patient had either piloted or flown in an aeroplane in action and knew that these instruments could, in an emergency, mean the difference between life and death. They rarely made mistakes.

When news reached the unions of the new development they dispatched an organizer. 'It is interesting to note,' Archie wrote, 'that the production of many patients with crippled hands and good mentality often exceeds that of workers with undamaged hands but of duller intellect.'

The union organizer, stop-watch in hand, was rather more blunt: 'They're working too bloody fast.'

There were complaints to the Ministry and the threat of trouble in the home factory if the 'unfair competition' from East Grinstead was not curbed. An arrangement had to be made whereby the members of the therapeutic unit were paid union rates and adopted union rhythm of production.

Between them, Archie and Blackie were already thinking of the future of the men who had come into their charge. The idea for the vast rehabilitation programme which eventually developed from the formation of the Guinea Pig Club was germinating in their minds. For they knew what the Guinea Pigs did not: that these repeated operations, successful though so many of them had been, were bound to have an effect in later life; from each man some of the juice of longevity had been sapped each time he went under the knife. They would have to be watched and tended like rare plants for most of their future life; brought back regularly for 'service' to their hands, noses, ears and chins; watched for any deterioration in their general bodily condition—and not only that. Archie was determined that not only physically but also materially and mentally must their needs be looked to.

'After what these boys have been through nothing is too good for them,' he said. 'The State should keep them in comfort for the rest of their lives. But you know what the State is like after it is all over. They forget about them. Well, if I can help it, they are not going to forget about the Guinea Pigs. No man I've ever worked on is going to end up playing a cornet in Oxford Street. And if the State won't look after them, we will.'

He told Blackie to start building up the funds of the Guinea Pig Club in preparation for the demands of peace. Meanwhile, he wrote a note which he sent to the Health Ministry which read:

'With this extensive programme of rehabilitation, it is obvious that the surgeon in charge develops a deep interest in the welfare and progress of his patients. When the time comes for return to service or industry, he is likely to see to it that the man who is reconditioned mentally and physically is placed in the correct niche and not thrown willy-nilly on to the labour market. Employers of labour and heads of service departments are only too eager in these times (1943) to adjust the job to the man, or vice versa. Hence close touch must be maintained with the patient and with his employers until it is clear that he can stand on his own feet.'

He added:

'It must be remembered that these conditions may not always persist when the demand for labour is not so acute, hence it is vitally important to maintain an efficient follow-up scheme and to check from time to time the patient's progress. It may be found for instance that a new form of work is desirable, and that vocational training is required. It is, I believe, not part of the duty of a hospital to undertake work of this sort, and it is much better handled at a training centre. It would be in the best interest of the patient, however, if the hospital and training centre maintained intimate contact so that all available information concerning the patient is directed to the same desirable end.'

This was his plan for *all* the patients who had been through the Queen Victoria Hospital, but so far as the Guinea Pigs were concerned he said:

'These are our boys, and we must look after them ourselves.'

He spoke for the rest of his staff in voicing these sentiments. Those nurses and doctors—particularly Mary Rea and the anaesthetist, Russell Davies—spent most of their scant leisure hours looking after the Pigs, and they were beginning to face the fact, but willingly, that they had undertaken a spare time task that would keep them busy for the rest of their lives.

It was perhaps because of his deep and abiding interest in the welfare of the Guinea Pigs that a rumour began to be spread that no one not of the RAF who went to East Grinstead could expect the 'full works', as his boys called it, from Archie McIndoe. It was not true, of course. It was not easy to get into the Club. You did not become a Pig unless you were a burned flying member of the RAF. But it was the Guinea Pigs who made the rule and not Archie, and it certainly did not prevent him from doing his own personal, post-operation therapy on his other patients, whether they were soldiers, sailors or civilians.

At a time when his wards were overfull with burned airmen, he received a visit from the mother of a twelve-years-old girl who had been badly disfigured about the face as a result of an injury at birth.

'As we knew how busy he was,' her mother wrote to the author, 'we offered to wait until he had more time, but his answer was immediate and quite definite, that it must be done as soon as possible because of the psychological effect of a facial injury on a sensitive girl. He had her in his hospital at East Grinstead and there she spent an unforgettable and incredibly happy fortnight among all his "Service" men. What struck us most forcibly was the free and easy, happy atmosphere of the hospital. After a couple of days in bed my daughter was allowed up and used to go to film shows in the men's wards, learnt to make toys with them and was frequently found to be playing games or chatting with men whose disfigurements or injuries were, like her own, taken in a calm, matter-of-fact manner.

'When we went to say goodbye to him I thanked him and commented on this extraordinarily happy atmosphere and his reply was: "But I am making faces. What is the good of making them if they do not set in happy lines?" '

The girl went home and grew up to be a doctor herself, kept up a correspondence with the man who had mended her face, and treasures a letter from him which said:

'Dear Jane,—I am delighted that you enjoyed yourself at the hospital and that it was not quite such a terrifying experience having your new face made as you might have thought. There are hospitals and hospitals but I hope you will always remember this one as not being a hospital at all. Certainly we enjoyed having you here and if at any time in your future career you want some odds and ends trimmed off I will have a special room all ready for you.'

Nor would Ben Coutts, an army officer who had his nose shot away in the Western Desert in 1941, ever complain that the Guinea Pigs got preference over him.

Coutts came back from the Middle East after having had fifteen operations done on his nose in a military hospital in Alexandria.

'I was thoroughly fed up with the whole business,' he said, 'as I could not see any improvement. On the way home I was torpedoed and my papers were lost. As an army officer I should have been sent to a plastic surgery in Scotland which is where I was landed. However, as I had lost my papers I fooled the medical board that I was to go to Archie McIndoe of whom I had heard a lot from a dental surgeon in the Middle East. The chairman of the medical board telephoned East Grinstead and it was typical that Archie should answer the telephone. At that time he used to do a lot of this. He inquired briefly about my case and said "Send him on". I went down there after having been given a month's leave and arrived the week between Christmas and New Year in 1941.

Archie came in, took one look at my nose, and said after a few moments' pause: "We will do so-and-so, and it will take two years." I was out of hospital with a complete new nose in just exactly two years. This I felt was one of his greatest characteristics. He inspired confidence in you and yet he didn't minimize the length of time it would take.'

Coutts mentions a typical example of the McIndoe psychology with his patients. Having learned he was a Scotsman, he said:

'It's no use starting to operate on a Scot with New Year coming on next week. You'd better get it out of your system. Take another week's leave and we'll start on you after Hogmanay. And don't drink too much, because when we begin you'll bleed like a pig.'

It can hardly be said that he neglected Coutts' after-care because he was not a Guinea Pig.

'After my operations were finished,' he said, 'Archie decided that it would be extremely stupid for me to go back into the fighting forces even though I had done a good deal of instructing between operations. In 1944, much against my will, he advised me to go in front of a medical board to be discharged from the Army. In his write-up for the medical board he stated that he felt that I had certain advantages which would help the farming industry in Scotland. I must say that I little realized what I was to do and expostulated with him that my experience pre-war had been very much of physical work in farming and I had done very little on the managerial side. He brushed that aside. He said he was quite convinced that what he had written was correct. Although I can't remember the exact words, I remember that he said that my knowledge of stock was such that it would carry me to the forefront of British agriculture.'

Coutts added:

'All I can say is that he knew more than I did. In 1956 I bred a Smithfield champion which still carries the record price of £1,600 for a fat animal. I was also lucky enough to manage the well-known Millhills beef Shorthorn herd when we sold bulls to the Argentine and America for very high prices. All this makes me very humble when I think that Archie should know so much in advance of what he felt were my potentials—and he did this constantly with many other people.'

Towards the Queen Victoria Hospital itself Archie McIndoe now felt a proprietary attitude which often irritated the hospital committee and was to infuriate the Health Service authorities after the war. But he could not help the way he felt about it. He did not mean to hog all the credit for what had been done there; he knew as well as anyone else that it was a team of surgeons and nurses rather than a single man which had wrought the miracles in Ward Three. But what those who were jealous of him could not or would not understand was that it was Archie McIndoe whose methods, personality and dogged fights with bureaucracy had put the Queen Victoria on the map.

He was determined that it should stay that way. To his Canadian colleague, Ross Tilley, he said:

'What I should like to do is leave this hospital bigger and better than when we found it. I don't want it to lapse back into a little cottage hospital again.'

Tilley had an idea. 'Why can't we get the Canadian Government to help?' he asked. 'We've been written up in the Canadian papers for our work. The people over there would like to help. I wonder if I can persuade the Canadian Army to build us an extra ward.'

He made inquiries at Canada House and found a sympathetic reaction forthcoming. He pointed out that without any help from the Canadian Army the Queen Victoria had already treated many burned and mutilated Canadian airmen.

He came back to Archie and said:

'They want to know how many Canadians we've treated here. If the number's big enough, they'll play.'

Archie turned to his clerk, Bernard Arch (now Secretary of the Guinea Pigs), and asked him to find out exactly how many Canadians had passed through his hands and those of his colleagues. Arch produced the figure that evening and it was seventy-eight.

'It's not enough,' said Archie. 'They'll never give us a new wing on the strength of that.'

Bernard Arch said: 'May I make a suggestion, sir? These are all plastic cases, which means that they've all been on the slab more than once. Couldn't we——?'

'We can,' replied Archie and started to laugh. 'Now you go away, there's a good boy, and multiply the number of cases by the number of operations they've had and let me have the figure.'

At this Guinea Pig Reunion McIndoe was photographed between John Hunter (with moustache) and Edward Blacksell (Right) A less-publicized, but just as important, aspect of the Reunions was the Maestro's careful checkup on his patients' progress

(*Above*) The Duke of Kent was one of McIndoe's patients—notice how he holds his hand in this photograph of him, with McIndoe and some of the nursing staff, outside the East Grinstead hospital

(*Left*) Digging the first sod for the Children's Ward with Mrs Kay Clemetson

A few days later Ross Tilley was able to point out to Canada House that no fewer than four hundred and twenty operations had been performed on Canadian servicemen at the Queen Victoria Hospital. Canada House was impressed. So was Canadian GHQ. So were the Canadian Government and people. Shortly afterwards, the builders moved in. Splendid equipment began arriving from Canada. The new Canadian Wing began abuilding. Archie knew that, for the duration, it would care only for Canadian servicemen; but afterwards the Queen Victoria would have it for its own.

Nor was he satisfied with that triumph. What about the Americans? Surely a rich nation like the United States could not stand by and see its much smaller neighbour make such a tremendous effort without a reciprocal gesture! By a combination of blandishments and sly remarks about national prestige—plus some heavy hospitality—he got a theatre wing from the Americans too.

Those who watched Archie McIndoe closely during those busy days of 1943 noticed that he was always clenching and unclenching his hands. They put it down to a nervous reflex, a kind of 'surgeon's twitch', but it was much more than that.

For some time he had been aware of a growing stiffness in one of the fingers of his left hand and a 'deadness' in his right. It did not at first interfere with his operating technique, for he worked mostly with his thumb and forefinger when he cut, but it caused him both pain and fatigue when he wrote. Secret sessions squeezing a rubber ball of the kind which his patients used for their 'frozen hands' did little to ease it. He was not surprised at that. It did not take him long to diagnose what was wrong, and for a surgeon it could hardly have been more serious. To Edward Blacksell one night he confessed that he was developing what was known as Dupuytren's contracture of his ring finger 'and if I don't do something about it quickly Archie McIndoe is washed up as a surgeon'.

He was indeed. The Dupuytren's contracture was named after the senior surgeon at the Hotel Dieu in Paris who, in 1831, demonstrated to his surgeons the hands of a coachman named Demarteau. The ring finger of each hand had contracted insidiously and spontaneously towards the palm. In Archie's case only one finger was beginning to bend inwards, but he knew that the others might soon follow. He himself had once written, in a study of the affliction:

'The course which any particular case will run is difficult to assess and there are many variations on the theme of a slow, inexorable contracture. Occasionally a case may begin with a contracture of comparatively rapid onset and then the disease appears to become arrested, perhaps for years . . . In other patients, however, the onset and rate of contraction are so rapid, with the events of years becoming telescoped into a few months, that operation becomes a matter of urgency if irrevocable joint changes are to be avoided.'

His gifted hand was threatened and he knew he must take steps to ease it without delay. If the condition spread to the distorted finger it would produce the so-called 'frozen finger' with which he would be saddled for the rest of his life, with normal function of his hand never possible again.

But the only remedy was surgery, and it was a delicate operation during which something might well go wrong; not perhaps serious for an ordinary man but tragic for a surgeon. An incision must be made in the palm of the hand, skin hooks applied to the edges and then a sharp and meticulous dissection until the skin of the palm is retracted and the nodular Dupuytren's tissue which causes the contraction is revealed and cut away.

A surgeon performing the operation must identify each digital nerve and cut with care. At each stage of the operation there is danger of a kind which only a pianist, an artist or a surgeon can possibly understand.

Archie went to his friend and partner, Rainsford Mowlem, a specialist in this kind of surgery and, in a sense, handed him his future.*

'Get it over with,' he said.

The solid and dependable Mr Mowlem looked at him, grinned, and said:

'There's no need to be nervous. I've done this sort of thing before.'

* Hand surgery is one of the most important specializations of a plastic surgeon.

'Maybe,' said Archie. 'But not on *this* hand. Take care of it. It's the only thing between me and the bankruptcy courts.'

Two days later, his bandaged hand elevated on a pillow beside his bed, he received a telephone call from Jill Mullins. Disaster had struck East Grinstead. A German bomber, on the run from RAF fighters, had jettisoned its bomb as it fled and it had dropped smack on the Whitehall Cinema in the centre of the town. The cinema was full of children as well as grown-ups and there were scores of dead and badly wounded.

Mowlem had warned Archie to treat his hand with care. His examination had revealed that the operation had been done only just in time; another few months and the golden hand which had served him so well would have been ruined for ever. It needed cherishing for some time to come.

He fretted in his sick-bed at the London Clinic and cursed his helplessness. In fact he need not have worried. The Queen Victoria Hospital responded magnificently to the emergency, housing the dead bodies until they could be identified, ministering to the burned, wounded and shocked. Under the guidance of Percy Jayes and his team, the staff worked throughout the day and night in all the operating theatres which could be set up. But Archie had to be there. In the middle of the night he rose and took off his bandages and put his hand in a sling. He went down to his car and drove out to East Grinstead and arrived in the early hours of the morning.

He had reason to be proud of his staff for they were coping wonderfully, but he would not have been Archie McIndoe if he had not chafed at his uselessness and realized morosely what life would be like for him if ever the day came when he would not be able to operate at all.

This mood of pessimism remained with him after his hand had completely healed, and his friends began to worry about him.

He was no longer full of the bounce and bonhomie which enlivened so many of his sessions in the operating theatre. He bit his staff savagely whenever anything went wrong. He confided to no one except Edward Blacksell that although the pain in his hand had now gone one in his stomach had taken its place. Was it psychosomatic? He tried to believe so at first and put his distress down to bad digestion and overwork. When the pain persisted, however, this suspicion gave place to a fear that he was suffering from something far worse. He was a stomach surgeon of great skill and experience and he knew all the symptoms.

'Don't tell me I've got a carcinoma of the liver,' he said on one occasion. 'I'm about the only surgeon in the country who can do that operation properly, and I'm damned if I'm going to start cutting up myself.'

It is perhaps not surprising that relations, both domestic and professional, were not easy during this period. Uncharacteristically, he could not decide what to do about himself; he did not confide in Adonia, although it subsequently became clear that he had told Jill Mullins; he nursed his ache and went on with his work, but the smile was gone and so was the resilience.

In the circumstances, it is not surprising that a letter he received from the Air Ministry on September 21, 1943, touched his raw spot. It came from Wing Commander George Philippi, an old friend, and it dealt with the behaviour of some of the Guinea Pigs at Marchwood Park.

Marchwood Park, near Hythe in Hampshire, had been opened a week earlier as an official training centre for injured and disfigured RAF aircrew. It consisted of a commodious country house and four workshops which were later to be run as a satellite factory and assembly point of the British Power Boat Company, whose main workshops were a few miles away. The injured airmen would make the boats under expert supervision and some of the injured pilots would be allowed to test them—a good way of coaxing back their confidence. The accommodation was comfortable and commodious; once Archie had pulled a few strings at the Ministry of Food the meals would be more than adequate; and he had enthusiastically recommended its use for 'allied personnel, Poles, Czechs, etc., and for patients from overseas who are without homes in this country.' The training centre was under the general command of Wing Commander Philippi, head of P.5 (Rehabilitation) at the Air Ministry with Wing Commander Harris in charge at Marchwood itself.

Archie sent a number of his Guinea Pigs to the training centre as soon as it was opened and offered his personal cheque of £100 towards their comforts fund. He was furious to hear, at the end of their first week, that his Pigs, far from developing into the star-boarders of the new establishment, had turned it upside down.

'I now wish to draw your attention,' Philippi wrote to him, 'to a matter which is worrying me not a little and is giving Wing Commander Harris grave concern at Marchwood, namely the somewhat riotous behaviour of four of your East Grinstead patients. I think I realize why you give these men as much latitude as you do and of course there is much to be said for the principle of giving men as much freedom as possible, but surely there is a limit and that limit is reached when they do themselves injury. You will appreciate that it is very difficult to lay down stricter rules and regulations than you do at East Grinstead . . . The matter to which I refer now is that of men who are allowed to go out by themselves and return at all hours in an inebriated condition. I am told that they are permitted to do this at East Grinstead and indeed that patients still living in Ward Three frequently return so drunk that they have to be put to bed by the nurses. My attention has been drawn to this by the behaviour of four of your men who were given leave-out passes from Marchwood last week and who returned between twelve and one o'clock in the morning so intoxicated that the sergeant had to help carry them upstairs and put them to bed. One of the men had damaged his hand to a considerable extent and Mrs Grant who dressed it is very worried because she has returned him to East Grinstead considerably worse than when he arrived at Marchwood. Further, you will realize that behaviour of this kind is bound to give Marchwood a bad name and it is only a question of time when these men will be picked up by the military or civil police in Southampton and we will have something of a scandal.

'What I would be grateful if you would do is to discuss this matter with Flight Sergeant Blacksell and, if you think fit, tighten up your rules and regulations and let me know what you have done or propose doing so that I can amend mine to coincide with yours.'

This was nasty enough. But there was more. In addition to his offer of his own money for the comforts fund he had also been to some trouble to find out which of his rich friends had houses in the district from which they could start schemes—as they had done at East Grinstead—to entertain the patients in their leisure hours. It so happened that most of the ladies whose names he sent on were Jewish.

'Now I would like to refer,' Philippi went on, 'to the letter which you sent to W. C. Harris, regarding the help which your Welfare Committee have very kindly offered to Marchwood. I feel that we have not been established long enough to benefit from the assistance of the ladies mentioned. We have not yet come to the end of our own resources and I rather hesitate to bring in anyone from outside until we ourselves know exactly what we do want. Also I am doubtful as to the wisdom of accepting help from the ladies named by Mrs Laski, as they are all of the same persuasion. One of them no doubt would be very helpful but you know what prejudices there are in a county and we must avoid cliques at all costs.'

Rarely had the staff at East Grinstead seen Archie McIndoe so angry. He summoned Blackie and said:

'Go down to Marchwood at once and give those bastards hell for disgracing us.'

He called a meeting of his Service patients and harangued them for thirty minutes, calling them every name under the sun, threatening them with dire punishment.

'Normally, at the end of it,' said one of them, 'he would have finished it up with a smile and said: "Well, that's it, boys. Now go away and for God's sake behave yourselves." But not this time. It was pure venom all the way. He looked at us as if he hated us. We came away feeling ashamed of ourselves but also very sorry for Archie. We knew there must be something wrong with him.'

He went back to his office and tore up the cheque for £100 and then he wrote to Philippi:

'Dear George,—Thank you for your very straight left of September 21. The incident of September 14 was reported to me and I took immediate action by sending F/Serg. Blacksell down (*a*) to investigate the behaviour of the four patients who came from East Grinstead, and (*b*) in conjunction with W. C. Harris to take the strongest disciplinary action possible. His report to me on return was that the position was essentially as you described, namely that the four men had in fact returned riotously drunk and stated in defence that they had enjoyed this privilege at E. G. and saw no reason why they should not behave similarly at Marchwood. This of course is absolutely *not* the case . . . To make the matter perfectly clear, in case the position at E. G. might be misunderstood by any patient there, I had every serviceman before me on Wednesday morning and delivered myself of a vitriolic diatribe on the behaviour of the men at Marchwood, reiterated the rules that are in force here, and re-informed them that drunkenness would be dealt with in the following way:

'On the first offence, offenders would almost certainly be relegated to hospital blues and be subject to penalties laid down in King's Regulations, and on a second offence they would be immediately transferred with a letter accompanying them detailing their offence for their CO.

'Now as to the rules in regard to this matter, it is quite obvious that you have been grossly misinformed. All patients in Wards One and Three must be in by 10 pm and passes till 11 are only issued in special circumstances. Spirits have never been allowed within the precincts of the hospital, although an issue of beer is allowed. Leave at the annexe, consisting of men fit and about, is more generous. The evening pass is till 10.30 and if there is a dance the leave is extended to 12.30 once a week . . . There is no question that the men at E. G. understand the position now with crystal clarity and I should be obliged if Harris will return forthwith any further offenders in this way. I can assure you that a month or two at Uxbridge can have a most sobering effect.

'In regard to the Welfare Committee, please forget it; it was a suggestion which followed a conversation I had with Harris. I am sure it would be far better if the local situation developed in its own way.'

When he had finished the letter, he read it through. It was far from being the blistering document he had intended to send. But now he was tired. He wrote 'A poor reply' across the carbon copy of the letter and put it in his files.

How differently he might have written is indicated by a letter which he sent to the new Commander of Marchwood a year later, when that officer complained that the undisciplined and boisterous Guinea Pigs had stolen his squadron flag and his sunglasses:

'Dear Squadron Leader Warlow,—As the result of profound and far-reaching inquiries I have at last run to earth your Squadron Leader Flag, which by now you will have received. But all my most hard grilling failed to reveal the whereabouts of the sunglasses and I am driven to the conclusion that this time my lot were not the guilty ones. However, to even things up, I am sending you one pair of new American sun-glasses. In the course of my investigations I am informed that "one only" pair of non-Service ladies' breeches are missing from one of our lot. Whether these are to be regarded as the legitimate trophy of the race, or whether they are to be returned, I leave to your discretion.'

But by then, of course, he was in a different mood.

Perhaps his greatest solace at this time was his daughters. His life was unhappy at home. With East Grinstead and the Guinea Pigs he had grown stale. It was not that he had lost his touch or even his dogged efficiency, but he noted in his minute-book that he had performed no less than 2,300 operations in the previous two years, and it was, of course, too much. He would have felt a numbness in his hand even if he had not undergone an operation for contracture.

Someone who watched him working noticed that one of his operations disappointed him. 'He seemed tired, deflated, a little irritable, and worried about how his patient would take his new face. I wondered if he was becoming too involved, whether the crushing strain was beginning to tell. A visiting doctor mentioned X-rays. "We're too slap-happy with X-rays," he snapped. "How do we know the effect of so many X-rays?" The doctor started to apologize. He gave an expansive wave. "The fault is mine. Please excuse me. I've had a tiring day. A boy I know—a good-looking boy—I'm afraid I haven't been able to make him as good-looking as he was." Then suddenly he was in control again, and it was as if a drawbridge had gone up on his mind, hiding his feelings from us. He began to tell a story. He dominated our little group.'

His daughters, however, seemed to fill a gap in his life, even though they were not with him. Adonia junior had gone off to university: a slim, fair-haired, serious girl who seemed to be so self-contained that he could say: 'That one will be keeping me in my old age. There's no telling where she'll go.' The younger daughter was Vanora, just going on fourteen years old, with just the sort of mischief and quicksilver temperament about her to remind him of the excitement he had once known in the early days of his marriage to Adonia. She had gone off to school in Buckinghamshire whence she bombarded him with letters. He called her 'threepence three farthings' and she called him 'twopence'. She would write:

'My darling Pop,—How are you? I hope you are well. I was wondering if you could get me a new prayer-book. The one I have at the moment is Mummy's and is starting to come apart. She asked me to take care of it as it had a lot of sentimental value or something of the kind. Don't get anything too expensive but see that it will last please. Also could you please send me some marmalade and some rum-flavoured chocolate spread. I -ang yow. I don't want to make this letter one long gimme so now I will tell you some news. Yesterday. Got up early, was ready long before the gong. Surprising ! ! ! Did nothing in particular, just had lessons. Today. Got up early, lost my coat, missed chapel. Swopped my fountain pen with Anne de Rothschild, a new girl. Mary Limb and I both joined the Secret Service Society for the Suppression of Sinister Subjects, Sinical Sinners and Strong Sentences. Well that's all for now buddy all my love, 3¾ alias Vanora. PS—Please could you send me a jar of marmite. PPS—Do you mind me taking confirmation classes. PPPS—When was I baptized and where.'

These letters always came from 'The Lunatic Asylum, Winslow, Bucks,' and he adored both them and their writer. He had shown so little evidence of being a proud parent before that his friends could hardly credit his enthusiasm.

The physical pains, however, did not improve and after months of procrastination—and several weeks when he took to his bed—he decided that there was only one thing to be done. He picked his surgeon with care. He was now a serving officer but one of great skill and distinction in Harley Street. Archie conducted his last series of operations, brought his records up to date, and went up to London to be, as he put it, 'probed for the leak in the gas mains'. He made only one request when the arrangements for the operation were being discussed, and that was that Jill Mullins should assist in the theatre.*

After all his fears, the actuality was something of an anticlimax. The cancer that he feared did not exist, and all that happened was that his appendix was whipped out, and he was stitched up and told that he was now as good as new. In fact, there had never

* Though she was actually only an onlooker.

been need for an operation at all, and that was ironic in the circumstances. A couple of weeks of convalescence and he could go back to East Grinstead and start work again.

This he did. Three weeks later he was back in Ward Three, chatting with the boys, making plans, pencilling in operations at the Queen Victoria and 149 Harley Street. When anyone asked him how he felt, he would answer:

'Splendid, boy. Never felt better. Always pick the right man to operate on you and you can't go wrong.'

But when he thought no one was looking he clutched his stomach again and the expression of pain on his face was not pleasant to see. Soon everyone was aware that something was amiss. He had never been anything but ruddy of face but now it was noticed that he had a pallor. There was one occasion when he stopped in the middle of an operation and went out to be sick.

The climax came on the evening when Mr Leon Goossens, the oboist, was due to visit East Grinstead to give a concert for the patients at the hospital. Adonia had been spending more and more of her time alone at the cottage, but this was a treat for which she had been waiting eagerly. Two hours before the concert was due to begin, Archie announced to her that he would not be able to go and suggested she go alone. There was a great quarrel. He had not told her that he was suffering from the most severe pain, so that she could not be expected to understand why he was so suddenly refusing to go with her, and she insisted. He dragged himself to the Queen Victoria Hospital and sat it through, though for most of the time it was sheer agony.

A few days later he was put on the operating table again and opened up once more. It was discovered that the great surgeon who had performed on him in the first place had left a surgical swab inside him and it had been festering in his gut ever since.

He kept the swab as a souvenir. And some time later, when he flew out to the Middle East on what had been planned as a tour of inspection but was now a convalescence, he took the swab with him. In Cairo he presented it to the surgeon whose staff had left it in him with the words:

'I think you'll find, old boy, that this belongs to you.'*

* It is, in fact, the theatre staff's responsibility to see that all swabs are removed.

There were many of his friends who afterwards maintained that the 'incident with the dirty linen', as he came to call it, caused him so much strain as well as pain that, physically, he was never the same man again.

CHAPTER EIGHT

'SOMEONE OF IMPORTANCE'

THE WAR WAS ON the ebb.

For Archie McIndoe and his staff at East Grinstead the knowledge that we were sweeping forward into Europe and that it would soon be over helped to relieve the strain but did not take much of the pressure off their work.

'Thank God all this beastly business seems to be approaching its end,' he wrote to his mother towards the end of 1944. 'But then the new problems of peacetime will arise, I suppose, and for some of the boys here it is not going to be funny. I don't suppose it is going to be funny for me, either, not for a time, anyway. I am feeling very tired. I calculate that I have operated about four times a day for every weekday except holidays and trips to Town since 1941 and I sometimes feel that I never want to cut another flap again. But we go on working—and only occasionally do we despair. Such an occasion occurred today when they brought a boy in from Italy. You should see what the fools did to him there.'

He was referring to a young man who has since become one of the most famous of the Guinea Pigs, by name Jimmy Wright. Flying Officer James Wright had won a DFC for his part in the raids over Holland and Belgium and was then posted to Italy. Early in 1944, on the start of his forty-fifth mission in a hundred days, his Marauder crashed and caught fire: most of his crew were killed, and Jimmy Wright was dreadfully burned about the face. He was taken to hospital at Taranto and there—because instructions about coagulating substances had not yet reached them from England—the staff covered his face and his burned eyelids with gentian violet.

The grim process started. The skin hardened and then began to crack, particularly the skin of his eyelids. He lay in bed, unable to close his eyes, and suppurated.

By great good fortune it happened that his father was serving in the RAF in Italy and he visited his son, was appalled at his state, and got him on a hospital ship for England. He arrived at East Grinstead in the late spring of 1944.

'God almighty,' said Archie McIndoe after he had examined him, 'what have they done to him?'

Cornelian ulcers had developed on his eyes. He was staring, eyes wide open but sightless. The amazing thing was that despite his condition he was smiling with what was left of his lips, and he came to be known later as quite the most cheerful member of the mutilated in Ward Three. Archie set to work on the job of giving him a new face. At East Grinstead now an eye unit had been opened; and they tackled the eyes.

Here was a Guinea Pig for whom the end of the war would mean little. Work on him would have to go on for years, as the face was rebuilt and the fight went on to save his sight. (In fact, Jimmy Wright had forty-six operations on his face and eighteen corneal graft operations. He has lived to go out into the world again and is today running his own film business at Shepperton Studios. But treatment on his eyes came too late; the gentian violet had done its work, and he is blind.)

'One thing we can be certain of, Blackie,' Archie said to his welfare officer one day. 'Whatever happens, these boys are going to be with us for always. When I'm ninety-nine, they'll still be coming in for repairs.'

'And advice,' said Blackie. 'You've inherited quite a family. They'll never leave you now.'

It was true. In fact, only one of his Guinea Pigs ever did leave Archie McIndoe, and that against his will. His name was Vladimir Razumov and he was a Russian fighter pilot who had been shot down over the German lines on the Eastern Front in 1943. His face had been well-nigh burned away, but he received scant attention from his captors. They flung him into a Russian prison camp and left him to suffer. His ordeal was not a short one. His compatriots had no drugs to ease his pain and there were no surgeons to tend his burns.

It was not until his camp was overrun by Allied troops that he was transported to a British hospital at Bad Oyenhausen, where a surgeon did a makeshift operation on his eyes. A few weeks later, clad only in a shirt and trousers, he was flown to England and taken to East Grinstead.

Archie was away at the time, so Jerry Moore did an emergency operation on his eyelids, for the grafts had not taken. When Archie returned he took over and started to work on his face, a long and meticulous job.

Raz could speak no English at first and he was both morose and suspicious. He could not understand why the other inmates of Ward Three were so cheerful. He had been indoctrinated with the Russian belief that to be taken prisoner is to be disgraced, that it is better to die than to be caught. As he picked up his first few words of the language, he began to say:

'When I go back to Russia—poof—finish!'

Slowly, Blackie and the boys began to win his confidence. They took him with them on their pub crawls and on their visits to the great houses in the neighbourhood. They had no Russian uniform, so they bought him an RAF uniform in Soho and, with Archie's permission, gave him a Flight Lieutenant's bars and pay. They taught him to drink beer and even, occasionally, to smile.

'This nice place,' he said about East Grinstead, and then hastily added: 'But Communism better.'

The Russian Embassy in London had been informed of his arrival. One day a small group of baggy-trousered men arrived to see him and, clustered around his bed, talked with him a long time. When they had gone Raz would not say what they had talked about, but his comrades noticed that he was very gloomy. He did not go out with them any more.

'What are you worried about, Raz?' Jimmy Wright said to him. 'You've got a cushy billet for at least another two years.'

One afternoon a few weeks later, when the nurses came round to serve tea, it was noticed that Raz's bed was empty. No one had seen him go out. It was only afterwards that someone remembered having noticed a large car draw up at the hospital and the baggy-trousered men climb out. Everyone thought that he had gone for a walk on his own.

But he never came back.

Blacksell went up to the Russian Embassy and asked about it.

A blank-faced servant told him that he had no information at all. Archie wrote to the Ambassador but received no reply. A copy of his membership certificate of the Guinea Pigs was sent to him at the address in Russia which he had given to the hospital authorities, but there was no acknowledgment.

He was never heard from again. Beside the name of Vladimir Razumov in the membership list of the Guinea Pigs is written:

'Gone away. Address unknown.'

There had been failures, of course, of a different kind. Death had taken several of the Guinea Pigs.

There were those whose operations had made them well again but hardly whole. There are some human skins which do not take kindly to grafts. There are others which will not knit together again without leaving behind ugly keloids, scars which all his efforts failed to make sightly. These men were no longer faceless, but what faces they now had often looked like mockeries of a normal visage. All Archie could do for them was coax them, bully them, out of their depression and stress once more that they must learn to live with their mutilations and never, never, never hide themselves from the world.

His attitude towards those who tried to encourage the Guinea Pigs to do so is shown by an exchange of letters between him and the Senior Pensions and Welfare Officer of the Royal Air Forces Association. This officer, Mr G. F. Roper, had written:

'I have been in correspondence with Major Shelagh Howe of the Women's Royal Army Corps who has been closely associated with Group Captain L. C. Cheshire, VC, in the formation and running of one of his homes for the disabled in Cornwall. Major Howe herself owns a large farm at Predannack near the Lizard in Cornwall, which is being run by two women, both of whom are trained nurses with experience in general and mental nursing and of plastic work. Major Howe wishes to make her farm a centre for the employment and housing of badly disfigured ex-Servicemen many of whom, as you know, find it difficult to mix with their fellow men owing to their grave disfigurement. She has asked me to approach you . . .'

Archie replied:

'I must say right away that I think this is a pretty forlorn project.

Disfigured men do not take to colonization as, for instance, tuberculosis patients do, and, quite apart from that, all the people with whom I am concerned and who have been badly disfigured are excellently well set up in the normal community and all making adequate livings. In the past I suppose at least a dozen schemes of this sort have been put forward but, of course, none of them has the slightest chance of success. The answer is perfectly simple. Disfigured men spread about the community become someone of importance. When all put together they tend to dislike each other with the curious snobbishness of disfigurement that only those who have lived in close contact with them can really understand. This is not apparent in hospitals where they are undergoing treatment but it is obvious in places where they work and establish their homes. I think it would be very wise of you to dissuade Major Howe from any project of this kind. It simply could not succeed. I hope you will forgive my frankness.'

Men of importance! That, he always stressed to the Guinea Pigs, was how they should regard themselves.

To another proposer of a hideaway for his boys, he wrote:

'These boys are not lepers. They do not suffer from contagious diseases. They are learning to live normally. You may be interested to learn that some of my most badly injured are already married to the prettiest wives, and quite a few of them have offsprings on the way.'

It was true. Holebrook Mahn was not the only Guinea Pig to have grabbed himself a good-looking nurse as a wife. William Simpson, with stumps where his hands had been and a mended face, was now married to one of the most beautiful nurses in Ward Three and building a family. He had learned to make two dwarf fingers on his right stump do the work of ten normal fingers and needed the help of no man. He was in process of getting himself a discharge from the RAF and would soon be air correspondent of the *Sunday Express*, the best that air-minded newspaper had ever had.* His wrecked first marriage, if not forgotten, had ceased to be a bad memory.

'It's not the men's faces I worry about too much,' Archie said to Blackie. 'It's remarkable how soon you can get used to even the

* He subsequently became Director of Public Relations for British European Airways.

ugliest and most fearsome-looking physog. Women, bless 'em, don't seem to notice it after a time. They drool over film stars, but they marry men. And thank God most of my boys are men. No, what I worry about most is the hands. If a man has injured or mutilated hands, those are what you never stop noticing—when he lights a cigarette, when he tries to do up his flies, when he holds out his hand to be shaken.'

Blackie knew only too well what a problem injured hands can be. He had just returned from Glasgow where he had attempted to patch up a pre-war marriage of a Guinea Pig who had lost all his fingers.

'It isn't that I don't love him any more,' the wife said. 'I do. I'm sure I do. But there comes a moment when he touches me with those hands, and I can't help it—I cringe.'

So Blackie was schooling his charges not only in the art of mixing with the world but of forcing them to accept *all* their mutilations.

'When you meet someone,' he said to those with injured hands, 'always shake hands with them. Don't tuck your stump behind your back. Offer it proudly. Make them get used to it. Make them learn to know the feel of it. You'll be surprised how soon they will begin to accept it.'

But oh yes, there were failures.

Triumphs, too. Archie McIndoe wrote to Tom Gleave, who had been a fried wreck of a man only two years before, on June 13, 1944:

'My dear Tom,—I was delighted to see your name in the honours list and I do congratulate you with all my heart. A long time ago I remember a review of your little book concerning your celebrated "Row" which appeared in *The Times*.' [Gleave had written a book called *I Had a Row with a German*, which, with typical modesty, he had asked to be published under the pseudonym 'RAF Casualty'.] 'The critic said that here was a gallant story of a man who had fallen from victory to defeat. I have always felt how incredibly wrong that was. If ever anyone achieved victory over defeat it was yourself, and someday you must write the story which followed the final chapter. Some of us know it already but there are many whom it would benefit. Anyway, everyone sends congratulations. Yours ever, Mac.'

Squadron Leader Gleave had gone back into action with the RAF and risen first to command a squadron and then a wing in intensive battles over enemy territory. His rank was now Group Captain and the honours list had made him a CBE.

Just before Christmas in 1945, the BBC asked Archie to broadcast from Ward Three about his patients and he consented on condition that the Corporation added its own contribution to the food and drinks which friends from all over the world had been sending to the hospital.

'It is a great day in this hospital,' he broadcast, 'but then it always has been. This is the sixth Christmas the boys have celebrated since the war began and it won't be the last. They come from all over the world and they keep on coming. To many of them it is as near home as they have known for a long time. Yes, the war is over for most people but not quite yet for these lads. Don't forget this . . . Over there are Frigger Foxley, Wanker Wilkins, Frankie Trulah, George Taylor and Bill Wormans. This is their second or third Christmas, I forget which. Next year they will be out and perhaps they will join the old hands like Henry Standen and Geoff Page and Jock Morris and Tom Gleave and Ben Coutts, who come back today to see how their pals are progressing, to wish them luck and join in the fun. At the other end of the ward is Dickie Richardson and Geoff Paine and lots of others. This is their first Christmas here; some of them will probably set the pace next year as men of considerable experience in these matters. I know that I am voicing the general feeling here when I send to all our friends—whether patients or just friends—our best wishes for their happiness. In particular to all Guinea Pigs scattered over the world in seventeen different countries; to hundreds of them in Great Britain; to Ross Tilley and his lads in Canada; to Ken Gilkes and Wishie and Strick and Dusty Rhodes and King Cole in Australia; to Bob Penman in New Zealand; to Graham Lawson in South Africa. To them we here in Ward Three say thumbs up and a merry Christmas.'

In his manuscript of the broadcast the name of Dusty Rhodes has been added in pencil, as if as an afterthought. In fact it was put there at the suggestion of John Hunter, for whom this young Australian had become something of a talisman. 'If I can keep this little so-and-so alive,' he used to say, 'no one need die under anaesthesia.' For Rhodes, terribly burned about the face, not only had no wish to live after he caught the first sight of his burned face but was one of those cases who reacted dangerously to drugs. After his first major operation he was being wheeled back to the ward when John Hunter, who had performed as anaesthetist, caught sight of him on the trolley.

'Get him back to the theatre at once,' he shouted, and rushed away to scrub himself. The moment the boy was back on the slab, he took a knife and slit his throat, pushed a tube down it, and began to breathe into it.

'Another two minutes and the bugger would have been dead,' he said. He had had a landoul spasm.

After that, he took especial care of Rhodes. He was a tiny, sensitive little man, acutely aware of his lack of inches, desperately unhappy about his looks. Thanks to Hunter's vigilant care, he had no more trouble under anaesthesia, but somehow, no matter how hard Archie tried, the new face he was building on the young man failed to take the right shape.

Shortly before the end of the war he was told he would be repatriated to Australia. John Hunter urged him not to leave too quickly. 'Archie says you need a lot more work on your face,' he said. 'Don't have it done in Australia. They make flaps over there like kangaroo's pouches. Stay on here. I can fix it.'

He had become very fond of Dusty Rhodes. He worked hard to persuade him to stay, and when he insisted on leaving he gave him a last warning. 'Don't let anyone meddle with that face of yours. If you want anything done, get in touch with me.' He was convinced that only he could look after the boy under anaesthesia.

A few months later Archie received a letter from Mr Basil Riley, a plastic surgeon in Sydney, which said, in part:

'You will, I am sure, be upset to hear that Dusty Rhodes died quite suddenly within twenty-four hours after our having done a dermatome graft on his face. It would seem that the pentathol anaesthesia was in some way responsible though he actually regained consciousness.'

Archie wrote back:

'While I am sorry that you had this misfortune, I could not help feeling that it was, in the long run, a good thing. He really had had a terrible burn, but his rehabilitation was a stormy and trouble-some business. I do not think he would ever have become psychologically resigned to the fact of his severe injury; largely I think because he was small in stature and the burns were peculiarly distributed and gave him a kind of gollywog appearance which he deeply resented. He used to give John Hunter a terrible time with landoul spasm and I have no doubt that is what he got.'

But John Hunter said:

'Why didn't he write to me? I'd even have gone to Australia if he had asked me.'

'Go on, John,' said Archie. 'You'd never have lasted the journey.'

John Hunter shook his head. 'I saved his life once. I could have saved it again.' He sighed. 'I used to like that silly bloody boy.'

Peace. All the colonial and foreign Guinea Pigs were now being repatriated. Archie's two favourite Czechs, Frankie Trulah and Joseph Capka, announced that they would soon be leaving for Prague, and he threw a large and liquid party for them at the Whitehall Restaurant. Trulah was an effervescent and irrepressible young pilot who had been burned twice by the fires of war. His face was burned during the Battle of Britain and Archie patched it up. He went back to fly again and crashed again. This time the burns were even more severe and the labour on his face and body was long and difficult; nor was it made easier by Trulah's habit of stealing out of the ward to go on parties in the town. Capka was a bomber pilot who had escaped to Poland after the Nazis occupied Prague, and then kept one jump ahead of the enemy through the Balkans, North Africa (where he joined the Foreign Legion) and France until he reached a bomber squadron in England. There he had fallen in love with the Waaf who directed him in the air from the Ops room and married her. He was shot in the face while on a bombing raid by the rear-gunner of an American Liberator plane which had been captured by the Germans. Archie was proud of the job he had done on him.

Now these two were on their way home. And neither they nor Archie guessed that, when the Communists came into power, Frank Trulah would be killed and Joe Capka would be arrested as a British spy and incarcerated for ten years.

They said goodbye in the best rough-house tradition of Ward Three. Towards the end of it, Archie was carried to a table, relieved of his collar and tie, lathered with soap, and put through a mock operation. He got his own back by creeping away, first locking the jokers in the room for the night.

'Lots of them are going,' he wrote, 'and even an old cynic like me sometimes thinks that they are taking a part of me away. But that doesn't mean that our work is slacking off. We are extremely busy here, particularly at East Grinstead, which has become a very big show, and it looks as if something in the way of a post-graduate school will be formed. I will have half a dozen fellows under training constantly on a two-year basis. There is a terrible shortage of plastic surgeons in England now with the amount of work to be done. It just seems impossible to cope with the flow of cases and there are far too few trained hands for it. However, things are shaping well in the field of plastic surgery and one great advance will be the establishing next week of a plastic society which will be affiliated to the College of Surgeons. I think there are about fifty people interested in the field, so that we start with a goodly number of aspirants to plastic honours; either Gillies or Kilner will be the first president.'

Not only were the Guinea Pigs departing from East Grinstead, but the surgeons too. Archie's team was breaking up. The brilliant young doctors who had learned the skinner's art at his elbow were looking for new jobs where they could lead instead of being led. Ross Tilley had returned to Canada. Percy Jayes and Jerry Moore, his two most brilliant subordinates, had already applied for positions in other hospitals, and he wrote, lobbied and cajoled the powers-that-be to see that they got the appointments they wanted This was one of Archie McIndoe's most admirable qualities: his active loyalty to anyone who had ever worked beside him (worked well, that is). His files are stuffed with letters of recommendation not only for his surgeons but for his nurses, secretaries and assistants as well. They scattered all over the globe, but when letters came in from South Africa, South America, the United States, Europe and the Far East asking for recommendations or help, he never failed to respond; and he responded with letters which are far from the usual stereotyped references. He dictated an average of five such letters a day, and never repeated himself once; and he did this on top of a vast correspondence about the welfare of each individual Guinea Pig as well as his own professional correspondence. Nor was he often unsuccessful in his advocacy. 'What's good enough for McIndoe is good enough for us,' seemed to be the view of hospital authorities everywhere.

His team was not ungrateful for these efforts; at the time, anyway, though the gratitude did not always last. Percy Jayes remained for all time constantly loyal, constantly aware of Archie's aid. And the brilliant, erratic Jerry Moore wrote to him soon after the war:

'This is a letter I meant to write before. It is to express to you my deepest and sincere thanks for all the things, little and big, which you have done for me. I hope as the years pass you will think your labours on me have been worthwhile. I was delighted with King's, but East Grinstead and yourself will still receive my 99·9 per cent energy and support. The 0·1 per cent is reserved for temperamental peculiarities of myself. I feel deeply indebted to you and time again will give me the opportunity to repay you.'

Of all the departing doctors, Ross Tilley, the Canadian, was perhaps the one whom he most missed. It was Tilley who had proved his strong right arm in his fights with authority. It was Tilley who had got him the Canadian Ward at East Grinstead and, when the Canadian troops departed, persuaded his Government to turn it over to the hospital as a gift. It was Tilley's charm and drive which had helped to promote the Americans to donate an extra wing—the wing now almost ready for occupancy.

Archie wrote to him on January 11, 1946:

'I have been exceedingly loath to write, first of all because I have been, as usual, up to my ears in work, and secondly, your departure left me with a certain hopeless feeling that I found difficult to overcome. However, here is all the news. We invaded the Canadian Wing after your departure and by slow degrees managed to get ourselves installed. It was hard work getting everything reshuffled, at the same time fighting off the numbers of cases clamouring for admission. Cherry Hall took over and I must say has done a magnificent job. The place is full and has been so since you left—practically entirely RAF but the Army infiltrate every so often whenever Percy (Jayes) gets his hot hands on a bed. The place is running well, and as we have few calls for private rooms—the severe burns tailing off—I have taken over the whole nine rooms for private work and believe it or not keep them filled . . . The American Wing next door is now complete and we move in next week. It is by long odds the most magnificent thing in the country. The theatres are beautiful and the arrangements superb. It took £10,000 to finish it which we managed to get out of the British War Relief Fund, so that the total cost of building and equipment is just under £100,000. We had some awkward moments towards the end when we found that we were completely down the drain, but we took the matter straight to Bertram Kruger who simply reached for the cheque-book and signed his name. It is almost certain that the Queen will open it and the only person I would wish to be there beside myself is you.'

He added:

'I had to increase my operating times to four days a week and for the last six months I have been cracking about thirty a week . . . As for our friends. Jerry Moore is doing well, but requires a swift kick in the tail about once every two months and I can tell you he gets it. Percy [Jayes] married Kate Harrington two or three weeks ago and is now living out. He is still as good as ever and works like a Trojan. John [Hunter] has been ill for some time; first of all with the old jaundice, and although no one suggested opening his tummy—which was a pity—he made a stir by taking some sulphanilamide and developed the worst sensitization rash I have ever seen. He was a raw and bleeding mess from head to foot and that's a lot of rash! It has not improved his temperature any but it has shaken him off the bottle for a while. It will do him no harm.'

The close-knit union between Archie and John Hunter was, in fact, coming to an end. New techniques were developing in anaesthesia; like everything else in surgery, it was striding forward as a result of the emergencies and experimentations of war; and the bluff, too-human John Hunter was in no physical condition to keep up with them and not mentally willing to accept them. Archie McIndoe was only too well aware of them, and not for the first time he had begun to weigh his friendship with a man against his professional skill. In such a contest, there was never any doubt about the result: no ties, no affections, would ever weigh heavier with him in surgery than sheer competence. 'This job,' he used to say, 'has no place for passengers.' It would be a long time before John Hunter ceased to march into the wards with his famous smile and his famous slogan: 'Just a little prick,' but already Archie had begun to take the first moves which would result in edging him out of his team. He had already approached young Doctor Russell Davies and offered him the job of his principal anaesthetist if and when he decided that Hunter was no longer capable of doing the work, and he coupled the offer with the promise that he would not have to wait long for the succession. For a man in Davies' position it was an offer which carried with it prestige in his work and considerable financial reward, for he would be working with Archie not only at East Grinstead but also in the more lucrative operating theatres in Harley Street. He turned it down not out of any sympathy for Hunter—for he too believed that the back of the old horse was bending—but because he believed in the National Health Service and was not interested in money.

Archie dismissed him with the comment: 'You're a fool. You don't know what you are missing,' and turned to another newcomer, a remarkably cool and efficient young man named Hale Enderby. Enderby accepted what Davies had refused, and a remarkable partnership was born which was to do much for the craft of plastic surgery in the years to come.

These overtures were, of course, secret. Not for anything would Archie have deliberately hurt the feelings of his old friend and associate. But East Grinstead is a small place. The gossip began to get around, and Hunter heard what was afoot. The seeds of estrangement were sown . . .

Perhaps even more than Ross Tilley, the man whom Archie McIndoe most missed in the immediate days after the war was Edward Blacksell. He had been the friend in his blackest hours. He had been counsellor, comfort and support not only at the hospital but in the lonely hours at home. For Blackie, Archie cherished two ambitions—to get him adequate reward for his painstaking and devoted work as the father and mother of all the Guinea Pigs, and to persuade him to stay on at the hospital as superintendent of welfare.

He wrote to him on July 11, 1947:

'There comes a time in every man's life when he has to make a decision. I think this is yours and it is now or never! Last night I dined with a person whose name is known all over the world. He makes it possible for the following offer to be made to you: that you return to East Grinstead on a five year contract at £1,000 a year, this to be divided into salary and expenses according to how it would work out from the income tax point of view. I need only say that the reason for the five year term of contract is that no one can foretell what will happen in five years and no one will want to bind you if you want to spread your wings in other directions. I may say here that Sir Ian Fraser of St Dunstan's is behind all this. The money would come to us either through the Guinea Pig Club or the hospital. The donor's only stipulation is that he remains anonymous and for ever more! He assures me that providing the aims and objectives which we have at heart are achieved future expenditure is of no moment to him.'

It was an offer which might have tempted Blackie had he not been so eager to return to his first love, schoolmastering. He had already taken his discharge from the RAF in order to take up a schools appointment in Barnstaple, Devon (where he is now a headmaster). Reluctantly, for he hated to hurt Archie, he said no. 'I will look after the affairs of the Guinea Pigs just as long as you and they want me to,' he said, and accepted the honorary position of Resettlement Officer to the Club.* But he was imbued with a mission to educate the young, and nothing would deflect him from it.

So Archie turned his efforts towards getting him recognition for his wartime work, without, of course, telling him he was doing so. In this he was backed to the hilt by the Guinea Pigs, who had reason to bless the humanity, understanding and enterprise of their welfare officer. His rank had been merely that of warrant officer but his strength and influence had been that of ten air marshals. Archie put his head together with Group Captain Gleave, the most senior of the Pigs, and the result is seen in two letters, one written to Archie by Gleave and one written by Archie to Air Marshal Sir John Slessor at the Air Ministry. Gleave's letter, written on July 21, 1945, said:

'Dear Mr McIndoe,—You are undoubtedly aware of the esteem and affection held by past and present RAF patients for the RAF staff at East Grinstead. For some time past two of the RAF staff in particular have been singled out in their respective spheres of activity for special comment, to wit:

1198648 W/O J. E. Blacksell, Welfare Officer.

370823 F/Sgt Salmon, NCO in charge of Saline Bath Unit.

* A position which still takes up most of his spare time today.

'With regard to W/O Blacksell I have yet to meet, in fifteen years' service with the RAF, an NCO or W/O possessing such personality, capable in his line of work and ability to mix with all ranks, commissioned or otherwise, as he does. He has applied himself to his job in a whole-hearted and commendable manner which, in my opinion, thoroughly deserves recognition.

'With regard to F/Sgt Salmon the number of past and present RAF burns patients of all ranks who have received unstinted and devoted service from him are too numerous to mention. Now that he is due to leave the service, I feel it would be a great pity if he did so without some recognition of the excellent work he has accomplished. I am writing to you in this form as I have been unable to ascertain who is directly responsible for honours and awards in respect of the RAF staff at East Grinstead, and as I am anxious to avoid stepping on anyone's toes perhaps you may wish to do something about it. I can assure you that from the many comments and expressions of gratitude directed to me in respect of these members of the RAF staff by numerous past and present RAF patients, the subject of this letter will have their whole-hearted support.'

Archie tucked this letter into an envelope with one of his own to Slessor which said:

'I have received the enclosed letter from Group Captain Gleave which is self-explanatory. Gleave, as you know, has been a patient here on and off since 1940 and is well aware of the worth of these two men. I have long wished that something could be done to recognize the sterling work which they have put in for so many years. I feel very deeply that some tangible expression of their grand work over the past five years would be deeply appreciated, not only by themselves but by so many members of the Guinea Pig Club who have passed through their hands. I cannot speak too highly of both of them and I am sure it would give the greatest pleasure to all our members if the suggestion in Group Captain Gleave's letter could be carried into effect. As you can see we are rather out of the swim of RAF organizations here and lead a peculiar life as an RAF Establishment within an Emergency Service Hospital—a sort of parasite which tends to escape notice in matters of this kind. It is in fact difficult to know to what authority such matters should be submitted, hence I am sending it direct to you. Although I know little about such affairs I should have thought that a MBE or a BEM would be a very suitable recognition.'

It took some time and many more letters than that, but on June 11, 1946, Archie was able to write to a friend:

'You may not know that Blackie was awarded the MBE for his work during the war and well earned it was too. I had recommended him for this at the end of last year just before his demobilization. Nothing happened until three months after he was out and as a result of a considerable damning and blasting around the Air Ministry. It was a poor way of doing it but better than not at all.'

He had received a CBE himself for his wartime work, and that was a poor way of doing it too. Many a serving doctor had got much more for doing much less. But a Labour Government was in power and it was not being generous with its awards to civilians in those day. It was only another reminder that the exciting times of war were over and the bumpy and difficult roads of peace lay ahead.

He knew that his most urgent task now was to fit himself for the trials he felt were coming. 'Things over here are in a great state of uncertainty,' he wrote to Ross Tilley. 'The Government have not revealed their hand or their intentions and the result is we are all hanging on waiting to see whether we become State servants or whether there is a chance left for the old buccaneering spirit.'

To a friend, Vincent Hurley, in New York he wrote:

'I have not been out of England except for various visits to the Middle East and Germany on business throughout the war, and, therefore, I have no idea what a civilized country looks like or a town which is not bombed flat. We live here like savages and, not entirely as a result of our socialist government, seem to be getting worse every day. My brother, who had just arrived after seven years' absence, has taken one swift look round and decided to leave the country to the aborigines. We of course think it is all right; it is going to take a prolonged holiday in a country which approaches normal to get over the war mentality which is heavily engrained in all of us . . . I have been more than busy for the past six years, and what with one thing and another seem to have done little else except chop young men around who might well have been left alone.'

Now he was going back into the competitive world of cosmetic surgery. He had written only a few months before to Ross Tilley that his wards were still filled with RAF casualties, but now he reported to a colleague, Selwyn Kenrick:

'The vast majority of our severe burns are coming to an end and the wounds of soft tissue and bone are also disappearing. I notice in my own hospital that the ratio of men to women of 80 to 20 is now beginning to get back to the 20 to 80 ratio of peacetime. This includes all the congenital deformities, the road, rail and air crashes, the civilian-type burns, industrial accidents and so forth.'

It also included the film stars and models with noses to be reshaped, the old women in search of face-lifts, the seekers after beauty where there was none and shape where there was shapelessness.

It gave every indication of being a busy life, but with a Government in power pledged to a National Health Service, not an easy one for a surgeon eager for the comfort and financial rewards he had missed during the war. He would have to fight to get them.

That meant he must first put his house in order.

CHAPTER NINE

McINDOE VERSUS BEVAN

IT WAS ALMOST INEVITABLE that the famous partnership of Gillies, McIndoe and Mowlem, split by the war, should fail to come together in peacetime.

Each of them had increased in stature during the war and Archie himself had become world-famous. He was no longer willing to take second place to anyone; he suspected that Gillies would be inclined more than ever to favour the golf club or the fishing rod over the scalpel, and though the old man had richly deserved all the leisure he coveted, Archie was no longer willing to do three-quarters of the work for only half the profits.

'What you have to remember,' said one of his rich friends, Neville Blond, 'is that Archie came out of the war a poor man. He had managed to sandwich a few cases in between his work at East Grinstead, but I know that he had been able to put very little by. Some people thought he was inclined to be stingy, but it wasn't so. He was always making private loans to some of his Guinea Pigs, and he never expected to be paid back. But he had to look after the pennies.'

Archie himself made no secret of the fact that now the war was over he wanted to make money as fast as he was able. He still dreamed of a more leisurely life and a home somewhere abroad in the sun; the advent of a Labour Government had, in fact, quickened his ambition to make his pile and get out. 'For that I need independence,' he said.

So by mutual agreement the old partnership was wound up. 'Now we all run our own shows,' he wrote to Basil Riley, 'but still at the same address. This is the effect of the war which has separated us into different parts of the country for six years. Under such circumstances partnership became impossible. On the whole it has worked very well, and I think has dispersed the widely accepted but quite erroneous view that plastic surgery was in the hands of a ring. Certainly the competition is keen and healthy now.'

But how much should he charge his patients now that he was independent and famous? At first he was so unsure that he would write to the doctors who sent him cases and ask for their advice.

'Dear McIndoe,' one of them wrote towards the end of 1945, 'about charges. Commander —— is a damn good fellow and his Missis may be too. She at least will value your services in proportion to your operating fee, if any, and your consulting fee should be five guineas, I suggest. He is, as I told you, rolling in wealth, his cars vary between Rolls and Hispano Suizas and a plethora of others. As regards an operating fee, I really do not know what to think, but I suggest the highest you can decently charge anyone less than a duke. *At least* one hundred guineas. As to Mrs ——; the family live in a comfortable house. They are very decent people and will not plead poverty unnecessarily, but if you suggest a hundred guineas they may have a fit and ask you be be good enough to reduce it to seventy-five or fifty, but I think you should try and make it seventy-five. After all, what is the use of being McIndoe if one cannot charge more than the common herd? For God's sake do not leave this letter about!'

He was not to be anything like as hesitant as this in the years to come, but for the moment he was feeling his way.

It was not only his professional life which he was in process of adjusting. At home, his relations with Adonia had gone from bad to worse. It is difficult to say which of them was to blame for the inexorable estrangement which had begun shortly after Adonia's return from America. There were faults on both sides. As may have been indicated earlier in this story, the war had freed Archie from his wife's apron strings and he was no longer willing to accept the strong-minded guidance which she was always eager to give him. He resented her interference in his affairs. He could not put up with her temperament. They had begun to live in two different worlds, physically, mentally and emotionally. Archie was not entirely blameless for the arid quality of their life together, for after the first few attempts to introduce Adonia into the new world he had created for himself he gave up. There were too many quarrels as a result. He could not stand public scenes. He resented the interrogations he had to undergo when he came home of an evening after a hard day's work. He did not help Adonia's sense of grievance by leaning more and more upon the soft and sympathetic shoulder of his assistant, Jill Mullins, after he had had a row.

There was, of course, another side to it which cannot be gone into here. Adonia's increasing sense of isolation, her feeling that she was being squeezed out, reacted upon her in a way which was least likely to improve the marital relationship. Resentment, jealousy and tantrums were not the moods in which to win back a husband who was drifting away, especially one whose only ambition at the moment was to forge ahead with his career. For more than a year before it happened, most of Archie's friends accepted the fact that the break would have to come; and when it did come, towards the end of 1946, only Adonia believed that it was because of another woman. She blamed the separation on Jill Mullins. In fact, the cause was simply a cessation of communication, a loss of sympathy, a weariness with rows and misunderstandings. The tragedy was particularly poignant because these two had once had so much in common, had fought so many battles together, and had somewhere lost touch with each other.

It was decided that Adonia should go to London and try to make a new life for herself. Archie made her an allowance of £133 a month and installed her in a flat at Chatsworth Court in Kensington. There was no question of her taking the children with her. It is doubtful whether Archie would have let them go if she had insisted, but she did not insist. She got herself a job as a consultant in a beauty parlour and hoped that sometime, somehow, a reconciliation might be brought about. It was a forlorn hope because Archie was abundantly happy to be free.

'You may not be surprised,' he wrote to Mrs Meredith Jack on January 20, 1947, 'that Adonia and myself are now separated to our mutual benefit. The children are grown up and they live with me and both seem to be pursuing their education with fairly sound results.'

She wrote back:

'I am glad to hear it. We all know what this thing can be like and it must be a tremendous relief to you.'

But if those eligible women who welcomed his separation from his wife thought that this was an opening for them, he swiftly disabused them.

'Your touching little Valentine,' he wrote to one of them, 'is to hand. With the sentiments contained in the doggerel on the obverse side I entirely agree. Long may it continue. But I had better warn you that my own pump is of the sweet but completely indifferent order as experience should have taught you long ago: it is a purely mechanical circulator. As far as I can make out, it has no emotional significance whatsoever.'

It is true that after the separation from his wife his relationship with Jill Mullins moved on to an even more intimate plane. He continued to live at his cottage, Little Warren, outside East Grinstead, and the red-headed assistant was a frequent visitor to his home—especially when the children were on holiday, for they were extremely fond of her—as well as at his parties. Shortly after the separation, he wrote a letter to Lady Kindersley, who presided over the hospital committee at East Grinstead.

'I would be grateful if you would raise the following matter at the next meeting of the Finance Committee. Sister Mullins, who, before the war, was my private assistant, has now served the hospital for six years. During that time she has lived in, carried out her duties and at the same time in her off-duty hours has continued to act as my private assistant. It is now her intention to live outside the hospital and to relinquish her post of sister-in-charge of the American surgical centre. She will also resign from the CNR. But she wishes to retain an association with the hospital on a part-time basis, to continue as an assistant in my theatre, and to control and organize my own particular entourage. As I have a heavy teaching programme to carry out, many private patients, and my theatre technique is much on view to visiting surgeons and students, this arrangement would ensure that degree of efficiency which is necessary. She would thus be employed three days per week at East Grinstead and the hospital would receive the same enthusiastic support from her which it has had in the past.'

Thereafter, Jill Mullins moved into a cottage close to the hospital which he bought for her. It would be hypocritical to suggest that they did not see more of each other than ever, but that there was any thought of marriage in Archie's mind would be as untrue. Of his daughters, Vanora would have liked it to happen, for she

These two pictures of Kay Kendall, taken before and after McIndoe operated on her nose, are a striking illustration of his skill

McIndoe in Africa: (*Above*) with Jack Penn, and (*below*) inspecting his farm

adored Jill, and Adonia would not have minded. But when Vanora wrote to ask him whether this was what he contemplated, he replied:

'I am not going to marry anyone. I may tell you that I have had a sickener of your sex. About the only two left I like are you and Doni.'

To which Vanora replied:

'You are quite right. The female of the species is a terror, particularly the ones at this school. Here is an example of the day they give me here. Get up at 7.30. Breakfast at 8. Make our beds and tidy our rooms until ten minutes to nine. Chapel, roll call, then more work. Lunch, rest, walk, tea, work, then preparation until 7.15. Supper, bed and so on. And all through the day someone is yelling out: 'Don't talk!" "You can't read now!" "Move on please!" "Walk in single file!" And as a result of this I am in bed with a terrific sty, a dreadful cold, and feeling so dead that I can hardly write this letter now that I have (at last) the chance. I seem to do nothing but get infected with spots and styes and sore fingers. I am just one ruddy spot, and I tell you, right now, Archibald H., this is only the beginning of the term and *I can't* go on like this. I was run down when I left home but you should see me now! (Oh damn, my sty has burst! Just a second——) I know that you think I am complaining and I assure you that I am. I am going to grow up a bitter neurotic spinster if someone doesn't *do* something. Nothing has happened here except that I had a long row for being naughty (well, when you can't do anything *of course* you are naughty). And I was a good girl and did *not* answer back (which put a severe strain on me!).

'Please, darling, don't work too hard and look after yourself, won't you? I hate to think of you all alone there and now I am bothering you with all my worries—but feel I must tell someone!!! Loads of love sweetie pie, Vanora.'

He found himself a service apartment in Drayton Gardens in Chelsea and henceforth divided his week between East Grinstead and Harley Street. He was not as busy yet as he would be in a year or two, but the queue had already begun to form at the London Clinic and he had all the nose and breast reductions and face-lifts he could cope with for the moment. He was busy with Gillies and Mowlem in the formation of a British Association of Plastic

Surgeons, from which he was determined to exclude all the quacks and mountebanks who had crept into the profession during the war.

'The council, of which I am a member,' he wrote, 'has the job of scrutinizing prospective candidates for election. There are three types: (*a*) full members, (*b*) associate members, and (*c*) honorary members. This last difficult proposition was forced on us by one —— —— alias The Healing Knife, who, in a barefaced attempt at horning in, demanded there and then the declaration that he be admitted as a *full* member. With one accord the boys said balls and referred their own credentials to the Committee. It looks as though —— —— is about to get the chop. The axe will be swung by yours truly against all comers.'

The letters he wrote in this period would seem to indicate that he was restless and bad-tempered about everything around him, but this was not strictly true. It was a fact that he found conditions in Britain at the moment highly uncongenial.

'The very best for New Year and I hope you had a good Christmas,' he wrote early in 1947 to a former pupil, Jack Penn, now a plastic surgeon in South Africa. 'At least you would have sunshine and warmth for it. Here the warmth was entirely internal and had it not been for friends (like yourself) would have been spartan indeed. The weather has been bloody awful and the atmosphere of austerity and self-imposed misery in which this bloody country loves to bask takes a bit of bearing.'

Archie McIndoe had always been an instinctive tory at heart. He believed in the aristocracy of merit, the power of wealth, and the right to spend his money as he thought fit. He abhorred the Labour Government not so much because it was socialist as because it seemed so determined to level down the standards of living in the country. He feared the consequences if the Government went ahead with its promise to introduce a National Health Service in no selfish spirit, for he knew that his own private practice would not be affected. But he honestly believed that medical standards would be lowered, and he was apprehensive about what would happen under State control to his beloved Queen Victoria Hospital. For the independence of that institution he was prepared to fight tooth and nail.

For the moment, however, the Queen Victoria seemed to be in no danger. Far from it.

To Edward Blacksell, who had succumbed to a bout of jaundice in Devon, he sent his old friend Sir Dan Davies together with good news about the hospital.

'To make life difficult for your unfortunate physician,' he wrote, 'I have stimulated Dan Davies whom you remember looked after my own carcase to pay you a visit. He has at least experience of my own case behind him and the least he can do is to protect you from the surgeons and their bloody swabs. I hope he can help. . . . This place moves steadily forward. The New Wing is well open and in daily operation, even though it isn't yet finished in certain particulars. It excites both professional and lay admiration. No lack of patients and the RAF still heavily productive . . . From this you can see we are headed somewhere—just where no one could predict—probably the city Jail—but anyway there is still fun in life and you had better get well quick and climb on the wagon. When you are about again you and Joan must come down here and have a week at the cottage. There is only myself now with the girls at school and I enjoy my solitude—and peace! Adonia has moved to Town and complicates my life no longer. We have agreed to a separation—two great forward steps, first to agree, second to separate. I think she is happy. I know I am! So you can see I have at last turned the heat on my own little problem without the intervention of the Welfare Dept.'

For his holiday in 1947 he planned a trip to Africa. One of his patients, Robin Johnston, an ex-fighter pilot, was now established in East Africa as a district officer and had invited him out. So had Jack Penn in Johannesburg. But how to get permission from the Labour Government which would allow him to book a passage? Wartime restrictions were still in force. To obtain a place on a plane one needed official sponsorship, or an invitation from an official body overseas. He asked Jack Penn to arrange it with his local university.

'If you can stand one short lecture of say half an hour on any plastic topic—say circumcision—I can run the cost of the trip on to expenses and tell Mr Dalton to take a short run. After the lecture we can repair to the nearest local and get down to cases.

After one week in Jo'burg I propose leaving for Tanganyika where the real job of loosing off a few assegais at the indigenous fauna will be energetically pushed. So count on me for that, laddie, but the university must do its stuff or I'm in the workhouse. All is well here and we are swamped with work—there seems no chance of getting it all done. I am adopting a new motto—really the reason for the South African trip: Enjoy yourself, it is later than you think.'

The invitation was duly arranged to lecture on mid-facial injuries at the University of Witwatersrand, but the booking on a plane was not forthcoming. 'It seems either that there are no planes flying, or that if they do fly they crash,' he wrote. 'Hence BOAC were unable to guarantee anything until 1950 and even if they could they would give me no guarantee, except at the last moment, that I could even leave the country.'

That was written in May. A month later the name of Archibald H. McIndoe appeared in the honours list as the recipient of a knighthood. It could not have come at a better moment. It was a tardy recognition of Archie's tremendous wartime efforts and his persistent and devoted work at East Grinstead and for East Grinstead in the bleak days of peace. His ticket for a passage to South Africa appeared like magic. On the eve of his departure he was, as usual, president of the annual dinner of the Guinea Pig Club which was held at the Felbridge Hotel in East Grinstead on July 19, 1947. It was probably the most raucously happy and nostalgic celebration which that organization has ever held, for each burned airman felt that he shared in the Maestro's recognition. He stitched up the wound in the leg of one Pig who had somehow managed to fall from the roof of the building and was poured on to the plane with a bottle of champagne under his arm.

Between Archie and Africa it was a case of love at first sight. The moment he set foot in Tanganyika it was as if he were back in New Zealand again. Medicine was forgotten. So were his marital worries, his finances, even the Guinea Pigs.

'I am enjoying myself immensely,' he wrote to Jack Penn. 'We go out on safari for 3–4 days at a time and what with the sun and exercise I've lost about 12 pounds already. Messrs Nathan Son and Mick Davis would be horrified to see how the natty suit looks now. I have sweated off much Cape brandy and cream cakes and feel exceedingly fit . . . In the last two days Robin Johnston and I achieved our ambition and slugged the biggest bull elephant in the district. He gave us the fright and the thrill of our lives. After tracking him up hill and down dale, over trackless (and very hot and dry) African bush for ten days for a distance of 150 miles—30 miles per day—we arrived at his port side and only 20 yards away. At this point I began to feel that the whole thing was a bloody foolish affair. However, there being no other course I smacked him with 2 45/50 express bullets and offered up a slight prayer. Instead of falling dead at my feet I found I had touched off an atomic bomb. He went wild, felled about half an acre of forest and trumpeting like a banshee came straight for me. I left the scene of operations smartly. I was relieved to hear him charge off into the bush. We gave him half an hour to recover from the wound and then went after him. It took six hours and 15 miles, but eventually we got him—a beauty!'

He arrived back in England with a moustache—which he wore for a month, until his irate daughters persuaded him to shave it off—and a strong infatuation for Africa. He vowed he would go back and make his home there. It was a dream which, as will be seen, almost came to pass.

'I return to a vast accumulation of work,' he wrote, shortly after his return, 'my book choc-a-bloc till mid-December and no possibility of seeing a patient before then. Blowed if the best way of building a practice isn't to go big-game shooting in Africa. Certainly makes you think. Anyway, it means I'll be out again as soon as possible.'

But meanwhile, he had a fight on his hands.

He had realized from the beginning that if the National Health Service came into being the future of the Queen Victoria Hospital was in jeopardy. 'If Bevan wins,' he wrote, 'we will be up the local creek without a paddle.' He was convinced that if he could get Bevan into a corner and talk to him he might make a case for East Grinstead's independence no matter what the Government might do to the other hospitals; and he engineered an introduction to the Health Minister at a medical reception, following it up with a written invitation to Mr Bevan to come down to East Grinstead to see the Guinea Pigs.

The Health Minister replied through his secretary on December 8, 1947:

'I am desired by Mr Bevan to thank you for your letter of the 5th December and to say he would be very pleased indeed of having an opportunity to come down to East Grinstead. Unfortunately he has already made arrangements for the Christmas holiday and he cannot disappoint his wife's family with whom he has promised to spend New Year's Eve. If you found it possible to repeat the invitation early in the New Year Mr Bevan would look forward to the opportunity of coming down then.'

Archie wrote again and repeated his invitation. But by this time Aneurin Bevan had been warned that Archie McIndoe was a persuasive advocate and what he was out for. His secretary replied:

'I have shown Mr Bevan your further letter of December 22 and he thinks he had better wait until the early spring before promising to come down to East Grinstead. He has several Bills and other business in the House which will make him very busy for the next few months and he would rather wait and be sure of being able to keep the engagement. Would you like to write to him again, say, at the beginning of May?'

By this time, Archie guessed, the Health Service would be in force and the fight might be lost. He organized a party of Guinea Pigs and arranged for them to visit the House of Commons in charge of a local MP and urged them to do some vociferous lobbying. From every point of view but the important one the visit was a great success. But how had his Pigs affected the Minister of Health? They did not meet him. Instead, they took tea with, among others, Miss Jennie Lee, and the leader of the delegation sent Archie the following report:

'Miss Jennie Lee, wife of the Minister of Health, Aneurin Bevan, yesterday showed her complete grasp of up-to-the-minute news. On meeting some of the patients of this hospital at tea in the House of Commons, and being informed that they were all under treatment for plastic surgery, came forth the following enlightening remarks:

' "How very interesting! You know, I'm very interested in plastics. I was down at Imperial Chemical Industries only the other day."

'The patients in question would very much like to hear the Maestro's views on this subject, and whilst appreciating the advantage of this most wonderful hospital, respectfully suggest that indenting at ICI for a new nose is a far more simple procedure than plastic surgery as we know it.'

Whether Miss Jennie Lee could have been quite so obtuse as this would seem doubtful, but it certainly did not improve Archie's opinion of the House of Commons. 'You can guess what the temperature here is like,' he wrote, 'from Bevan's description of us as a "set of raucous-voiced squalid politicians masquerading as medical men," who have deliberately misled our colleagues and induced them to flout the "will of the people". That is the "51 per cent who keep Mr Bevan in power" and who are very shortly, unless we don't sign on the dotted line, to get the chop in the biggest possible way. There will be a 90 per cent vote among doctors against the National Health Act, and tempers are rising on all sides. Unfortunately the economic sanctions which Bevan can draw against us are grim in the extreme and I am not at all sure that there won't be a considerable degree of ratting when the appointed day comes along.'

He was right in his suspicions and most of the doctors did give way, despite assiduous campaigning by him and many of his friends—none of whom, incidentally, would really lose by the introduction of a National Health Service.

'What fools they are,' he wrote to Jack Penn, on June 18, 1948. 'The introduction of a National Service in which everybody can get everything for nothing will put, of course, an immense premium on the overcrowded industrial areas where the doctors can accumulate very rapidly a practice of up to four thousand patients at fifteen bob a nob per year. As you well know, doctors in industrial areas of this kind have always been of the inferior sort. They now become the élite of the profession simply because they command more fifteen bobs. On the other hand in the rural areas where the better class people are to be found, attended by more doctors, and incidentally where practices are far more widely scattered, there will not be enough financial return to justify more than one-third of the doctors remaining in practice... If the scheme is not a success it means that black marketing methods will have to be used, or alternatively the medical profession will institute such a ca' canny policy that the same people who paid the doctors before will be forced in self-defence to pay them again.'

He saw a bleak future ahead for the young specialists who were beginning to emerge now that the war was over.

'Specialist and consultant work is allegedly to be made easy for the young man,' he wrote. 'He is going to be paid six hundred a year on graduation and encouraged to progress along the paths of righteousness until he earns two thousand five hundred a year. There is an extra bait of another two thousand five hundred for the top line exponents of the Bevan policy. So that a few, possibly ten per cent, will receive inducement prizes of a maximum of two thousand five hundred per year on top of their original salary, half of which will very smartly be scooped back in the form of income tax and super tax, so that our gallant consultant, or specialist, is exactly where he was when he started. If you can see any sense in all this you're a better man than I am, Gunga Din.'

It was this deeply-felt concern for the future of the young doctor which shaped his feelings towards the National Health Act.

'He was convinced,' said Edward Blacksell, 'that once it began to operate a young man would never be able to do what he had done. I believed in the National Health Act and he was against it, and we argued about it for hours. "Where will the young plastic surgeons come from under the new conditions?" he would ask. "If I had to start all over again in these circumstances I could never have got where I am." What he could not see was that he would never have got there, anyway, if it had not been for the war. Without the war to dramatize his battles, plastic surgeons would still be justifying their trade and Archie might well have gone elsewhere.'

But what troubled him even more was the threat to East Grinstead's independence.

'Already the planners and centralizers are at work,' Archie wrote, 'and there is a move to incorporate the Queen Victoria Hospital, with its highly selected band of London consultants, with a local hospital with a lousy set of general practitioner-specialists with few qualifications. Naturally it has been given a very hot reception, and we are looking at each other over ten miles of Sussex countryside with considerable doubt and suspicion! All this adds up to the fact that medicine in this country is going to go through a period of immense reconstruction which will in the long run, I believe, result in no improvement but a general lowering of standards of service with the advent of the State as a third party. It will be a modification of Service medicine and all its attendant evils. Again I am sure that it is a political move to get the vote of the great unwashed, and damn the men who stand on the bridge. The new service will not affect me materially, the only adverse feature being the high rate of income tax. Whether there will be any reduction of this in the future is, I think, doubtful. The Socialists are well established, and unfortunately the Conservatives have so far not produced an attractive alternative policy. Churchill, however much one may admire him, is literally banging the big drum up and down the country and producing nothing of an attractive nature. The slow progress of the Socialist party to the right will, I think, in time really mean that you could exchange the terms Socialist and Conservative and get little change out of either.'

Despite all this grumbling and despite his constantly-expressed wish to get away from it all, Archie McIndoe was, in fact, more active, and more happily active, than he had been at any time since the war. He could not, of course, succeed in his fight against the National Health Act, nor could he keep the Queen Victoria Hospital out of the hands of the planners; it came under the control of the regional board at Tunbridge Wells. 'They have got their hands on the hospital at last,' he wrote, 'but they haven't got their hands on me and they never will. And so long as I am independent and so long as I continue to work at East Grinstead, I shall see that the tail wags the dog.'

There were so many new clients queueing for attention in his Harley Street rooms now that he was forced to open an extra consulting room, so that he could move swiftly from one patient to another. Rich old ladies, actresses, models, children—they all came in for the McIndoe treatment, a reshaped face, a new kind of nose, the removal of scars, birthmarks and chronic acne. He had always made mammaplasty (the reduction of breasts) one of his specialities and nothing infuriated him more than to see the operation deprecated or sneered at as 'pure cosmetic surgery'. The medical world was still inclined to regard pendulous breasts as phenomena which women must learn to bear, in more than one sense of the word, and an article along these lines in the *British Medical Journal* aroused his ire.

'Dear Doctor Ware,' he wrote to the assistant editor, 'I thought I should draw your attention to the somewhat idiotic answers given in last week's BMJ on the question of pendulous breasts and what should be done about them. The rather old womanish answer suggests that either they should be properly supported or the patient should go in for breast-stroke swimming; which is precisely what a woman would not want and is invariably the reason why she seeks relief from the condition. Of course the answer should have been that a surgical breast reduction should be performed by a competent plastic surgeon. This is an everyday operation and gives excellent results.'

The BMJ obediently printed his letter. But to a question to the same journal asking what he would advise a woman who wished to increase the size of her small breasts, he gave a different answer.

'The point at issue,' he wrote, 'is whether foreign bodies should be used for the purpose, and many people have attempted to more or less stuff the breasts out with Terylene wool. The pooled experiences of some seventy surgeons have proved conclusively that this was a very bad thing to do and the method was roundly condemned; but unfortunately it seems to have got into the papers and there are some people of the quack order actually doing it in London. I would therefore recommend that you give the following answer: Injections of the various gonadtrophic hormones, while they may increase the size of the breasts, have undesirable effects on other parts of the body; and surgical attempts are not less unsatisfactory, in particular the insertion of foreign bodies beteen the breasts such as Terylene wool. At the present moment unfortunately there is no treatment that can be whole-heartedly recommended.'

But he was strenuous in his defence of all the other kinds of beautifying surgery in which he was so busily engaged; and he never had any doubt in his own mind that cosmetic surgery was always justified if it increased the happiness of the patient whose looks it improved. Later on he wrote a letter to an old friend and plastic surgeon, B. K. Rank, in which he clarified his attitude to the whole subject. Rank had written him from Australia and enclosed a clipping from a magazine there in which his name was mentioned as the surgeon who had operated on a number of famous people, including a popular writer, a very beautiful model, an actress, and an enormously rich Indian prince. Rank added this comment:

'I know we have to take a fairly broad view of public rights and news information these days. It is a matter in which I have a fairly liberal mind, but I must say I find the crap talk in the gutter press, such as this, most embarrassing to our cause and our patients . . . I know I would be very cross and at least send them a damned sharp letter if my name was used in the way yours is here . . . I think one's patients have certain rights of privacy too.'

Archie wrote back:

'Your anguished howl from so far away has just reached me. I sympathize with you. I sympathize with myself! It is interesting that this sort of thing is just beginning to happen in Australia. It has been happening here for years. The worst I ever saw was the one you sent me just after the war, when our little friend X hit the headlines. We are blessed or cursed with the best and worst press in the world, and medicine is just being discovered and plastic surgery has been more than discovered. I don't know who operated on Mrs K (an Australian quoted in the article). It certainly wasn't me. The novelist was operated on by a quack called Y and publicized by him heavily in the local press. Kay Kendall was operated on by me and the lovely ex-model by my partner Gillies. They both publicized their operations, no doubt for a sufficient sum to cover their fees. The actress certainly wanted a pert tilt to her nose. She got it from a quack in London and came to me for a bone graft; but she happened to be on her way to New York so I sent her to Tom Rees, who is one of my best pupils, and he did her with an excellent result. The pert tilt is now removed but she immediately leapt into print.'

He went on:

'There is nothing you or I can do about this. The fabulously rich young Indian prince, was certainly operated on by me. He had a terrible cleft lip and palate which actually turned out to be a very nice result. He too jumped into the public press and I had no recourse but to accept it. A crafty reporter got every single detail of the operation from him, including the cost, and put it in the *Daily Mirror*. What one does about these things is hard to say but the answer is not a lawyer's letter. At the present moment I am trying desperately hard to bring sense and sensibility into the public relations of medicine in the widest sense. It is absolutely no use trying to beat the ears off a press which is far tougher than you or I can ever be. The only thing to do is to feed them good sound information, because the public wants to know and is not going to be put off with yarns . . . No one deplores the sort of thing you sent me more than I do, but I believe that entirely the wrong way to go about it is to attack it savagely in print. Answering defamatory articles never gets anyone anywhere; the mud sticks twice as closely. Fortunately, the kind of article you sent me is possibly today's news but tomorrow it has other uses.'

And he ended:

'If I could really stop this sort of use of my name I would need to be able to get up in public and say that I neither reduce noses nor do face-lifts. I do both, and I think they are both, in the right cases, justifiable operations. But I do other things too which the public prints are not in the slightest degree interested in. So there is a slight dilemma here and I am sure the answer to it is eventually a programme of education. Meanwhile, if you are really going to try to stop it, you have a busy time ahead of you!'

He did not mind—in fact, he kept a copy carefully among his papers—when some anonymous versifier circulated Harley Street consulting rooms with a doggerel which was called 'Uplift' and read as follows:

Carlotta, such an ancient hag,
 Whose face was like a crumpled bag,
Declared 'The fates I mean to swindle,
 I cannot see my boy friends dwindle.'
And so she bought a large *Who's Who*,
 Looked up the famous McIndoe,
And calling on him said, 'I'm told
 You are the Mecca of the old,
Having that rare and precious gift
 Of giving fallen girls a lift.
Quite unreservedly I place
 Into your magic hands my face,

And beg that you will do your best.
  But please don't make me like Mae West.'
And now to cut the story short
  That genius did just what he ought.
Carlotta who had been a fright
  Is now an object of delight,
From being a passée debutante
  She's now a damned hot cuty-pant.
Her beauty's fame outstrips by far
  That of Garbo or Lamarr
Or Rita Hayworth—what is more
  She snatches husbands by the score!

He did not mind because he knew, if the public did not, that cosmetic surgery was only the visible part of the iceberg, and work was going on in his operating theatres which did much more than put vain women back in circulation. Not only that. If he could not destroy the National Health Service, he could, by joining it, help to make it better than it might have been. He wrote to his old friend and helpmate, Doctor Balfour, at the Mayo Clinic:

'My new centre here has been much admired. It is, of course an example of co-operative planning. I have a very able group of people around me who have really put their backs into producing something of value to this country. Like everything else, however, which one builds to any size, it becomes a juggernaut or treadmill, and it is now very difficult to leave it to run of its own accord. My aim here is to develop a post-graduate teaching centre of plastic work; a subject very badly catered for throughout the world. The world war threw into high relief the crying need for good plastic surgeons, and like America we were very badly caught out at the beginning. I have returned to the fellowship system, based entirely on my experience at the Clinic, and propose to take six young men of promise, with a background of general surgical experience, and turn them out as accomplished plastic surgeons after two years of intensive training. This is, I think, about the only contribution I can make to the future of medicine in this country.'

He was being modest. He had much to give yet, and he knew it; and it was unusual for him to hide his light. But then Doctor Balfour was for him almost a father-figure with whom he did not need to push or show off. With others, especially when challenged, he was apt to be more forthright. There was one characteristic which he had inherited from his Scottish forebears and his New Zealand upbringing, and that was a sturdy determination always to stand up for himself and to say what he thought, frankly and straightforwardly. If anyone tried to trick him or deceive him, he had a bite which was painful. 'There are times in life when you *must* be unpleasant or you will never get anywhere,' he would say. To one assistant who twice bungled a task which he had set him, he said:

'Young man, there are two basic qualifications for a plastic surgeon. First, you must be an artist. Second, you must have a pair of hands that do not shake. You are no artist and you have hands like aspen leaves. Get out!'

Once, when he was driving away from the Derby, he was sitting in the back of his Rolls-Royce as the chauffeur tried to edge ahead through a crush of traffic. A policeman came up to the car, angrily berated the unfortunate chauffeur with a rudeness unusual in a British bobby. Archie sat back and listened with slow-burning anger; and when the policeman finally said. 'Don't think you can get away with it just because you're driving a Rolls. Stop trying to get ahead,' he could not contain himself. He opened the window and said:

'If I had not been trying to get ahead all my life I would probably be standing where you are now.'

But such rough language to a subordinate was rare. Usually he fought only men of his own size. One young woman doctor interrupted him on one occasion and felt the sharp edge of his tongue as a result. The incident happened at a meeting. After it was over, Archie sought her out and took her into the mess for a drink and apologized profusely. He asked her to forgive him.

'There's nothing to forgive,' she said. 'You were quite right.'

'No, I was not right,' he said. 'I was not right in attacking someone who couldn't hit back. What can I do to show how sorry I am?'

The woman doctor pointed at her nose. 'It's the only thing on my face I don't like,' she said. 'Could you alter it for me?'

He took her to the theatre a week later and operated on her nose. After it was over, he went to visit her and asked her how she felt.

She said that the dermatol which she was being given was making her see people in the form of hallucinations.

Archie looked at her owlishly. 'Do you like the people you are seeing?' he asked.

The girl shuddered and said she certainly did not.

Archie grinned. 'Well,' he said, 'I can do something for you that will really make up for my rudeness.' And turning to his registrar, he said:

'Change this young lady to morphine. She'll meet a much better class of person.'

The woman doctor is now one of the most attractive and successful members of her profession in London. 'I have never met a man,' she says, 'who could say he was sorry in such a charming way.'

Four, and sometimes six, operations a day. Meetings, meetings, meetings—with his colleagues, with new governmental committees, with the Guinea Pigs to thrash out their problems, with the RAF Benevolent Fund. Long sessions, dictating letters to his tireless secretary, Joan Dunkerton. Lectures, speeches, dinner parties . . .

With restless energy, he tried to cram a week into a day and a month into a week. The file headed THE PIGS in his papers is packed with letters he wrote to bankers, business men, tycoons in all parts of the country asking—cajoling—pleading with them to find jobs for his beloved burned airmen. He rarely took a simple No for an answer and in ninety per cent of the cases he got the Guinea Pigs the jobs they wanted. He asked nothing from them in return except that they should not let him down; and even with those who did so he always kept on trying.

It was still on behalf of the Guinea Pigs that he fought most strenuously in this period, and, as usual, it was with Authority, this time in the shape of the Ministry of Pensions. Despite his exhortations to his burned airmen that they must go out into the world and live normal lives, he never lost sight of the fact that these were men who had been grossly injured. They would always need attention. They would never be free as most men were free (they must never, for instance, expose themselves too long to the sun, for solar rays play havoc with grafts and pedicles). Their life expectation had been shortened by continuous operations. And he was determined to secure the maximum pension possible for them from the Government. 'A man who has had his face burned away—even if I have given him a new one—still deserves a one hundred per cent pension,' he said.

During his first trip to Africa, both the Ministry of Pensions and the Air Ministry got to work on his men. The first began to cut down the pensions of those Guinea Pigs who had left the hospital and gone back into civil life. The second brought out an order reducing the rank and pay of all Guinea Pig aircrew still in Ward Three to that of Leading Aircraftman—even sergeants and warrant officers.

When he reached home, the following letter from Blacksell was awaiting him when he returned to England:

'I have written to the Ministry *re* the pensions and I am arranging an interview so that we can stop this fantastic nonsense of giving Jock Morris a fifty per cent pension and cutting Ross Stewart's pension down to seventy per cent. I am hoping to have an interview with them, when Russell Davies (Hon. Medical Officer), Bernard Arch (Hon. Secretary) and I really go to town on them. If they remain bloody-minded, you and Sir Ian Fraser can scare the political daylights out of them when you come back. Russell has worked out a chart, which is on the line of five per cent pension for one finger. We had a long discussion over this and I think it is the only way in which the Ministry will play . . . As to the Air Ministry Order reducing pay: There are now a series of very frightened bodies lying around East Grinstead, with one of the men, Ward Bowyer, now actually making a bigger allotment to his wife than his actual pay is and already well and truly in debt. The Welfare Committee of the Club have dealt with that, and I have written to Lord Portal for assistance with regard to the Air Ministry Order.'

Archie picked up the telephone and got straight through to Portal. He did not need to bully or wheedle with that staunch and sympathetic brass hat. Portal went to work immediately and the AMO was put in abeyance. But the Ministry of Pensions was a harder nut to crack. The battle raged fiercely over the weeks until at last a meeting was called in Whitehall. There Archie rose before the assembled civil servants and blasted them until the windows shook. And when they still persisted in their attitude, he said:

'I am determined that these men shall get their full dues from the Government. They are Guinea Pigs. They were dreadfully burned while flying for their country, and I will not have them cast out with starvation pensions because you now have no more use for them. Nor will I allow them to go on their knees and cringe for help. So let me warn you: if you persist in this petty, niggling attitude, I shall bring the problem before the public themselves. I will call the Guinea Pigs together and with me at their head we will march down Whitehall, showing our faces, and we will demonstrate for justice.'

The bureaucrats swallowed and gave in.

These were the tangible evidences of his efforts, but there were others he kept secret. Paul Hart, one of the most badly injured of the Pigs, remembers the time when Archie came to his rescue at the most crucial moment in his career. He had been discharged from hospital now, with half his stomach grafted on his face, and he and his wife were struggling doggedly to establish themselves as bulb growers in Lincolnshire. But money was in short supply and the banks were unfriendly. Archie wrote a cheque for £1,000. He was far from affluent at the time and his resources were stretched to the limit.

'For God's sake don't spend it unless you have to,' he said, 'or I'll be on my beam ends. But wave it in the bank's face and impress them.'

The money was returned to Archie less than a year later. Hart never spent any of it, but it gave him confidence enough to go on to become one of the most successful bulb growers in the country.

Archie had been spending much of his time promoting a scheme to send the Guinea Pigs on free convalescent holidays to Switzerland. The Swiss Red Cross and the Swiss people paid for the men while they were there, and Archie squeezed his friends at home for the money for their fares and pocket-money. He went to the station to see the first batch off and warned them to behave themselves; but for one or two of them, the Swiss air proved a little heady and one night a few of them ran amok in the roughest East Grinstead tradition. He flew out and angrily accused them of letting him down. He was extremely hurt at their misbehaviour.

'For God's sake, boys,' he said, 'how could you do it—before foreigners!'

He wrote to Blackie:

'Since your letter arrived I have been in Switzerland seeing the chaps over there. I wish to God you were back here and could give us a bit of help on the situation. Like idiots the British Red Cross Society sent them over expecting them to be good boys without control. Of course they merely kicked Montreux into the Lake of Geneva. There has been a hell of a row about it and we are now looking for two welfare officers to go out and take charge of the show, one at Geneva and one at Lucerne. You know the kind that is wanted. Do you know anyone who will do it?'

The welfare officers were found but they were not really needed. The boys behaved like lambs thereafter.

It is perhaps not surprising in one who pursued a profession so closely concerned with the repair and reconstruction of the human body that Archie McIndoe should be fascinated by the characteristics of the skin. This was the principal, though not the only, raw material of his art. He cut it in strips and squares and transplanted it from one part of the human carcass to another; he had learned to tend and nurture it like a plant; and he knew only too well where it would take root and thrive, and where it would never be persuaded to grow.

Just as the alchemists of old dreamed of making gold from dross, so have plastic surgeons dreamed of the day when they would be able to use skin like blood plasma and transfer it from one man's body to another. It would solve most of their problems in the most dreadful of the cases with which they have to deal, when the burned or scalded patient is brought to them with not enough left on his body to enable them to graft his own skin over his wounds. Plastic surgery has advanced sufficiently for its technicians to be able to build up skin banks in the same way as blood banks, and from these they can take enough material to cover the open wounds of a grossly injured patient. But it is only a temporary measure. The human epidermis, like the fingerprints on it, is unique; a graft of one man's skin on to the body of another will grow for so long, and then—after a period ranging from fifteen to thirty days—antibodies and allergies will get to work and the skin will slough off like the rejected covering of a snake. If the patient has not grown enough of his own skin in the meantime and is too weak to withstand yet another temporary loan of a foreign homograft, he will die.

The day may come when scientists will learn how to defeat the forces in the human body which still so successfully fight all attempts to introduce permanent grafts from one body to another. It was Archie McIndoe's ambition to see it happen in his lifetime, and he was one of the principal backers of research into the problem. But though laboratories in the Queen Victoria Hospital at East Grinstead are leading the experimentation today, they have not discovered the secret yet.

In 1948 they were far away from the solution. Plastic surgeons knew only this; skin grafts from the same blood groups would not 'take', neither would those from mother to daughter, father to son, or twin from ordinary twin. But with *identical* twins it was different. In 1927 a doctor named Bauer transplanted a strip of skin from one small boy to the injured finger of his identical twin, and it 'took'. In 1945, a nineteen-year-old French soldier was brought to hospital with extensive skin loss on both legs from a phosphorus grenade wound, and his injuries were complicated by gross suppuration. The patient was weak and it looked like a hopeless case, but the surgeons covered the burns by a foreign graft. That evening, as they were walking to their mess, they saw what appeared to be their patient walking in the grounds, fit and well. On being questioned, he turned out to be the injured soldier's identical twin. He was taken into the hospital and it was his skin, transferred from his body to that of his brother, which saved the man's life. The complete stability of the homograft was confirmed by examination two years after the operation.

It was his knowledge of these events which enabled Archie McIndoe to achieve one of his most remarkable successes. In 1947, the Swiss parents of six-year-old twin boys, Victor and Pierre, became aware of a striking difference between the two in looks, manner and temperament, but remained unsuspicious of it until the twins participated in an Easter parade in which all the village children dressed up in costume.

Among those taking part in the procession was another boy, Eric, from another family. They were at once struck by the remarkable resemblance between Victor and Eric, so much so that the father of the twins went to the authorities and maintained that a substitution must have taken place; and his assertions were taken seriously when it was discovered that Pierre, Victor and Eric had all been born in the same hospital on the same night in the same ward.

A doctor named Franceschetti was called in and told to make an examination of the three boys, and his task seemed to be a simple one. All he needed to do was to make an examination of the blood groups of the trio; if two boys were of one group and the third was of another, it would be easy to prove whether or not a substitution had taken place. Unfortunately, it did not work out that way. All the boys belonged to group Ai and MN. To break down the blood groups further in search of indubitable proof Franceschetti would need to examine the blood of both sets of parents, and that could not be done because Eric's supposed father was dead. He compared the colour of the boys' eyes, their hair, the shape of their ears, their fingerprints and the capillary structure of their finger-nails, and in each case Eric and Victor strikingly resembled each other. But was this sufficient evidence to convince everyone—especially Eric's mother, who had come to love her child—that two of the boys were in the wrong homes?

It was at this point that Archie came into the picture. He had read some details of the case in a journal and at once got into touch with his medical friends in Switzerland; it seemed an ideal case to carry a step further his research into the skin characteristics of identical twins. He was asked to fly to Switzerland and take over the examination. He cut two one-centimetre-long full-thickness skin grafts from Victor's arm and exchanged them with similar ones taken from Pierre and Eric.

'Then,' he wrote afterwards, 'we waited. It was a curious situation—really rather like feeding facts to the oracle and waiting for an answer. My curiosity was purely scientific. But think of how the parents must have felt. I felt sorry for them.'

Three weeks later, the grafts taken from Pierre sloughed off Victor's arm and Eric's arm. So did the grafts from Victor and Eric on Pierre's arm. But the grafts exchanged between Victor and and Eric were not only growing; they showed, in addition to normal skin pattern and texture, persistence of the same patterns of hair growth as had been characteristic in their original situations.

There was a complete survival of all elements of the transplanted skin.

Archie was convinced at once that the point had been proved. A substitution *had* been made and Victor and Eric were the true identical twins. But it was another ten months, when the boys were examined again, before the authorities agreed. The grafts on Victor and Eric had become a normal part of their body, and there were only cicatrices left where Pierre's grafts had once been.

The boys were exchanged and settled down in their new homes. 'This story, unique both from the scientific and emotional point of view,' Archie wrote afterwards, 'had an interesting epilogue. The authorities ordered the exchange on July 1, 1948. They were three splendid kids and I was interested in what would happen to them in their new environment, so I kept in touch. I am glad to say that they settled down happily.'

It had been obvious for some time that John Hunter was a very sick man indeed. He tried hard in the wards at the Queen Victoria Hospital to be as cheerful as ever and he still cracked a risqué joke as he leaned over his patients with his needle and said: 'Just a little prick!' But his Pickwickian figure had shrunk and his eyes were yellow, and Archie was not the only doctor who realized that the diabetes would soon take its toll.

I have mentioned before that Archie McIndoe was not the kind of man to accept inefficiency in his operating theatre. To those who made mistakes he would react with livid anger; and though he would put his heart into the recommendations he wrote for aspiring young surgeons whose work he approved, he would not hesitate to damn in downright language a doctor whom he considered stupid or incapable. There is no doubt that he was right in this. A doctor may be a friend, even a beloved friend, outside the operating theatre, but once inside he must be judged only by his skill; and the truth was that as an anaesthetist John Hunter was losing his touch. No longer did he work in instinctive co-ordination with Archie and Jill Mullins, and his occasional hesitations made both of them nervous.

Even so, Hunter might well have continued to work as a member of the team until the last had it not been for a clash over anaesthetic technique. Archie McIndoe had always been an innovator, always eager to try out new methods, and he had been stirred and excited over a daring discovery which had been made by some of the younger anaesthetists at East Grinstead, notably by Doctor Hale Enderby. It has been given the name of hypotensive anaesthesia and it was a method whereby a patient, once under drugs, had his or her blood pressure lowered (or 'frozen') until temperature was drastically reduced and the blood hardly flowed at all.

The advantage of this to a plastic surgeon was enormous. Most plastic operations take place in those portions of the human body where the blood flows most freely once the surgical knife has cut. It pours from the nose which is being bobbed. It clogs the mouth of a patient whose cleft palate is being joined. Under ordinary anaesthesia, the floor of an operating theatre is covered with blood as soaked swab after swab is discarded; and still the blood wells up, obscuring the surgeon's view as he cuts or chisels or stitches.

Hypotensive anaesthesia promised to end all that, and Archie enthusiastically adopted it. But when he asked John Hunter to use the technique on one of his patients, he was met by a blank refusal.

It may have been that the old dog decided that it was too late for him to learn such new tricks. What he said was that he considered the technique dangerous. 'I don't like it,' he said. 'You can hardly feel the pulse. The temperature makes the patient practically moribund. I'll never know whether they are alive or dead. I'm not going to do it.'

Archie looked at him in silence. There were no angry words. All he said, quietly, was:

'In that case, I'll have to get someone else to do it for me.'

It was not quite the end, but it was the beginning of the end, of their association. Archie went to work with two other anaesthetists, and at first it was not all plain sailing for him.

'I am delighted to hear that you have started with hypotensive anaesthesia,' he wrote to a fellow surgeon shortly afterwards, 'but for the love of Pete be careful about this blood pressure business. It is very attractive to have them completely avascular on the table but there is a snag here. I recently had a patient whose heart stopped at 45 millimetres of mercury and it took me eight minutes to revive her, including heart massage. She lived for thirteen days completely unconscious and the post-mortem showed she was cerebrally decorticated.'

But he learned to perfect the technique and there were no fatalities after that; and hypotensive anaesthesia is today a normal technique in plastic surgery.

There was never an open quarrel between Archie McIndoe and John Hunter, but since they worked less and less together it was natural that they should meet infrequently after this. Hunter took the separation badly. His health began to deteriorate rapidly. He still came to the hospital regularly for his insulin injections and he loved to go into the wards and reminisce about the good old days of the war when the Team did such glorious work for the Guinea Pigs.

He died while Archie was on holiday in the South of France, and he was too late to attend the funeral.

'Poor John,' wrote Archie to one of his Guinea Pigs, Bob Wright, who had written to commiserate with him. 'Unfortunately I was in Cannes when it took place and did not myself hear about it for some days owing to the strike of post, telegraph and trains. I think everybody is relieved now that this terrible year has ended.'

The Guinea Pigs assembled and gave their beloved pricker a sentimental send-off. Archie came back and at once went to work to help his widow to straighten out the woeful financial mess he had left behind. If they had drifted apart in the previous two years, at least he proved himself a real friend now.

CHAPTER TEN

HAVEN ON KILIMANJARO

THE AFRICAN BUG HAD bitten Archie badly, and each year after his first visit in 1947 he went back. There was something about the African sun which invigorated him as nothing else could.

'When he arrived,' said Robin Johnston afterwards, 'he was usually exhausted after a heavy year's work. He seemed almost like blotting paper to the African sun and turned from pale to dark mahogany within a few days. He seemed to pick up from the sun quantities of renewed energy. Africa unquestionably rebuilt him year after year so much that, greatly as he loved it, I could sense at the end of each visit an eagerness on his part to return to his patients and their problems. I was told that East Grinstead almost dreaded his return, for in place of the tired, pale man who had left for Africa they could scarcely recognize this man who looked more like a Pacific pearl-diver than a wan London surgeon.'

In 1950, when the undeveloped land on the north face of Mount Kilimanjaro came up for sale, he made a pact with Robin Johnston to acquire it and go into partnership to farm it. They acquired 963 acres on a lovely site overlooking some of the wildest flora and fauna in Africa and settled on a plan to cultivate it with cereals, pyrethrum and coffee. Archie would put up most of the money—some £15,000—and Robin Johnston would do most of the work, with Archie coming out to help whenever he could make a break from his surgery.

'I left the Tanganyika Administration,' said Robin Johnston, 'and we began to farm. At first we lived in the open, sleeping under a tarpaulin, then in a tent, then a mud-and-wattle hut, and finally a small wooden house. When Archie saw our water supply, which was a chocolate colour covered with algae, dead frogs, bones and other forms of more active life, he paled visibly and began supervising the boiling and filtering of the water—to which he added liberal quantities of gin, which, he said, was the only agent that could possibly kill off the germs. He loved any form of physical work and drove combines, tractors and a Land Rover, supervised the laying of pipes, clearing of land, the building of a house and laying out of a garden. Always he worked stripped to the waist and wearing a jelly-bag on his head. A Water Development man once, after seeing Archie at work in the bush, wearing nothing but shorts, a jelly-bag and a gun on his shoulder, weakly reported he had seen a pixie in the forest.'

The word spread through that part of Kenya that a medicine man of more than ordinary skill had arrived in the land, and he was set upon by the local inhabitants with all manner of ailments from headache to hookworm, festering sores, sick babies, broken limbs and occasional burns. He attended to all of them with one exception, he refused to deliver babies.

'He never grumbled about inadequate medical supplies or modern drugs,' said Johnston, 'and though he often had to use rusty scissors and a really unhygienic set-up, he gave his black patients as much attention as he gave his rich patients in Europe. His patients would mime their ailments. One man had a pain, he said, that started at the back of his head and came out of the tip of his nose; another had a snake twisting around in his stomach; a devil was sitting on another's chest—all highly original, but they had to fall into certain categories of diagnoses that could be cured with iodine, aspirin, epsom salts, cough mixture or male fern.'

On his visit in 1950 he was riding through the brush when he came upon a badly injured Masai warrior. The Masai had been charged by a rhino and tried to hide behind a bush, but the rhino had caught him and pierced his horn right through the man's back to the front of his stomach and gone on to transfix his lower thigh.

'Archie always carried a small emergency pack with him wherever he went,' said Johnston; 'it contained a small phial of drugs and he gave the Masai some morphia. He washed out and dressed his dreadful wound as best he could, and we sent the wounded man off in our Land Rover forty-five miles to the nearest hospital, and not even Archie thought he would survive the journey. A year later, during his next visit, to our amazement the same Masai appeared. He was in one piece. His only complaint was that when the wind blew from the East he felt a slight twinge in his back.'

It was these invigorating bathes in the African sun which enlivened him and gave him the power and the drive which he needed increasingly in his work at home. For his professional horizon was widening. The patients increased. They now included such visitors as the Duchess of Windsor, who wanted a scar removed, and Princess Marie Louise, who had a minor face-lift. The famous *McIndoe Nose* was in demand among actresses, models and society women. His wartime friendships were beginning to bear fruit in more than one way. Through Mrs Neville Blond—whose husband had always been one of East Grinstead's greatest benefactors—he had met her brother, Sir Simon (now Lord) Marks, who had decided to express his interest in plastic surgery in a tangible way. He financed a series of Marks Fellowships to train new surgeons, under Archie's control, in the intricacies of plastic surgery; he opened the doors of his emporia to the Guinea Pigs, who became buyers and managers in his organization; and he and his wife henceforth advised Archie on his investments.

'You will receive a letter of introduction from my friends Sir Simon and Lady Marks,' he wrote to Jack Penn in South Africa. 'They leave for Cape Town in a couple of days and are coming your way. I do not remember whether you met either of them but they are, of course, the head of the Marks and Spencer clan and are quite the best representatives of it. Simon, who, of course, is responsible for the Marks fellowships, is most anxious to meet Sir Ernest Oppenheimer and Harry Oppenheimer. He has lately acquired an interest in Woolworths of South Africa and is going through South Africa assessing its possibilities from the distribution angle. I like him immensely and Miriam is a grand soul. I have written up your shares very highly, boy, but you can keep your fingers off his money bags or I'll clobber you.'

Archie McIndoe had discovered a great gift. He could talk money out of anyone—so long, as he ruefully remarked, as it was not money for himself. His persuasive powers had already swelled the funds of the Guinea Pig Club until they were able to lend something between £10,000 and £15,000 a year to their members to enable them to improve their civilian positions. Loans went out to buy them cars, set them up in business, even finance their divorces.

'Dear Archie,' wrote Blackie, on March 12, 1952, 'the word has gone round that you are back in the country and the wheels have begun to turn again. The ——'s want £520 for essential repairs and renovations to the back of their property. I suggest they put up £100 themselves and ask for a grant of £200. John X. We are still in the process of doing something about this young man's divorce. As a man I think he has very little to recommend him but as a person who should be responsible for other people I feel we ought to do what we can to help. I think the answer is to put a limit on. If the Benevolent Fund are willing to pay £2,500 or so by means of loan and grant and let him find a place, that will keep him busy for a time, anyway.'

But Archie, always well aware of the value of money, did not automatically pay out to the Guinea Pigs everything they asked. 'I shall want full details of ——'s needs and I should think a statement of his financial affairs,' he wrote. 'I am very doubtful about John X but anyway let's have details of what he wants to do with £2,500. If this is not enough, Henry Y now wants £10,000 to buy a pub. So do I! I think we will have to do something about this, but I am trying to dissuade him from this particular pub as I think the outlook is bad and the tenure uncertain. Furthermore. I am not going to back a proposition whereby Y simply asks for £10,000 without putting in a bean of his own accord.'

But as the money he cajoled from his friends flowed in, so he paid it out to his boys. They were now swarming over the country as car-hire drivers, newsagents, coal merchants, club and pub-keepers, all financed by the Guinea Pig Club.

But this was not the only fund over which he exercised a proprietary control. There was the £24,000 collected by subscribers to the Peanut Club, and to keep his hands on that he found himself once more in the position he liked, butting his broad head against bureaucracy.

The Peanut Club had started life in a local newspaper, *The Kent and Sussex Courier*, of Tunbridge Wells, as a children's column run by someone who called herself Aunt Agatha. Its motto was 'Happy Smiles and Helpful Deeds', and for a subscription to its funds—which were to be given to charity—members received a blue-and-yellow badge and an exhortation to enrol their friends. During the war its membership bounded upwards as children in the two counties circulated their fathers and friends in the Services and asked them to join. By the end of the war, the Peanut Club had sixty thousand members in all parts of the world.

Archie McIndoe had always had his eye on the Peanut Club funds. He knew that from them had come several contributions to Tunbridge Wells hospitals. He felt that the Queen Victoria Hospital should have its share. He went to see Aunt Agatha and discovered that she was a very pretty and redoubtable young woman named Mrs Kay Clemetson, the wife of the chief of his photographic unit at the hospital. Mrs Clemetson and he took to each other at once; they had the same driving temperament* and contempt for bureaucracy, and by the end of their first meeting they were in agreement: the Peanut Club would start a fund to build a children's ward at the Queen Victoria Hospital. Thanks to Mrs Clemetson's unflagging propaganda, the fund topped £10,000 at the end of 1946 and was rising steadily.

Then came the National Health Act. 'It became obvious,' said Mrs Clemetson, 'that our money was in danger. The hospitals were being taken over. If we did not move quickly, it might well be that our money would be taken over too. Archie and I met and decided that it would be dangerous to hand any of it over to the hospital authorities, as we had done in the past, and we formed a trust fund so that we could hold on to it.'

But would they be able to hold on to it?

The amount in the fund by 1950 was £24,000 and the Ministry of Health stretched out its hands to grab it for itself, on the specious grounds that it had been collected for the hospital and was therefore part of the hospital funds, which now belonged to the State. Archie and Mrs Clemetson went into action and proved a formidable pair. Archie wrote and telephoned and badgered his friends. Mrs Clemetson opened the columns of her newspapers.

The battle culminated in a huge indignation meeting in East

* Which has since taken Mrs Clemetson to the top of her profession. She is now Editor in Chief of the *Courier* series, and President of the Guild of Editors.

Grinstead and speeches from the two leaders which not only roused the audience to a frenzy of enthusiastic support, but caught the ear of the national newspapers, who took up the cause. The Government havered, procrastinated, and then gave way. One morning in 1951 a letter arrived from the Ministry of Health to say that if the Peanut Club would be willing to hand the money over to the hospital authorities the Ministry would guarantee that a children's wing would be added to the Queen Victoria and that it would be called the Peanut Wing.

Archie and Kay Clemetson met at the Queen Victoria Hospital to celebrate their victory. It was a Sunday morning and no one was about, but they felt that this was too good a moment to miss. They took a spade from the gardener's toolshed and Archie polished it up. Then he and Mrs Clemetson cut the first sod on the site of the children's wing, while Mrs. Clemetson's husband took a photograph.

It would be a mockery of the word to say that Archie McIndoe was a lonely man in these years, for he simply did not have the time. At work or at play, he was always busy, always surrounded by people, always working on some new plan or idea. He now had more friends than he could cope with, and invitations from admiring hostesses lapped in a flood around his doorstep.

If he needed a woman's companionship, he could always call upon Jill Mullins. She was always willing to be beside him in his off-duty hours, a whisky-and-soda in her hand, sympathetically silent while he spoke about his problems. He had his mother living near him now. She had come to England after the war for a short visit but decided she would stay; and Archie had found her a house at East Grinstead and made her an allowance, to supplement her own income, of £10 a week. And there was the delightful relationship with his younger daughter, Vanora—the elder, Adonia Junior, had married—to lighten the darker or duller moments of his life, for she had grown up to be both beautiful and harum-scarum.

'Dear Daddy,' wrote Adonia Junior, 'Vanora showed me the letter you sent her so I gather all goes well with you and that you are having a thoroughly good time. I hope you are behaving yourself and getting your health and strength back. All that matters to me is that when you return I shall see a replica of the man I saw two years ago when you last returned from Kenya. So see to it, please! . . . Vanora returned at about the same time as we did and has been staying with us ever since. She's very well though a little Bohemian at the moment. The telephone has never stopped ringing and I have put my foot in it by attaching the wrong name to the wrong boy friend which never goes down well. Simon and I arrived home late one day last week in time to meet her returning in company with three boy friends (all pretty lousy), one of whom was attired in a pair of most glorious semi-pyjamas . . . I enclose a clipping of our dear friend L. W.'s wedding. All your girl friends are getting married. She's done herself proud this time. I think that's about all, so don't worry. Much love, Adonia.'

It was a full life, and yet something was missing.

'You are a terrible cynic about women,' wrote Vanora. 'Personalities apart, are we always quite so awful as we seem when you sound off about us?'

It was a moment in his life, as his daughter had divined, when the female sex seemed to be closing in upon him. His mother, always a dominant type, was nagging him to get his domestic life in order. She had never ceased to feel an antagonism towards his estranged wife, Adonia, but his present mode of living depressed her. In her opinion it would be better to make up with her and set up some sort of tolerant régime rather than continue his footless domestic arrangements, which might satisfy his momentary needs but left him rootless and uneasy. If the idea ever entered Archie's head that he should ever marry Jill Mullins, it certainly never entered hers; she knew instinctively that it would be wrong for both of them, and, of course, it was true. The moment for that, if there ever had been a moment, had passed; and though Jill Mullins may not have recognized that it had passed and still hoped that they would marry, she was certainly conscious of the fact that Archie was not in love with her. He admired her tremendously as a nursing assistant and he was deeply fond of her as a woman. During the war he had nursed her with sympathy and understanding through an unhappy love affair, and there was no question but that he would do anything for her that she asked; except marry her. When that topic came into the conversation, he had a convenient retreat. The break with Adonia had now solidified into a separation agreement under which he paid her £1,600 a year; but he was still married to her and Adonia would not give him a divorce.

There was, in any case, someone else who was beginning increasingly to take possession of his thoughts, as Jill Mullins was only too well aware. He never concealed that fact from her.

It was as far back as 1947 that Mrs Constance Belchem had first come into his life. In that year he took his daughter Vanora and Jill with him on a holiday to the Riviera, and with them went Mr and Mrs Osmond-Clark. (Osmond-Clark was an orthopaedic surgeon who was both a friend and a collaborator; in many of the accident cases which came to him, Osmond-Clark first mended the bones before Archie mended the faces.) It was there that they all met Mrs Belchem, though it was Archie who saw most of her thereafter. They swam together or went on rides together along the coast in the afternoons when the others had retired to their rooms for a siesta. Two years later, in 1949, they met on the Riviera again and this time Mrs Belchem drove Archie and Jill back to Le Touquet in her car.

Constance Belchem was married at this time to a British general serving in Germany. In the circumstances, Archie did not tell her so but she was the kind of woman he had always wanted to know. She was a woman of great beauty, devastating charm and high intelligence, and they shared a sense of fun which both of them found infectious. What neither of them shared at this time were the secrets of their domestic life, and though Mrs Belchem knew that Archie was separated from Adonia she did not confide the news that her own marriage was breaking up for reasons which cannot be gone into here. The friendship ripened into something much deeper, and whenever Mrs Belchem came back to England from Germany she saw Archie frequently. They did not have to tell each other they were in love.

It was not, however, until 1952, five years after their first meeting, that they decided to do something about it. Mrs Belchem returned from Germany and announced that she and her husband had parted and she was taking steps to secure a divorce.

'In that case,' said Archie, 'I must secure my freedom too. I want you to marry me.'

With a determination which he had never shown before, despite the urgings of Jill Mullins, he embarked upon the long and difficult negotiations with Adonia which would change their separation into a divorce, and it was not until 1953 that Adonia filed proceedings and, following the divorce, Archie made all the necessary arrangements for her to have a home and adequate financial support.

It seems difficult to believe that Jill Mullins cannot have known what was afoot, nor can she have deceived herself into believing that the divorce proceedings were being taken in order to allow Archie to marry her. She was on terms of close friendship with both of Archie's daughters and they kept no secrets from her.

Vanora wrote a letter to Mrs Belchem, which said:

'You must know how much I loved being with you and what a wonderful time I had. And for the rest—you must know how much my father loves you and how incredibly, suddenly and completely Right it seems, and I believe with all my heart it is. Two people who deserve happiness more than I can say and who I love as one now . . . Take care of yourself because you are very precious. All my love, Vanora.'

Now that Archie and Constance Belchem were both in the process of obtaining their freedom a difficult period had to be endured. At all costs he was determined to avoid scandal; he was too jealous of his surgical reputation to allow even his love for his wife-to-be to threaten it. He told Constance that until their decrees were made absolute they must not meet again except in the most casual and public circumstances.

It was easier for him than it was for her. When their enforced separation in the same city became too much to bear, he set out for his beloved Africa and engrossed himself in the affairs of Ol Orien, the farm on the slope of Kilimanjaro. To a letter from a sad and lonely Connie, he replied:

'Your quite startling letter made me feel a bit of a heel. Because I am really enjoying myself enormously though not with that peculiar abandon which I exhibited on former occasions. This time I see it through different eyes and wonder constantly whether you (who will have eventually to endure a bit of it) will like it as much as I do. These African scenes are primitive and savage and I know I have grown to love them well. I feel sure you will too for they have heat, distance, freedom and colour. There is rhythm in

McIndoe with HM Queen Elizabeth when she opened the American Wing at East Grinstead

The Duke of Edinburgh (President of the Guinea Pig Club) with Tom Gleave (Chief Guinea Pig)

Sir Archibald McIndoe and Mrs Constance Belchem, who was to become the second Lady McIndoe

the country and exhilaration in the air. This morning at 6 am I left Nairobi with Robin Johnston (my partner) and leaving that rather tatty city was within half an hour spinning down through Masai-land at sixty in the Land Rover. One hundred miles south we had breakfast at the Nimanga Hotel and then broke East along the Masai furrow for the foot of Kilimanjaro. I had some good shooting on the way and then up the side of the mountain to our farm (Ol Orien). In one year Robin has converted 1,000 acres of sage brush and African undergrowth into a beautiful farm complete with house, garden and 700 acres of terrific barley and wheat. The rest is animals—horses, cows, goats, dogs and a Siamese cat. Have just come back from a twenty mile ride and will take breakfast off the mantelpiece tomorrow. Robin's achievement is enormous and that is why I am elated. But all that does nothing to to take away my terrible feeling of incompleteness which, thank goodness, you share. My love, A.'

The undefended suit of McIndoe versus McIndoe came before the courts in the summer of 1953 and a decree nisi was granted. But there was still the question of Connie's divorce, and as late as February 1954 discussions were still going on between what Archie called 'the legal narks' as to the procedure. At one point it seemed as if another two years of separation might have to elapse before a plea was put forward for a dissolution on the grounds of desertion.

Archie was back in East Africa, and it was an Africa moiling in the Mau Mau terror campaign. 'It really is amusing at meal-times,' he wrote, 'with the third gastronomic instrument on the right side a loaded and cocked automatic. Apparently this is the favourite time for attack. Otherwise Nairobi is cleaner, quieter and more law-abiding than I have ever seen it and superficially one would never know anything was amiss.'

But in the hospitals where he was called upon to exercise some of his surgical skill there was evidence enough of brutishness and bestiality. Here he collaborated with one of his wartime colleagues, Mr Michael Wood, who had set up in Nairobi as a reconstructive surgeon; and though much of his work was of the cosmetic kind—from the proceeds of which he paid the expenses of his annual trip to Africa—both he and Wood did a large amount of free work among the native population. It was this team-work which was, later on, to result in the formation of the East African Medical Research Unit, one of the most important developments in sponsored medical research on the African continent. Archie and Michael Wood pioneered it between them.

'Have just completed a week's operation work in Nairobi,' Archie wrote, 'and I hope the mess is now cleaned up. Twenty operations in four days! Not bad going but I am fed up with this city and long to get back to the farm. On Wednesday I fly down to Lusaka, spend Thursday there at the hospital and return Friday. The work has been very funny-peculiar indeed—a mixture of "duffing up" for the Girl's Union (noses, eyelids, faces, etc.) and cleaning up some of the most horrifying Mau-Mau atrocities one could possibly imagine. I thought I had seen about everything that one person could do to another but these boys are artists in their own right. They take the cake with no runners-up.'

He added:

'Hope that some move has at last been made in your direction and that an end to the tension is in sight. I am beginning to get the jitters myself!'

The decree was granted and made final at last, and almost immediately Archie announced his engagement. It was not so much a surprise or a blow to Jill Mullins as the confirmation of her worst fear, and she reacted badly at first to the news; though she confided her misery only to her closest friends, and in the years to come not only went on working for Archie as his assistant but formed a friendship and association with his new wife that was one of mutual admiration and respect.

'At least,' she wrote to a friend at East Grinstead, 'he hasn't married a floosie.'

She worked beside him, and she was a welcome guest in his home, for another three years until she met and married Mr Stanley Denton, who took her back to his home in Johannesburg. By that time she knew, and Archie knew—though her husband and Connie did not—that she was a sick woman.

'Dear Connie and Archie,' she wrote from there, 'I hope you will both understand that for the last six months I have been really unhappy, not of course with Stanley, but with this town. How right you were, Archie. Everyone here is intent on only one thing, money. I know that's not a bad thing but these boys and girls are really tough . . . I've taken up painting and am taking some lessons, starting with water-colours and then going on to oils. This I enjoy. I do hope you are both well and enjoyed your visit to the US. Please let me hear from you. Love to you both, Jill.'

Archie wrote back:

'I have so often wondered how things were going for you in your new country and had the uncomfortable suspicion for a long time that you would not find it very much to your taste. It is, as you say, a pretty tough city and the boys and girls have only one god and are quite prepared, should anything get tough, to pick up what they have and beat it for wherever may look safer. But I am immensely glad that next year you will find things easier and that no doubt you will be back home . . . Well, since you left, I could not have been busier for the reason that firstly the new rooms have made work so much easier that I simply don't know how we ever existed in the old ones, and, secondly, my job as Vice-President of the College has complicated things enormously. My new assistant, Mary Dean, is absolutely first-class and while no-one could ever fill your place she has been an absolutely second-class best. The patients like her and she is learning to be a really good assistant. But the nice thing is that we have room to move about and oddly enough the turnover has considerably increased.'

Jill Mullins came back to England a year later and Archie and Connie McIndoe put her up at their new house in Sussex. She seemed happy and content with her new life, and the Guinea Pigs who owed so much to her skilful and devoted attention did not fail to make her stay a happy one. She sailed back home, in October 1959, and had a stroke aboard the ship *en route*. Archie had departed with Connie for an appearance as principal speaker before an American medical congress in Miami, but his secretary, Joan Dunkerton, called him. He made arrangements for Jill, who was in a coma, to be landed and shipped back to England, where a room would be ready for her at the London Clinic. But it was too late. A second stroke killed her and she was buried at sea.

Two members of the Team from East Grinstead were now gone. First John Hunter and now Jill Mullins. They had done so much together, taken the art of plastic surgery so far, healed so many bodies and brought peace to so many minds. It was a blow to the Guinea Pigs and to Archie McIndoe, for in their way they had both loved her and were in her debt.

'My dear Stanley,' wrote Archie to her husband, 'it is not easy to write to you even yet under the distressing circumstances in which you must find yourself. I have never been so shocked in all my life as when Joan called me from London to Miami Beach to tell me of Jill's untimely death. It must have been a dreadful shock to you happening as it did in such alarming circumstances, where one feels so terribly helpless far from adequate assistance. Jill was a great girl and her passing will leave many behind to mourn her loss. There will never be anyone else like her in the extraordinary field in which she excelled with her kindness, thoughtfulness and gentleness in her handling of other people. She had, I think the finest pair of hands I have ever seen given to a woman. They were so infinitely gentle. She seemed to be able to inspire people with enormous confidence in her own sheer competence and in all the years she was with me she seemed to grow in stature as time passed. I knew, of course, that she had a fairly high blood pressure . . . When I last saw her she spoke with deep feeling of the happiness which you had given her and how much she looked forward to the future in Johannesburg.'

And in an article called *In Memoriam*, he wrote:

'Jill Mullins was more than a friend. For twenty-two years she was my personal surgical assistant, both in hospital and in private, with all the responsibility which such a position involves. I think those wonderfully gentle hands of hers were concerned in almost every operation I carried out on a Guinea Pig. There can be few of them who will not remember her green turban and titian hair, with the reassuring smile on her attractive face as Uncle John Hunter's "just a little prick" wafted them off to unconsciousness. Nor will they forget the gay parties at East Grinstead after the day's work was done, of which she was so often the instigator and usually the attractive centre . . . No one will ever equal her as a surgical assistant. Her hands were magic. They were long and strong, but infinitely gentle and steady. She used them with grace and easy facility. Whatever movements I made with my hands hers were never in the way. They seemed to advance and retreat simultaneously with mine as though intuitively guided. Neither of us ever spoke during operating but each instrument appeared miraculously as the need for it arose. Neither too soon nor too late and always the correct one.

'To work with her was a pure joy and she introduced a kind of rhythm into standard operations which gave them a curious sense of unreality. They appeared to flow without effort and to complete themselves. One scarcely had to think what came next.

'Sometimes I had to operate without her. To me it was hell.

'Her post-operative care of her patients was equally outstanding. Her knowledge of wound healing was uncanny and was based on the sound principle that cleanliness is next to Godliness. Stitches were individuals that remained without reaction in the tissues just until their usefulness was over. Then they came out—painlessly. The dressings were always immaculate. But more than this, her entry into a sick room did something to the person in the bed. She radiated cheerfulness and efficiency. She recognized immediately the signs of a restless night or a change in the physical condition of the patient. Within a few minutes she had everything under control—the doleful female smiling, the unshaven, tumbled male shaved, shining and looking at the green goddess with wide-eyed admiration. All were glad when she came, sorry when she went.

'So she worked with me for twenty-two years and in that time thousands of patients passed through her care. She made countless friends who will always remember her with affection. It is sad to reflect that just at the time when she could have enjoyed to the full a happy life she should have been cut down.

'We can be glad that she lived when she did. She was a real woman and we will not see her like again.'

CHAPTER ELEVEN

THE GOLDEN HAND

'ALL THIS BEGAN YEARS ago, but time, distance, and separation only make it worse. I miss you very much and really feel this is the last time you escape on your own to decorate houses.'

Archie McIndoe wrote this to Connie in 1956 when he flew out to Africa to the farm and she stayed at home to complete the decoration and furnishing of their new house, Millwood Manor, a few miles from East Grinstead. It was an old manor house with a minstrel gallery and, in the grounds, an ornamental lake and a forest of rhododendrons, and they were both in love with it.

It was two years since his marriage, and Archie McIndoe had never been happier. There was no doubt in his mind that he had found his ideal woman, and after a lifetime of women who bickered, of temperaments and domestic disasters, he cherished his new-found contentment. He was fifty-six years old and at the peak of his career, but in the delights of his new marriage he displayed all the joy of a young man who has discovered female love, loyalty and devotion for the first time.

It had not been easy at first for the new Lady McIndoe. In spite of the companionship of Jill Mullins, his life since 1946 had been largely that of a free-wheeling bachelor, always dining out, always game for a trip or a weekend with a colleague or a Guinea Pig. And though they took pains not to show it, the Guinea Pigs were the ones who, perhaps, felt most cool towards her. Jill Mullins had always been one of them; Connie was not. They bristled slightly when they heard her addressing her new husband not by the names they used—Archie, the Maestro or the Boss—but by his middle name, Hector. 'If Archie is good enough for us, why isn't it good enough for her?' they said, and refused, at first, to understand the psychological need of a new wife to have a name for her husband that is intimately and exclusively her own.

'It is true,' said Edward Blacksell, 'that we were all a little jealous of her to begin with. She was a person of such elegance and wide interests that we feared she would drag him away from us.'

They reckoned without Connie's determination not to draw Archie away but to penetrate the closed circle of his friends. She used as her battering ram all the charm, enthusiasm and sympathy of which she was capable, which was considerable, and she worked ceaselessly but humbly, to win his reluctant friends to her side. The Guinea Pigs soon came to know that in her they had an accomplice, a door through to Archie's interest rather than a wall between them and him. She read up their case histories from the records and then set out to know the men, and she was tireless in listening to their problems. It took time, but slowly the opposition crumbled and she was accepted, as an ally and a friend.

The Guinea Pig annual dinners at East Grinstead took on a new zest for the wives who had never been allowed to attend them. Connie moved in, gathered the wives together, and turned the event into a comfortable hen-party. She came into her own in the spring of 1957. In that year a local brewery proposed to open a public house by the name of The Guinea Pig and requested that Archie should be present to draw the first pint. The Vicar of East Grinstead, the Rev. H. C. F. Copsey, misinformed about the exact date of the event and obviously fearing an orgy, wrote:

'Dear Sir Archibald,—You will know that I am no "Sabbatarian" nor am I against public houses, but it is disturbing to hear that you are formally opening "The Guinea Pig" on Whit Sunday at eleven o'clock. Your Christian upbringing will tell you that this must cause distress to many good people, and it is bound to reflect adversely on the Hospital with which you are so closely connected. I will say no more. If you can open this house at some time other than at service time on one of the great Christian festivals I am confident you will do so. And if you ask me to be with you I shall count it a privilege.'

Archie immediately wrote back:

'As a result of an attack like this in days gone by some men went to the stake, some to the gallows. As far as I know the Guinea Pig

Pub will be opened officially on June 11 (a Tuesday) at 11 am. Has anything happened to change these arrangements? It is likely that you will be invited on that occasion to draw the second pint.'

He added as a postscript the verse:

> 'To Banbury came I, Oh Profane one!
> When I saw a Profane one
> Hanging of his cat on Monday
> For Killing of a mouse on Sunday.

The Vicar came and drew the second pint, but Connie McIndoe threw the first dart in a game which has since become a ritual of the Guinea Pigs' annual meeting.

Socially and professionally, the marriage had done Archie nothing but good. In the sometimes frigid and always rarefied atmosphere of Harley Street, Archie McIndoe had always, in spite of his fame and his knighthood, been regarded as a brash and inconoclastic colonial with a messy private life. The powers-that-be began to change their minds once they met the new Lady McIndoe. Her presence at a dinner table or cocktail party, fair, elegantly good-looking and charming, was a sight to be savoured, and the senior men of the medical world came eagerly to savour it. One had only to see the smile on Archie's face as he watched her performing at social functions to realize how proud he was of her. She gave him solidity and a new peace of mind.

In his operating theatres at the London Clinic and East Grinstead he had never been busier. There were more women waiting in the lists for cosmetic surgery than ever and it was nothing for him to do six face-lifts or nose reductions in a day. Many of them were distinguished. Some were of such lineage that all manner of stratagems had to be adopted to conceal their identity; and even now it is not possible to identify the patient who afterwards wrote him the following verse, headed: To Sir Archibald McIndoe:

> Oh dear Sir Archie McIndoe,
> This grateful patient writes to you,
> Remembering on that day of grace
> She begged that you should lift her face.
> But forced to look upon the truth,
> The sagging muscles, wrinkled skin,

Ruined profile, double chin,
  She who once had 'what it took'
Knew no man bothered now to look.
  And then Sir Archie McIndoe
The sculptor and the artist—you!
  And after all her sweat and pain
She watches youth creep back again
  The bruisings and the swellings fade,
The brave new look can be displayed.
  The years roll back, the flags unfurl
The patient feels once more—a girl!
  And those who envy what they see
May say that it's illusionary
  But to your patient it is Truth
This lovely, concrete, second youth.
  Behold, in face of sad eclipse
A face to launch a thousand ships!

But this was far from the bulk of his work. There were still the unending lists of cleft palates, hare-lips, scars, moles, malformations. The post-war boom in motoring was reaching its height and the accident rate was mounting. Facial fractures were now coming in for treatment every day, and Archie would sometimes get furiously angry when he saw the cases with which he would have to deal, for the smashed faces so often belonged to young motor-cyclists. In 1952 he dealt with twenty such cases in one month, and in 1956, with eighty. 'I would like to sponsor a bill to designate the motor-bike as a suicide machine,' he said. He would mend a young face, accompany its owner to the door of the hospital, and sadly watch him ride away on the motor-bike which had nearly destroyed him.

'Poor fool,' he would say. 'He'll be back.'

During all this time his mother had been living at East Grinstead, and he and Connie had visited her regularly. Her favourite son's marriage had been a great comfort to her but it could hardly be said that she was happy in her declining years, for her eyes were failing her. One of them had already gone. Now the other was beginning to cloud. It was a calamity which she, who had revelled so much in her power to see and interpret the landscape, found hard to bear. She still painted, but with difficulty. Archie was inclined to persuade her to accept her lot and let the darkness close in upon her, but the indomitable old lady had other ideas. She did not care how dangerous it was, she was determined to see.

'Dear Archie,' wrote Sir Ben Rycroft on October 9, 1956, 'I am enclosing a copy of a report on your mother which is self-explanatory. I feel, along with my colleagues here, that operation is now indicated in spite of all the obvious risks. The vision has now reached a degree of incapacitation that if it is left any longer your mother's general health will not be as good as it is today. Naturally one does not operate on an only seeing eye before it is absolutely essential, but I believe the time has now come.'

Mabel McIndoe was moved into the Queen Victoria Hospital and the operation was done.

'Your mother's convalescence,' wrote Rycroft, 'has been uneventful with no chest, urinary or cardiovascular complications. She frightened us one night by getting out of bed and falling, but so far as I can tell there has been no bone damage. An X-ray was immediately done and it proved negative but I am having this repeated as there is still considerable discomfort in the intercostal area. The method of cataract extraction was of the two-stage extra-capsular method. This was done to avoid any predictable risk and for safety. I propose to complete the job on Friday by needling the capsule and this should give your mother good sight. The needling is a routine procedure and of no serious consequence. Glasses will be fitted in the following week. She has been wonderfully patient and brave and I am sure you will be pleased with the final result.'

Archie wrote back:

'I am once again deeply in your debt for your care and attention to my mother. She seems to be in very good condition and has come through with flying colours. I take it that you will require her in your wing for a week or so yet before she is fit to go home. Let me know whatever you want in the way of attention for her after she does return and I will lay it on.'

But he never had the opportunity to do so. There was a relapse while he and Connie were on a lecture tour in America.

He came back in time to see her before she died. He attended her funeral while suffering from a bad dose of influenza, and then retired to bed in a gloom which did not leave him for weeks. He had always rather resented his mother's dominating manner, but he knew well enough that her guidance had shaped him and made him the man he was.

'She was a tyrant at times,' he said, 'and she would interfere. But she knew me as no other woman has ever done. I shall miss her more than I can say.'

Slowly, his spirits lifted. It is true that his own physical condition was giving him cause for concern at this time. A doctor is in a difficult position when he feels discomfort or malaise within himself. He knows so much of what goes on in the bodies of his patients that he is only too well aware of the variations of his own condition. For some time Archie McIndoe, mentally exuberant, had been feeling physically extremely low.

'I am afraid both you and I have been slightly on the sick list,' he wrote to Edward Blacksell, in April 1957. 'For the past year I have had a good deal of trouble with my innards and finally got myself into the hands, quite inadvertently, of the cardiologists. These citizens managed to persuade me that I had chronic heart disease, but, after enduring their ministrations for some time, going to bed and resting for goodness knows how long, I came to the conclusion that the whole thing was nonsense. Then I returned from Africa and demanded a full investigation and the miserable truth eventually drifted out that I have a plain ordinary everyday case of gallstones, which, you may remember, should have been removed in 1945, but weren't. The result is now that I have to have my gall bladder out in the course of the next few weeks. It is not a very pleasant prospect and is going to interrupt my work a great deal, and beside which I shall be put on the shelf for a bit. The complaint, I find, is not a pleasant one and one wakes in the morning feeling as though one has had to drink a pint of rancid fat. Other than this, I am very well and so busy that there seems not enough time in the day.'

It is typical of his attitude towards his own ailments that he could add those words: 'Other than this I am very well. . . .' At the end of 1956, the elder statesmen of his profession made a gesture towards him that epitomized their new-found respect not only for his surgical skill but for his social virtues and he was offered the Vice-Presidency of the Royal College of Surgeons. He did not think of refusing it despite his aches and pains, and it is as well for surgery in England that he did not for he proved to be the most remarkably successful vice-president in the history of that distinguished institution. To those who congratulated him he casually replied that it had come to him 'solely by reason of seniority', but this was not true; he might easily have been passed over, and might well have been in other circumstances.

Archie McIndoe's tenure of office at the Royal College of Surgeons was a *tour de force* in every sense of the phrase. He took it upon himself to improve domestic facilities inside the college itself which turned it into one of the most splendidly equipped in the country, both as a place in which to study and research and a club in which to relax. But his goal was a much more splendid one than that. The college had been badly damaged by bombs during the war, and a certain amount of rebuilding had been allowed; but it was a charity and received no financial aid from the State. If all the new research departments were to be built that the Fellows envisaged—departments to research cancer, rheumatism, kidney troubles, opthalmology, dental science and all the diseases whose evils had not yet been solved—the college would need at least £500,000 for its building programme and £150,000 a year to keep it going.

At his first meeting to study the situation, Archie discovered that money was so lacking that even the limited building programme now going on would have to be stopped. He went at once to see his friend, Simon Marks. Sir Simon (as he then was) had long been a friend and donor and he could easily have said that he had done enough. Instead, he sat down and wrote out a cheque for £100,000. And from then on he was at Archie's shoulder, with help and advice. It was a glorious start to one of the most sustained and successful hunts for money ever conducted by one man. He was tireless and persistent. He wrote to the chairman or managing director of practically every big corporation in the country, and invited them to august and elaborate lunches in the council chamber of the college. There he talked, and talked so persuasively that the money began to flow in. In less than two years he raised more than a quarter of a million pounds and covenants for substantial annual payments were coming in at the rate of several a week.

He even tried to tap the wells of Lord Beaverbrook's heart by pointing out that he had once financed a Beaverbrook Research Scholarship at the college, and that the fund for it, now exhausted, might be renewed. Beaverbrook replied:

'Dear Sir Archibald,—I am leaving London next week to spend some time in the West. On my return, early in the spring, I will be delighted to see you and discuss with you the Royal College of Surgeons. St Matthew recorded: "For where your treasure is, there will your heart be also." My heart and treasures are in New Brunswick, Canada. And with good wishes, yours sincerely, Beaverbrook.'

This did not daunt him. He replied:

'Despite St Matthew I hope that you will find room in your heart to devote a little of your treasure to our needs. Throughout the long history of the College it has exerted a tremendous influence upon the medical life of the Commonwealth. It still does, and being vitally alive today, will continue to do so in the future.'

Nor did he allow the coming operation on his gall bladder to interfere with his whirlwind campaign—though he did, this time, take considerable pains to make sure that the surgeon who worked on him for this operation would not leave a swab inside him! To Lord Webb-Johnson, one of the elders of the College, he wrote on May 25, 1957:

'My dear Alfred,—Thank you very much for your kind wishes. I think I have found a surgeon who can count up to ten and has passed the eleven-plus examination! This time I really hope to be parted from my gallstones and be able to view them in a bottle . . . My voice in the building committee is a weak one at the present moment, for I was obliged to give it up as I simply could not keep committees going on building and finance at the same time and the finance with all this is a big enough burden . . .'

A month later he wrote again:

'Dickson Wright removed my gall bladder last Monday and I am going home tomorrow. It was the most uneventful affair and I practised these new-fangled ideas of getting up—it really works! I am going down to my house at East Grinstead on Friday for a few days and then off to the South of France. At least I am not going back to work too soon. You will probably know by now that I have arranged for the future finance of the College. We will not have to stop building and I am in hopes that the whole programme will go through as planned. There is, as you know, many a slip and I am being extremely careful now to keep my competitors in the donations field away from my prospects until they are nailed to the mast.'

Webb-Johnson replied:

'I am so happy and delighted to hear that you have thrown those stones away. I hope you minded the windows. Splendid fellow! You are the stalwart support of the College now. I have just heard about the Cerebos gift. That alone is fine, particularly after Willie Collins' gift of three hundred thousand out of his privy purse. Best love to both of you from both of us. Connie, my dear—tell Archie that good engines must have brakes as well as accelerators. Go slow! God bless, Alfred.'

But if Archie McIndoe had been winning friends by his ceaseless efforts on behalf of the College, there were still enemies lurking in the background, jealous of his success, eager to bring him down. The medical profession has always had more than its fair share of the envious and the malevolent, and there were those who resented the resounding triumphs of the campaign on behalf of the Royal College. To a fellow doctor, Archie wrote:

'I have raised a quarter of a million pounds for the completion of the College Phase II of the College building. We need another quarter of a million pounds, and in addition another £150,000 a year to run what we have built. We expect this from the public and the only way we can get it from the public is to explain to them what we are doing. We have begun with informed articles in *The Times*, *Daily Telegraph* and such newspapers as will accept informed articles.'

For perhaps the first time in history, one branch of the medical profession was making an attempt to end the secrecy under which they worked and to persuade the people that here were scientists and healers rather than witch-doctors and spell-casters. Under Archie's stimulation, the College opened its doors to editors and writers and showed them how they worked, what they were researching, the goals towards which they were working. It is true that the result was publicity for the College and its needs, but its effect was deeper and more important than that: it strove to bridge a gap between doctor and layman, to allay fears, to broaden public knowledge. One of the most salutary and successful revolutions it brought about was in the treatment of medicine on television. A programme was produced by one of the networks which showed, in close-up, surgeons at work on their specialities, coolly and calmly going about their jobs with none of the melodramatics and crises which usually clutter up such attempts to show a doctor at work.

But there are worms in the woodwork of the stoutest institution, and by sheer inadvertence they were given the excuse to nibble at the beams. The television company, without consulting the Royal College of Surgeons, printed the names of those surgeons who took part in the programme in the *TV Times*. A week or two before, a photographer had taken a picture of the distinguished guests at a lecture at the college and the names of those who appeared in it were printed in the newspapers. It is usually some obscure and unsuccessful doctor—and rarely if ever members of the public—who complains when he sees another medico's name in the public prints and rushes forward crying: 'Advertising! Unethical!'

In this case, the cries came anonymously to begin with in an editorial in the *British Medical Journal*. In an unsigned editorial headed *Top Surgeons*, the paper wrote:

'A photograph in a Sunday paper a few weeks ago showed the President of the Royal College of Surgeons of England (and others) listening to the Hunterian Oration. Leaning forward earnestly from a solitary column of type was the orator himself. The names of those in the two front rows were given in full so the reader should be in no doubt of their identity. . . . As the President of the Royal College of Surgeons is the most unassuming and modest of men, it was obvious that there must be something desperately wrong with the present state of the College for him to consent to this kind of publicity. Like many a private doctor suspected of advertising, it wanted, and wants, money—and apparently quite a lot. The college deserves it. It is a national institution built up by the labours of famous men. But many national appeals for money* have been launched before this without attempts to publicize the persons behind the cause of the appeal. The College of Surgeons could probably raise the money it

* The *Journal* did not specify which.

wants without losing its dignity and without giving publicity to the members of its council. No one could have felt at all happy at seeing the full-page advertisement in last week's *New Statesman* and *Spectator* announcing the presenting by "Granada" on ITV of *Surgeon*—printing the names of the President and the six members of the College Council . . . This Journal has a great respect for the present President of the Royal College of Surgeons of England. No one who knows him can doubt that his first concern is for his college and the last is for himself. He is not in private practice, and therefore does not stand to gain any professional advantage from the present series of publicity stunts of which he is the unwitting centrepiece. Doubtless they are as distasteful to him as they may be pleasing to the ingenious minds who have thought them up. We hope the College will raise the money it needs. We hope too that the President will look a bit more critically at the advice he is receiving from the promoters of the various schemes for raising it. It would be a pity if the College, in achieving its target of £3 million, found that in the process it has lost something more precious than money.'

There could have been no more baleful and spiteful attack, and there was no doubt at whom it was aimed. The papers of the Royal College of Surgeons Appeal are in the possession of the author and could easily be used to prove that each step in the campaign was discussed and approved by all members of the College Council, including the President. The suggestion made by the *British Medical Journal* that they were tricked into distasteful methods by 'ingenious minds' is wholly false; they helped to think up the schemes themselves and espoused them enthusiastically; and they had played no part in the publication of their names. Certainly, no member of the public, and no important member of any of the professions, voiced a protest or suggested that the campaign was doing anything but good for the community. But one doctor, a member of the Royal College of Surgeons himself, decided in his wisdom that his more august colleagues had sinned and must be punished for it. On May 26, 1959, he wrote to Archie:

'Dear sir,—I am enclosing a copy of a letter which I have written to the British Medical Association regarding my complaint about unprofessional conduct on your part when you permitted

Sir Archibald and Lady McIndoe with Princess Marina (then Duchess of Kent)

(*Below*) Archie's daughters Vanora (*left*) and Adonia

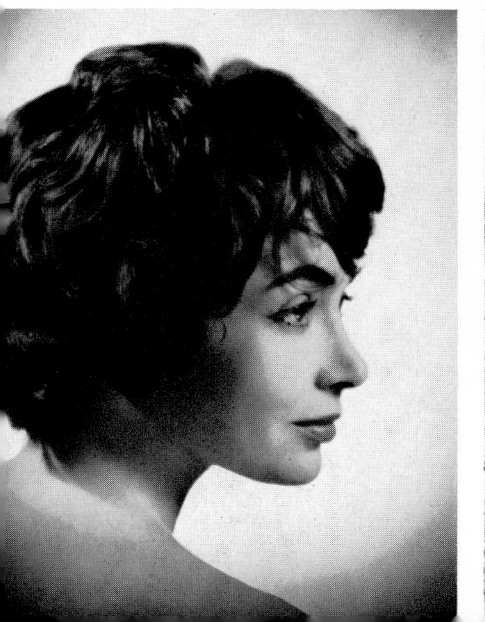

Archie, with Lady McIndoe behind him, on their return from his eye operation in Spain. He had had a heart attack during the flight

your name and qualifications to be published in the *TV Times*. I regret that the matter has reached this stage, and would have preferred it to have been dealt with in isolation from the individuals concerned; but it would appear that the only way to have the situation clarified is for me to formally complain about you personally. I am giving you this opportunity of offering an explanation, as requested by Rule 7 of the "Revised Rules governing procedure . . . ." before the matter is considered further by the Central Ethical Committee of the British Medical Association. Yours faithfully, E. W.'

The letter of which he enclosed a copy was addressed to S. J. Hadfield, Assistant Secretary to the British Medical Association, and read as follows:

'Dear Doctor Hadfield,—Thank you for your letter of 8th May; I have delayed my reply in order to give the matter further thought, and also so that I might quote from the *TV Times* the names of the medical practitioners concerned in the programme *Surgeon* to which I have referred. I have also now read in the *British Medical Journal* the report of the discussion of the matter by the Central Ethical Committee and I cannot agree that the line taken by the Committee in its deliberations was at all conclusive or satisfactory. I continue therefore to regard the behaviour of these eminent members of the profession, in allowing their names and qualifications to be publicized by the ITA, as a breach of etiquette and I feel compelled, not without considerable regret, to ask for an inquiry into their conduct. I shall be grateful if you will please pass this request to the Honorary Secretaries of the appropriate Divisions. As indicated in Rule 7 of the "Revise Rules governing procedure . . . etc." I have written to the members concerned giving the substance of my complaint and asking for their views. In conclusion I would add that I have drawn the attention of the General Medical Council to the television programme in question and am awaiting their reply. The medical practitioners whose names were quoted in the *TV Times* are: Lawrence Abel, Esq, FRCS, Professor Ian Aird, FRCS, Sir Archibald McIndoe, CBE, FRCS, Sir Arthur Porritt, KCMG, KCVO, CBE, FRCS, Sir James Paterson Ross, KVCO, FRCS, Sir Reginald Watson-Jones, FRCS, Arthur Dickson Wright, Esq, FRCS. Yours sincerely, E. W.'

It was rather as if the Archbishop of Canterbury and the Convocation of Bishops had been arraigned before the Church Council for their fund-raising activities on behalf of Coventry Cathedral. The legal adviser to the Royal College was called in and asked to draft a letter, which was sent to the Doctor at his home address in the country.

'Dear Sir,' the letter read, 'We have been instructed by the Royal College of Surgeons of England and the following members of the Council of the College in connection with your letters of 26th May addressed to the above-named individuals with which were sent copies of your letters of the same date addressed to the Assistant Secretary of the BMA. We are instructed to inform you that neither the Royal College of Surgeons of England nor any one of our individual clients was asked for or gave any permission or authority for the publication or use of the name or qualification of any individual in the *TV Times* or in the course of the television programme to which your letters refer, nor had any of our clients any knowledge that the name or qualifications of any individual would be or had been published or used until after the television broadcast in question. We are instructed to qualify the first part of the above statement by informing you that, in speaking to Mr Frank Duesbury on the history, activities and aims of the Royal College of Surgeons of England in connection with the College's appeal for funds to finance its rebuilding, Sir James Paterson Ross was aware that what he had to say on these subjects would or might be published as having been said by him in his capacity as President of the Royal College of Surgeons of England and that his name and description as President of the College would or might be published as the author of his statement to Mr Duesbury. Our clients further instruct me to say that they are astonished and indignant that any suspicion should be entertained by anyone that any individual among them should desire or attempt to obtain or permit or acquiesce in or be associated with any publicity for the purpose of obtaining patients or promoting his own professional advantage. Our clients regard with pain and surprise the fact that allegations of this nature should have been made against them without any prior attempt to ascertain from any of them whether the use of their names and qualifications was with or without their knowledge and assent. We are instructed to invite you, now that you have been informed of the facts, to withdraw the charges you have made and to apologize to our clients.'

There the squalid fuss died down, except for one heart-warming sequel. The affair had distressed Archie McIndoe deeply. He had always had a great respect for, almost fear of, the disciplinary powers of the General Medical Council, and there are scores of letters in his files refusing offers for articles or interviews on the grounds that publicity would be damaging. When the features editor of the *Sunday Express* once wrote to him and asked him if J. W. P. Mallalieu, MP, might interview him for an article on his work, he wrote back (on September 7, 1957, long before the controversy over the College Appeal came up):

'Dear Mr Robinson,—It is very kind of you to believe me worthy of inclusion in your series of profiles of eminent men. The subject, however, is not without a certain difficulty. As you know, no medical man knowingly presents himself to the public through the medium of such a great newspaper as yours without coming face to face with the General Medical Council. There are four great medical sins for each one of which expulsion from the Medical Register is the penalty. They all begin with A and they're Alcohol, Abortion, Adultery and Advertising; of these Advertising is considered to be by far the most serious. So you will have to wait until I am either dead or retired. I am so sorry.'

Now, in his distress, he was comforted by a note from his old friend and partner, Sir Harold Gillies. Giles wrote:

'Don't worry, my dear. We live and work in a sty and some pigs are dirtier than others.'

But he did more than that. He wrote a letter to the *British Medical Journal*, in which he referred specifically to complaints that members of the Council of the College had been named in a photograph published in the newspapers.

'How anyone can complain,' he wrote, 'of the ethics of that wonderful photograph of the College Council passes comprehension. X's only complaint is that X wasn't a good enough surgeon to be included. After all, we voted them there and good cess to them. At seventy-six plus I hope there are still a few friends who will credit me with a life that has been devoted to surgery—the surgery of the maimed, the wounded and the burned. It is unfair but inevitable that through the thrust of the Press the limelight should be thrown on such subjects as hole in the heart, insulin, penicillin, psychiatry, or even plastic surgery. Having had a hand in developing the present plastic surgery service of our country, of which the Health Service may well be proud, I can speak with feeling of the encouragement given to this young subject not only by the great medical journals but by such dedicated individuals as Lord Northcliffe, Beaverbrook, Owen Seaman, Squire Spriggs, and, later, Lord Nuffield. Their Press, their approval, helped on the work, educated the public and obtained facilities necessary to its progress to the benefit of many disfigured folk and to the credit of British surgery. Somebody outside the profession has got to put it across, somebody or bodies inside the profession have to be utilized, even against their interests, to further these aims by explanations and interview. One small note in the Press may influence in a few days the trend of medical treatment which might otherwise take months to percolate.'

At which point he referred to the mud stirred up by the TV programme.

'Far quicker and more potent,' he wrote, 'is the television technique. It educates the public in the truths of our lovely profession, and what harm if one or two men get a tiny puff? Cannot we be tolerant as well as clever and ethical? Unfortunately, Mr A who is written up by some thrustful journalist may be one of our worst qualified and shadiest of practitioners, while Dr B, with less glamour and more ability, stays hidden under his bushel of ethical modesty. Is not the answer to be found in educating the Press to our standards? I wonder whose pocket and whose dignity suffers from such an excellent television programme as that recent one depicting an operation for hare-lip [which was Archie's contribution to the series]. It could hardly have been more sympathetically shown, and must have given a great deal of comfort to parents and of instruction to their medical practitioners. There seems to be a false idea that as a result of such publicity all the hare-lip babies in Britain would immediately be rushed off to be operated or televised. My own experience of this type of publicity is that only a few rather hopeless individuals seek an appointment without a doctor's reference, and impecunious to boot. As a form of successful advertising it is therefore a washout. But as a means of spreading among the populace, including the medical profession, the great advances in British medicine and surgery, publicity properly controlled should be welcomed with an open heart.'

He ended:

'I think it is magnificent that the President of the Royal College of Surgeons and his councillors and counsellors should devote so much time and energy to raise money for the good of surgery and not for their own gain. These men have all deserved great credit for the unselfish work they have done, and is it not preposterous that they should be called to account by a vociferous group of people who appear to enjoy criticizing the ethics of others? Are not the Peter Mays and Denis Comptons of our profession better than the Press critics? On a Sunday soon and for the five following Sundays, the *Sunday X*, ambitious to capture the doctors as readers, had proposed to publish my life story written by myself about golf and fishing and all sorts of things I've enjoyed with my medical pals and, of course, my efforts at surgery. These articles would have been quite harmless, the offer prodigious—£6,500. On advice and after much brainwashing, I have wistfully turned it down. Am I right, or a fool? Could the General Medical Council be persuaded to moderate Clause 5B?'

Archie sent a note to Giles which was short but from the heart:

'Dear Giles,—What can I say but bless you, bless you, bless you?'

The appeal fund for the Royal College went on mounting until it had reached one and a half million pounds. And despite the controversy, or perhaps because of the way in which it had been manipulated against him, Archie McIndoe's prestige mounted too. The fellows of the Royal College of Surgeons began to talk about him as their next President, and there seemed to be nothing —or no one—to stand in his way.

CHAPTER TWELVE

DOES A DOCTOR KNOW?

IT IS TRUE THAT, as he wrote to Blackie, 'I can no longer hear the stones rattling around inside me,' but Archie McIndoe was only too well aware that his operation had failed to restore his health. The pain which he had felt so long diminished for a few months, and then began to nag him again, only this time in his chest instead of his stomach.

'The dreaded event is almost upon us again,' he wrote just before the Guinea Pig annual dinner in 1958. 'My knees are shaking already. These Guinea Pigs will be the death of me yet.'

He made similar remarks every year, and of course he did not mean them; but this year it could truthfully be said that the event would be something of an ordeal for him. He was not really in condition for it.

The Guinea Pig annual weekend has always been, and still is, something of an event. It begins on a Friday when the members begin to arrive at East Grinstead with their wives. Single men are put up in dormitories at the Queen Victoria Hospital. Those surgeons and anaesthetists, like Percy Jayes and Russell Davies, who worked with the Guinea Pigs during the war, open their homes to them, as do the Friends of the Guinea Pigs, like the ever-hospitable Neville Blonds and the Douglas Sterns. Those who can afford it stay at Ye Olde Felbridge Hotel, where most of the social functions take place, and the lawns and swimming pool of that pleasant establishment are soon filled with the Pigs and their almost invariably pretty wives in bathing costumes. No one, not even outsiders who happen to be staying in the hotel, seems to notice—and are certainly not disturbed—that the bodies of many of the men still bear the dreadful scars from their wartime burning. The legless discard their false limbs and hop like frogs onto the diving board and bounce into the water from a handstand. The handless paddle around like happy puppies. The hairless doff their wigs in greeting to newcomers. The blind are taken to the water's edge and then pushed in. And watching it all from the edge is the Club's most charming tough, Tubby Taylor, shouting ribald comments while he sips beer from his very own mug, shaped like a lavatory pan.

That evening there is a dance and a cabaret which goes on until the early hours of the morning. It is open not only to the Guinea Pigs and the staff of the Queen Victoria but also to any outsider prepared to pay for a ticket. Those strangers who come will notice three qualities that make up a Guinea Pig reunion: it never loses its high spirits, it is the scene of some monumental imbibing, and no one ever talks about the past. . . . Unlike regimental get-togethers, it is rare to hear one of these men say: 'Do you remember when old so-and-so . . . ?' The Guinea Pigs live in the present and they almost invariably talk of what they are doing now or what they plan to do in the future.

Saturday morning and afternoon are the times when those Pigs who need it return to the hospital to have their flaps examined by the surgeons, to make appointments for the repair work which many of them will always need, or to talk to Edward Blacksell and Russell Davies about their jobs. It all goes under the heading of Guinea Piggery, and it is here that a man who needs a loan to help his business or a gift to see him through a crisis gets the expert help he needs.

Lunchtime is a boozy ritual meeting at the Guinea Pig Arms in East Grinstead for the annual darts match. Saturday evening is the dinner party for Guinea Pigs only, to which certain guests—who have included Prince Philip and all brasshats of the three Services—are invited. (Lady McIndoe takes the wives away for a private dinner of their own.) And Sunday morning is given up to a farewell cocktail party after which the Pigs part for another year. They may drive away with physical hangovers but mentally and spiritually they are uplifted.

For Archie McIndoe this unique event had always been a pleasant ordeal: hard work, hard drinking, and little sleep. He was the hero of the occasion, and heroes are not supposed to rest. He had to mix with the boys, listen to their problems, entertain the honoured guests, make the main speech of the evening. In 1958 there were those who noticed that try as he might he did not succeed in being as ebullient as usual, and at the annual dinner he hardly touched his food and was highly nervous and perspired profusely during his short speech.

What they did not know was that for almost all of the weekend he was suffering pain severely, particularly while he was speaking. After it was over, he retired to bed for a couple of days while preparations went on for a trip to America which he and Connie were planning. It was while he was still abed that Mrs Ann Standen, a Guinea Pig wife who looked after the arrangements for the annual dance, wrote to him with the results of the evening—and pointed out that some Guinea Pigs had gone to the dance without paying for their tickets.

'Dear Ann,' he wrote. 'First of all, congratulations on the results of your efforts. They are absolutely first-class. Secondly, I am quite sure that if you know thirteen Guinea Pigs who with their wives went in without paying you should send them the appropriate bill immediately. This is the only way in which this evil practice will be stopped and the boys will get to believe that there is a bill for practically everything in this life after all! I am glad that the date for the next get-together has been advanced a little bit, for it means that the Guinea Pig "do" will be just that little bit further off next year. But it will come too soon! I am off to America.'

He was off to America for what, on the face of it, seemed a needless purpose, if a pleasant one. His colleagues in the United States had deeply admired his work as a plastic surgeon both during the war and after it, and many of his techniques had been adopted by them, and his Papers—on Burns, on Homographs, Mammaplasty, the Congenital Absence of the Vagina, on the Rehabilitation of the Mutilated, on Dupuytren's Contracture—had long been required reading for them. They decided unanimously to ask him to visit them at their annual Congress in Miami and accept as a reward an Honorary Fellowship of the American College of Surgeons. He wrote back and gently pointed out that he did not need to be made an honorary fellow since he had earned his ordinary fellowship while at the Mayo Clinic in the years before the war. They replied:

'In that case, come anyway. You will be unique—the only

surgeon in the world to be both a Fellow and an Honorary Fellow of our College.'

He sailed with Connie in the autumn and submitted himself to the vigorous hospitality of the American medical world with no sign that he found it overwhelming. But when he could, he relaxed with his two old friends, Miriam and Simon Marks, who were visiting America, and one of his favourite pupils, Doctor Tom Rees, now one of Manhattan's most successful plastic surgeons. Towards the end of his stay, he slipped away without saying where he was going and arrived at the Mayo Clinic in Rochester, Minnesota. It was the first time he had been back to what was really his *alma mater* since the early nineteen-thirties, and there were few of his old masters or fellow-pupils who remained there. The Mayo Brothers themselves were dead, and his good friend, Doctor Counsellor, had retired to practise in Arizona. But Archie McIndoe's name still meant much at this great institution and he was given a reception that was royal in its warmth and enthusiasm.

He had not, however, come to be lauded but to be examined. He asked to be taken to the Clinical Section and submitted to every test they could give him. 'After which,' he said, 'I would like to see a detailed report.'

His heart and his oesophagus were X-rayed, his liver was submitted to a brom-sulphalein test, his blood was tested, so were his stomach and his duodenum, and he was put to exercise on a treadmill. He sailed with Connie for home while the report on his condition—on his life expectation—was still being compiled, and it reached him towards the end of November 1958. It was written by Doctor Howard B. Burchell, one of the most eminent and skilful specialists in the United States, and it began:

'Dear Sir Archibald,—It was a privilege to see you in medical consultation recently but regret that I had to be the bearer of some bad news regarding your coronary insufficiency syndrome. It seemed clear that at times you had angina, and that on occasion the small diaphragmatic hernia might be a contributor to the distress and indeed acting as a trigger mechanism on occasion. When we had you exercise on the treadmill your characteristic distress occurred in a minute and a half, and with this there was moderate depression of the ST segment on the electrocardiagram in the left precordial leads . . .'

It ended, 'I do hope that your angina does not increase, and that you continue to have an active productive life for many, many years.'

In between these two paragraphs were two pages of details about every part of his body, given in clinical detail. The Mayo Clinic had paid Archie the compliment of taking him at his word when he said he wished to know everything. To a layman it may have meant little. To a doctor of Archie McIndoe's experience, it told him everything that he had expected.

'My dear Burchell,' he wrote back on December 2, 1958, 'I am most grateful to you for your very nice letter, even if it does carry news which could only be described as "sobering". It is clear that I shall have to be a little careful of my expenditure of energy and it will interest you to know that I have already taken steps to limit my activities, in view of what the fire-eating Hermann Moersch [the heart specialist] had to say as he breathed gently down the back of my neck. Oddly enough, from a scientific standpoint I am somewhat interested in the possible effect which the histus hernia may have on my cardiac reaction which varies quite enormously from time to time. Some years ago I found it much more comfortable to sleep sitting practically bolt upright and I had no trouble whatsoever in sleeping in this odd position. Since I married some five years ago I have adopted a more recumbent position and oddly enough I feel quite certain that this wretched histus hernia sparks off the symptoms which I told you. Nevertheless, your treadmill test was a bit of a facer and I am sure one must accept it as meaning that my coronary inadequacy is fairly marked.'

He added:

'Just how to hold the balance between the emotional and physical factors is not easy; but I am already beginning to learn how to live below the appearance of any stress feeling and am consequently much better for it.'

His own doctor wrote to him:

'Dear Archie,—Herewith the dossier on your life. I think the gist of the situation is that as long as you keep your weight down you will live to be a grand old man. There is a new cooking oil called sunflower seed oil with which your food may be cooked even fried. Yours ever, Cecil Eppel.'

But Archie did not need to be told that the only way that he might live to be a grand old man was to give up everything he loved doing—his surgery, his work for the College, his paternal control of the Guinea Pigs, his restless interest in all forms of life. He had kept no secrets from Connie about his condition and he did not keep secret from her now that, though he might try henceforward to lessen the speed of his life, he could not slow it down too much, because that way he would die anyway, of boredom.

In normal circumstances, this would have been the time when he would be off for his long break in his beloved Africa. In the clear air and invigorating sunshine on the slopes of Kilimanjaro he might have found the tonic he needed at this time, but, alas, his dream of an African home had faded in the past two years. It had begun to fade after his partner, Robin Johnston, had married and become the father of a family, and no longer had time to share the trips, the adventures and the enthusiasm which these two had enjoyed in the past. On one occasion, in 1956, when Archie proposed bringing three friends to stay with him in the guesthouse which had been built for him on the ranch at Ol Orien, he had been told that his visit would be inconvenient. He cabled back to Johnston:

'Flabbergasted your cable. Has our repeat our guest house burned down. Can promise only minor demands on Ol Orien hospitality. Situation slightly embarrassing here and would welcome explanation return cable as time short.'

The party went out anyway, but for Archie it wasn't the same ever again.

In December 1957, Robin Johnston wrote:

'Firstly, you will find that here there are every day evidences of hostile political trends which were unknown in 1950. I am not being depressing but I am being realistic . . . Our friendship I value very highly. For ten years I have looked forward to your visits. They have been a highlight of the year for me. Now with a growing family and strictly limited accommodation I can still give you the same welcome, but I obviously cannot (and here surely you must be sensitive to my reasons) extend an effortless welcome to many more than two of you. Here, if we differ, we must differ for I cannot concur that I am being unreasonable. If you feel I am being so, we are on new and, for me, sad ground for it must be the first time in our long years of friendship that we have been unable to resolve a difference of opinion.'

It was a letter which hurt Archie McIndoe grievously, and he rightly suspected that his partner's enthusiasm for the ranch had waned and that soon he would want to get out. It took another year before his suspicion was confirmed. He did not complain. When the question of selling out came to be discussed he wrote at once to tell Robin Johnston that he would gladly wait for his money until his partner could pay him and (though eighty-five per cent of the capital had always been his) would not ask for more than half a share of the proceeds. He even spent much of his time in London writing letters and dining the directors of a large African corporation in order to find his erstwhile partner a new job.

But he was deeply hurt. He had loved Africa with a passion which transcended all thought of political development. He did not care whether Tanganyika was white or black, for he certainly never had any sense of colour or colour prejudice. 'If Mau Mau couldn't drive me away,' he said, 'why should an independent African Government?' He kept up his interest in African affairs and was an indefatigable promoter of the African Medical Research Unit to the last; but with his home gone, much of the savour had gone too.

So that winter there was no Africa to strengthen his muscles, pare off his surplus flesh, and drive the clouds from his mind. His days as the great white doctor of Kilimanjaro were over.

And yet a few months later his spirits had risen again and he was his old, restless, busy self.

'My dear Blackie,' he wrote, 'we had a most pleasant time with Simon and Miriam in the South of France. It was only eight days but it did us a lot of good. The mad rush of work, as you call it, is now in full spate. Where it is all going to end up I don't know, but probably the looney bin! . . . I shall be writing you a little bit more about Guinea Piggery, for there has been a spurt in activity here and one or two pretty strenuous demands have been made. I had a nice letter from the Duchess of Kent the other day thanking us all for our co-operation with the RAF Benevolent Fund. To date they have passed out £57,000. Not bad.'

His fund-raising campaign for the Royal College of Surgeons continued, but now there was a new topic to cause talk among the Fellows. When the term of office of the President, Sir James Paterson Ross, came to an end in 1960, who would be voted by them into his place?

There is no doubt that more than any of the other members of the Council, Archie McIndoe deserved the honour, and he was certainly well qualified for it. He was a great surgeon, and not in plastic surgery alone; he could not only beautify but he could also mend with masterful skill, and had time and again proved his own contention that reconstructive surgery was 'the art of ordinary surgery raised to the *n*th degree of finesse'. He had charm and presence, with a beautiful and talented wife to stand by his side during the social activities which the Presidency entailed. His work in raising one and a half million pounds for the rebuilding fund of the College had put the Fellows—as well as the country—in his debt. And his record of service to the burned and maimed of the war meant that in every country in the world he would be looked up to with admiration and respect.

But there were rivals in the field, and not the least powerful of them was his fellow New Zealander and lifelong (although friendly) competitor for medical honours, Sir Arthur Porritt. Sir Arthur had let it be known that he would be standing for election. He had considerable backing, especially from those Fellows who affected to look down on 'skin deep' surgery and the publicity which sometimes went with it.

Still, it seemed likely that this time the man most fitted to wear the mantle would receive it from his peers. The strength of potential voting seemed to be on Archie's side—if, that is, he was fit enough to take the job. But was he fit enough?

His friend, Osmond-Clark, also a member of the council of the FRCS, telephoned him and asked him point-blank whether he was up to the demands of the position.

'Let there be no doubt in your mind about that,' Archie replied. 'You know me well enough to realize that if there is a job to be done, I will do it.'

In that case, Osmond-Clark indicated, he and his friends would throw their powerful support on Archie's side. This did not mean that election was a certainty, but it meant that half the battle was won. He relaxed, and settled down happily to tending the garden of Millwood Manor and staying at home with Connie ('just you and me and the telly', as he wrote once).

He had accepted his heart condition as one of those hazards of life which must be lived with, and though it still gave him a great deal of pain, he no longer worried about it. What did worry him was his eye. The eyes have always been one of the weaknesses of the McIndoe family; his mother had cataracts in hers and so did Archie's younger brother, Ken. For some time (from about 1957 onwards) Archie had been aware that one was developing on his own right eye, filming it over, making it difficult to focus during the more meticulous moments of an operation.

By early 1960 he was only too well aware that if he was to continue as a practising surgeon—and that was what he wished more than anything, the Presidency included—something would have to be done about his sight. The only thing to be done was the delicate operation by which the filmy cataract is scraped away from the eyeball.

Who was to do it? Archie had no doubt who was the best-qualified eye surgeon in the country, for he had helped him in his rise from obscurity to fame, and that was Sir Ben Rycroft of East Grinstead. But Sir Ben had already had one distressing experience with the McIndoe family when he had operated upon Archie's mother. The operation had been a great success and it was nothing to do with her surgeon that she had later died.

It is always distressing, however, for a surgeon to lose a patient even though it is no fault of his own. How could Archie ask Rycroft to risk the same thing happening again? And with his heart in the condition it was, there was a definite risk. It would be unfair to a colleague and a friend to ask him to face it. So instead, he asked Rycroft to give him the name of an ophthalmologist abroad who could be recommended to operate upon him with skill and dispatch. He was told to put himself in the hands of Doctor Joaquin Burraquer, of Barcelona.

There is nothing to be gained for a great surgeon whose eyes are his stock-in-trade to announce to the world that he is having trouble with them, and there was a certain amount of secrecy and deception about the departure of Archie and Connie for Barcelona early in 1960. They announced that they were off on a cruise and then slipped ashore at a southern port and journeyed up to Catalonia. The operation went well and during the difficult first period afterwards, when the patient must not move, Connie shared Archie's room and watched over him. He was very cheerful and relieved, and did a small dance of glee when he looked at himself in the mirror with a black patch over his eye.

But in the 'plane which flew them back from Barcelona he all but collapsed with considerable pain and had to be helped from the aircraft at London Airport. There, when he saw the photographers awaiting him, he straightened up and even managed to smile. It is difficult, looking at the picture taken on that day, to realize it is one of a man who has just had a bad heart attack.

CHAPTER THIRTEEN

HOW LONG?

ONCE DURING THE WAR, when Richard Hillary and Archie McIndoe were going round Ward Three at the Queen Victoria Hospital, they stopped by the bedside of an appallingly burned patient whose tortured body had failed to respond to all the ministrations of the surgeons. He was conscious enough to talk a little and to smile at Archie's jokes, but when they walked away from him, the surgeon said:

'Poor fellow. He'll be dead by the morning.'

Hillary's eyebrows lifted. 'Tell me, Archie,' he said, 'does a chap like that realize he is going to die?'

'No,' said Archie. 'They never do. That's the happy quality of the human mind, even in the last moments. It keeps on hoping for the best.'

For Archie McIndoe, in the first few months of 1960, the warning bell tolled repeatedly inside his body, and he was too good a doctor not to heed it. Yet no one save his wife, Connie, to whom he confided his fears, could have guessed that he was aware of a cold hand on his shoulder. He too seemed to be hoping for the best, just like one of his patients. In truth, he was discovering that the optimism which protects the layman from knowledge of death does not protect a medical man sensitive to his condition and capable of assessing the facts.

He knew he was going to die. All he did not know was when. And for him there was only one problem: how long could he cheat death and still keep going, without radically altering his way of life, without giving up the work he loved? For that he was determined not to do. The years since his marriage, despite his bodily setbacks, had been the fullest, the happiest, the most fulfilled of his life, and whenever Connie suggested that he had done enough, that perhaps now was the time to retire, he waved the suggestion away. 'I would rather go out with a bang than a whimper,' he said.

Not that he neglected elementary precautions. The eye-patch had come off now and a contact lens had been fitted, and this, plus his glasses, corrected the double vision which had troubled him immediately after the operation. He performed one or two minor operations at the Clinic, but gradually cut down his work until his eyes were nursed back to condition. To help their convalescence, he gave up one of his greatest pleasures, driving a car, and became, as both his wife and chauffeur discovered, a snappish and critical back-seat driver. He still kept up his voluminous correspondence, dictating scores of letters into his dictaphone for his tireless secretary, Joan Dunkerton, to type out. He could hold back the queue of patients at the London Clinic and East Grinstead, but his work for the College and the Guinea Pigs went on.

At least once a week, he still attended a meeting or a dinner or a conference in London, or at the hospital. He made plans for the future. But as much as he could, he remained at Millwood Manor, tending his garden, and waiting—waiting for his eyes to recover, waiting for the all-important meeting of the Council of the Royal College of Surgeons in July when the new President would be chosen.

He had been invited to America once more in the autumn of 1960 to attend a medical congress, and on February 8, he wrote to the organizer, Doctor Gerald H. Gray:

'Dear Ged,—All my plans for your October meeting are upset by the fact that there may be an alteration in my way of life—not serious—during that month, which will make it impossible for me to come to America. But I will give you a firm answer by July 31st.'

He was referring to the election of the President. If the position came to him, he would take office in October.

He had once been reluctant to take the Presidency, but he was eager for it now. He was only too well aware that if he failed to win it now he would not live to fight for it again. It had become vitally important to him to get it, for it would represent an honourable culmination to his life and career.

But how stood his chances? All his friends on the Council told him that the majority were on his side, that he was bound to win.

But he knew that his chief rival, Sir Arthur Porritt, had influential friends, too, and that his claims to the Presidency were just as valid as his own.

It was in this state of uncertainty that he drove to London on the afternoon of April 11, 1960, on his way to attend a dinner party given by the Saints and Sinners. He was to be one of the guests of honour, and his old friend and fellow doctor, Lord Evans, was to be the chief guest. Connie had a meeting at the Queen Victoria Hospital next day, and stayed behind at East Grinstead, since it was to be a 'stag' dinner, and as she and a few friends said goodbye to him they noted in him a gaiety and a liveliness of spirits which had been missing for several weeks.

It was a mood that continued throughout the evening. If ever Archie McIndoe had been off-form in public lately to an extent that anyone noticed it, he made up for it on this occasion. It was as if everything had suddenly come all right again. He ate a normal meal and drank toasts with the rest of the guests. His charm was persuasive. No one guessed that he had recently been ill, and no one noticed that he had had an operation on his eye.

It was as if, suddenly, a load had lifted from his shoulders. After the dinner was over, he repaired with Evans and a few others to White's Club and drank a brandy, after which Evans drove him home to his flat in Albion Gate. There they sat, drinking and talking, until the early hours of the morning. Their conversation is not one to be gone into here, but it was certainly one which left Archie in a mellow and contented mood as he closed the door on his guest and went to his bedroom.

He died in his sleep in the early hours of April 12, 1960. A maid found him next morning when she brought his tea. He did not look dead so much as enormously, peacefully comfortable.

It would be pleasant to think that he knew before he died something which others knew only much later: that two days before his death, his chief rival, Sir Arthur Porritt, decided to withdraw his name from the list of nominations for the Presidency of the Royal College of Surgeons, and thus made the election of Archibald Hector McIndoe certain.

CHAPTER FOURTEEN

EPILOGUE

ARCHIBALD HECTOR MCINDOE was dead. He had died in the way he would have wished, not lingering, without fuss, with (to use one of his favourite phrases) his 'drinking boots' on.

But few men in dying have left so much of themselves behind. Sir Harold Gillies, in a farewell message to his one-time junior partner, wrote of his enthralling career, his beautiful technique, and of his 'congregation of friends more embracing than is given to most'. There were certainly plenty of friends. They crammed into St Clement Dane's, the RAF Church, for a memorial service a month after his death and they came from all countries and every walk of life. There were the surgeons he had trained, now at work throughout the Commonwealth and in countries in every continent; there were his colleagues from the Royal College of Surgeons, for which he had begged so hard; there were the businessmen who had been bullied and blandished by him to rally to the cause of medicine; and there were, most important of all, his friends, the Guinea Pigs.

Archie McIndoe's achievement, however, is not to be measured by his knack of making friends or even by his brilliance as a surgeon, but in the unique quality he possessed of mending lives as well as bodies, of smashing fears and prejudices, of sweeping away bureaucratic cant, of quickening events when they were moving too slowly, and of inspiring enthusiasm wherever he went.

There is no need to recapitulate here the things he did for medicine and for people, and those who need to be reminded of them are recommended to turn back these pages. He has left his footprints behind him in all the places where he worked or lived and among all the people with whom he mixed, as a doctor or as a man. But perhaps most of all he left his mark upon the Queen

Victoria Hospital at East Grinstead. Once it was a small cottage hospital in a small Sussex town, and he gave it greatness; and it is not too much to say that he performed miracles there, miracles of surgical skill, miracles of human rehabilitation, of a kind that modern medicine has never known before. If ever a man can be said to have given his heart to a collection of buildings, Archie McIndoe gave his to the Queen Victoria; and though today it is just a part of the south-western branch of the National Health Service, you can feel the difference between it and other hospitals when you visit it, for his heart still quickens its rhythm and gives it a special warmth.

Many famous men spoke up in praise of Archie McIndoe after his death, and lauded him for all manner of things: for having made reconstructive surgery respectable, for having helped to win the Battle of Britain by saving its pilots, for having skinned and sliced so well. But perhaps one tribute to him is most worth recording here. It came from one of the young surgeons he trained, Mr Robin Beare, and he said simply this:

'Almost everything about him is unforgettable, but most vividly I remember his enthusiasm—infectious enthusiasm—for whatever he was doing. A cleft lip in a three-months-old baby or a face burned beyond recognition: to either problem he would bring the same inevitable sureness and delicacy of touch. He was the most inspiring surgeon I have ever learned from and always his enthusiasm was there.'

It was to Beare that, just before he died, he confided his greatest enthusiasm. He wanted to see at East Grinstead—if possible before he died—the building of a new research unit that would probe the great mystery of human skin and tissue.

'The next great era in surgery,' he said to him, 'will be when we learn how to transplant tissue from one person to another. It will be bigger than penicillin, bigger than antisepsis. I foresee the day when whole limbs, kidneys, lungs and even hearts will be surgically replaced.'

Such a surgical research unit, thanks to his efforts, is in operation at East Grinstead today. And though he did not live to attend its opening, he knew that it was building. He knew too that his idea for an African Medical Research Unit was in process of formation in Kenya and Tanganyika. He knew that the Royal College of

Surgeons of England would get their new buildings. He knew that, in the week that he died, every single Guinea Pig who had survived the war was in work, and, as he used to say, 'active in every sense of the word—two squeakers apiece, and more to come.'

In the circumstances, death when it came in the early hours of April 12, 1960, cannot have come with too much of a painful sting. In the words his friend John Hunter used to use to his beloved Guinea Pigs, it was probably no more than 'just a little prick, if you'll pardon the expression'.

INDEX

Adams, Maude, 27
Adson, Dr Alfred, 45–46
Africa, 83, 196–7, 216 ff., 230, 251–2
African Medical Research Units, 226, 252, 260
'Airman's Burn', 9, 91
Air Ministry, 90–91, 123, 126, 138, 164, 185, 187, 208
Aitken, Adonia, *see* McIndoe, Adonia
Albion Gate, 258
Aldershot, 56, 58
America, *see* United States
American College of Surgeons, 35, 248–9
American Protective Ass'n, 33
Anaesthetic techniques, 70
Arch, Bernard, 160
Auckland, NZ, 29, 53
'Aunt Agatha', *see* Clemetson, Mrs Kay
Australia, 16–17, 23, 179

Balfour, Carrie, 40
Balfour, Dr Donald, 31, 39–43, 47–48, 82, 205
Ball, Girling, 52
Barcelona, 254–5
Barnstaple, 185
Basingstoke, 79–80
Battle of Britain, 10–11, 77–92, 153, 180, 260
Bauer, Dr, 211
BBC, 178
Beare, Robin, 260
Beaverbrook, Lord, 237, 244
Belchem, Mrs Constance, *see* McIndoe, Connie
Bevan, Aneurin, 189–215
Blacksell, Edward, 95, 116–17, 120, 136, 139, 142, 144, 146, 153, 155–6, 161, 163, 165–6, 173–4, 176–7, 184–7, 195, 200, 209, 219, 230, 235, 246–7, 252
Blond, Neville, 116 n., 137, 189, 218, 246; Mrs Neville, 218 (*see also* Mrs Elaine Laski)
Bowyer, Ward, 208
Brighton, NZ, 13, 18
Bristol, 16
British Ass'n of Plastic Surgeons, 193–4
British Medical Ass'n, 73, 110, 130, 240–1
British Medical Journal, 202, 239–41, 243
British Power Boat Company, The, 164
British Red Cross Society, 210
British War Relief Fund, 183
Bruntisfield, Lord, 125
Burchell, Howard B., 259–50
Burraquer, Dr Joaquin, 254

Cade, Air Commodore Stanford, 128, 130
Cairo, 170
Cambridge Hospital, Aldershot, 56
Canada House, 160–1
Cape of Good Hope, 16
Capka, Joseph, 136, 180

Capone, Al, 45
Central Medical Establishment, The, 127–8
Cheshire, Group Captain L. C., 175
Chicago, 38–39, 43–45, 48
Christchurch, NZ, 27–28, 38
Clayton, Margerie, 71
Clemetson, Mrs Kay, 220–1
Copsey, Rev H. C. F., 231–2
Counseller, Virgil, 82, 249
Coutts, Ben, 158–9
Cripps, Sir Stafford, 146–7
Czechoslovakia, 76

Daily Mirror, 204
Daily Telegraph, 238
Dalton, Sir Hugh, 195
Davies, Sir Dan, 195
Davies, Russell, 136, 157, 184, 208, 246–7
Dean, Mary, 227
Demarteau, 161
Dental Society, The, 108
Denton, Stanley, 226, 228
Desmond, Florence, 124
Dewar, John, 109–10, 115–16, 118, 137
Dewar, Kathleen, 109–10, 115, 118, 125, 137
Douglas, Sir Sholto, 137
Drayton Gardens, Chelsea, 193
Dunedin, NZ, 13–15, 18, 27–29, 37, 76
Dunkerton, Joan, 207, 227, 257
Dunkirk, 84
'Dupuytren's contracture', 146, 161–2, 248
Dutton Homestall, 110, 115, 118, 123, 125

East Grinstead, 10, 69, 72, 80 ff., 226, 228, 230–3, 237, 246, 254, 257–60; *see also* Queen Victoria Hospital
Edinburgh, 75
Edinburgh, HRH Duke of, 247
Edmonds (RAF pilot), 121
Enderby, Hale, 184, 214
Eppel, Cecil, 250
Evans, Lord, 258
Evening Standard, 129–30

Ferguson, Sir Lindo, 28
Fiorovanti, 83
Franceschetti, Dr 212
Francis Holland School, Oxford, 81
Fraser, Sir Ian, 185
Fry, Sir Kelsey, 79–80, 144

Gable, Clark, 96, 153–4
Gardiner, Bill, 120
General Medical Council, 243, 245
George V, 56
Gillies, Elizabeth, 50
Gillies, Lady, 63
Gillies, Sir Harold ('Giles'), 11, 50–53, 55–67, 71, 76, 78–80, 84–85, 90, 108, 112–13, 181, 189, 193, 243, 245, 259
Gleave, Tom, 90, 101–2, 109, 113, 136, 146, 177–8, 185–6
Goossens, Leon, 170
Gray, Dr Gerald H., 257
Guinea Pigs, the, 11, 136–77, 180–1, 184–6, 189, 196–8, 207–9, 215, 218–19, 228, 230–2, 246–8, 251, 257–9, 261; Guinea Pig Anthem, 145; 'Guinea Pig Arms', 231–2, 247

Hadfield, S. J., 241
Hall, Matron, 99–100, 109–10
Hall, Sister, 83, 100, 106–7
Halton, 109
Hamilton, NZ, 26–28
Hammersmith Hospital, 53
Hampstead, 53, 55, 67, 74
Harley Street, 9, 49–50, 67, 69, 74, 76, 78, 80, 82, 85, 169–70, 184, 193, 201, 204, 232
Harrington, Kate, 183
Harris, Wing Commander, 164, 166–7
Hart, Paul, 104, 120, 153, 209
Health, Ministry of, 156, 160, 220–1
Hercus, Professor, 28
Hill, Charles, 16–17
Hillary, Edwina N., 134
Hillary, Richard, 89, 99–100, 105, 110–11, 114–35, 256; *see also* *Last Enemy*, *The*
Hill End, 79
Hitler, Adolf, 76
Hodgkinson, Colin, 123–5
Hoover, President, 41, 47
Howe, Major Shelagh, 175–6
Hughesden, Charles, 124
Hulbert, C. P., 17
Hulbert, Eliza Ann, 16–17
Hunter, John, 69–72, 80, 86, 88, 120, 137, 149, 153, 178–80, 183–4, 213–15, 227–8, 261
Hurley, Vincent, 187

I Had a Row with a German (Gleave), 177
ITV, 240

Jayes, Percy, 80, 111, 137, 144, 181–2, 246
Johnston, Robin, 195, 216–17, 225, 251–2
Jones, Stewart, 122 n.
Joslin, Miss, 81

Kahler Hotel, Rochester, 31, 40, 44
Kendall, Kay, 203
Kenrick, Selwyn, 188
Kent, HRH Duchess of, 252
Kent, HRH Duke of, 146
Kent and Sussex Courier, *The*, 219–20
Kenya, 217, 260
Kilimanjaro, 216–29, 251–2
Kilner, Pomfret, 52–55, 65, 79–80, 181
Kindersley, Lady, 192
Know-Nothings, the, 33
Kruger, Bertram, 183

Lane, Roy, 99
Laski, Elaine, (Mrs Neville Blond) 116, 120, 137, 166
Last Enemy, *The* (Hillary), 100, 110, 126, 129
Law, Yorky, 121
Lee, Jennie (Mrs Aneurin Bevan), 198–9
Little Warren Cottage, 125, 139–40, 192
Liverpool, 48
London, 41–42, 48 ff., 84–86, 131, 191, 252, 256
London Clinic, The, 50, 54, 65–67, 163, 193, 227, 232, 257
Lusaka, 226
Luxfords, 149

Magill, Sir Ivan, 70, 72
Mahn, Holebrook, 139–41, 176
Maida Vale, 48, 50–53
Maitland, F. E., 81
Mallalieu, J. W. P., 243

'Mancini, Mr', 44–45
Manson-Bahr, Philip, 52–53
Marchwood Park, 164–7
Marie Louise, Princess, 218
'Mark', 141–4
Marks, Lady, 218, 249, 252
Marks, Sir Simon, 218, 236, 249, 252
Mary Ann, 17
Mau Mau, 225–6, 252
Maxillo Facial Unit, 136
Maxillonians, the, 136–7
Mayo, Charles, 31, 34–35, 45, 249
Mayo Clinic, 27, 30–47, 49–50, 54, 150, 205, 248–9
Mayo, Will, 26–28, 31, 34–47, 249
Mayo, William Worrall, 31–33:
McIndoe, Adonia, 26–29, 37–42, 47, 50–53, 55, 74–75, 84, 90–91, 108, 111–13, 117, 119–20, 129, 137, 147–53, 164, 168, 170, 190–1, 195, 223–5
McIndoe, Adonia junior, 40, 44, 47, 51–53, 74, 80, 150, 168–9, 193, 221–2
McIndoe, Archibald Hector:
  boyhood, 13–16, 19–23; graduates at Otago Univ, 25; appointed house surgeon, Waikato Hosp, 26; first marriage, to Adonia Aitken, 29; at Mayo Clinic, 31–47; MSc in Pathology, 41; elder daughter (Adonia junior) born, 40; sails for England, 47; meeting with Sir Harold Gillies, 51; younger daughter (Vanora) born, 52; first studies plastic surgery, 61–66; first sight of Queen Victoria Hosp, 80; opening of Ward Three, 80; family departs to USA, 82; settles in East Grinstead, 86; battles with authority, 87, 91, 122, 145–6, 147, 197–201, 207–9; President of the Guinea Pigs, 137; operated on, 161–3, 169–70, 237, 255; broadcasts on BBC, 178; separation from Adonia, 191; knighthood, 196; first trip to Africa, 196–7; on Kilimanjaro, 216–18; divorce, 225; second marriage, to Constance Belchem, 226; death of mother, 234; Vice-President of Royal College of Surgeons, 235–6; return to US, 248–9; visit to Barcelona, 254–5; death, 258; Memorial Service, 259
  quoted: 10–11, 30–31, 77, 82, 84–86, 90–92, 94, 108, 111–13, 117–19, 149–50, 151, 156–7, 158, 166–8, 175–6, 181, 182–3, 186–7, 192, 199, 200–1, 202, 203–4, 228, 237–8, 243, 250, 252
  writings:
    Adult Hypospadias, Operation for the Cure of, 65
    Congenital Absence of the Vagina, Operation for the Cure of, 65, 248
    In Memoriam, 228–9
    on Burns, Dupuytren's contracture, Homographs, Rehabilitation of the Mutilated, 248
    Survey of a Group of Slum Houses (thesis), 25
McIndoe, Connie, 223–5, 227, 230–4, 247–9, 251, 254, 256, 258
McIndoe, Jack, 13, 20–24, 74–76, 78, 153; quoted, 20–21, 24–25
McIndoe, James, 50
McIndoe, John, 14–15, 18–19, 23
McIndoe, Kenneth, 14, 75, 254
McIndoe, Mabel, 14, 16–24, 25, 28–29, 74, 76, 221, 233–4, 254; *quoted*, 16–20
McIndoe, Mabel junior, 14, 75
McIndoe Nose, the, 66, 73, 79, 218
'McIndoe's Operation', 43
McIndoe, Vanora, 52–53, 80, 150–1, 168, 192–3, 221–4

INDEX

Melbourne, 16–17
Meredith Jack, Mrs, 191
Miami, 227, 248
Millfield Cottage, 117, 120, 149
Millwood Manor, 230, 254, 256
Minneapolis, 32, 38, 43
Minnesota University, 31, 41
Moersch, Hermann, 250
Montifeltre, Duke of, 58
Moore, Jerry, 114, 174, 181–3
Morgan, C. Naunton, 112–13
Morris, Jock, 178, 208
Mother Alfred, 32–33
Mowat, Harry, 17–18
Mowlem, Rainsford, 53–54, 63–65, 78–80, 84, 108, 112–13, 162, 189, 193
Moynihan, Lord, 43, 45–46, 48–49, 51
Mullins, Jill, 71–74, 80, 108, 120, 128, 152–3, 163–4, 169, 191–2, 213, 221–4, 226–30
Munich, 76

Nairobi, 225–6
National Health Act, *see* National Health Service
National Health Service, 184, 188, 194, 197–201, 205, 220, 244, 259–60
New Statesman, The, 240
New York, 41, 126
New Zealand, 13, 15, 17, 19, 29, 50, 118
Northcliffe, Lord, 244

O'Connor, Patrick, 98, 104–5, 116, 126
Ol Orien, 224, 251
Osmond-Clark, Mr, 223, 253
Otago Boys' High School, 22
Otago Univ Medical School, 25–29

Page, Geoffrey, 87–89, 99, 103, 105–7, 115, 120, 125–8, 134–6, 178
Peanut Club, the, 219
Penn, Jack, 194–5, 199, 218
Pensions, Ministry of, 207–8
Philip, HRH Prince, 247
Philippi, Wing Commander George, 164–6
Plastic Surgeon, The (Anon), 67–71
Plastic surgery, 9–10, 53–66, 93 ff., 201–2, 210–13
Porritt, Sir Arthur, 22, 26, 253, 258
Portal, Lord, 208
Port Sonachan Hotel, Argyll, 119
Pretty, Ron, 122 n.
Price, Joseph, 34
Principles and Art of Plastic Surgery (Gillies), 59
Properties Association, 38

Queen Victoria Hospital, East Grinstead, 10, 80, 83, 92 ff., 234, 246–7, 256, 258–60; American wing, 182; bombed, 162; Canadian wing, 161, 182; Industrial Therapy Dept, 155; Ward Three, 80, 83, 91–92, 93 ff., 208 256
Quetta, 65

RAF, 9–10, 78 ff.; *see also* Battle of Britain; Guinea Pigs; Queen Victoria Hospital; etc.
RAF Association, 175
Rank, B. K., 202–3
Razumov, Vladimir, 173–5

Rea, Mary, 97–98, 157
Rees, Sir Milsom, 56
Rees, Tom, 203, 249
Reid, George, 155
Rhodes, Dusty, 178–9
Richardson, Air Commodore A. V. J., 79
Riley, Basil, 179, 189
Robertson, Harold E., 36, 71
Rochester, Minnesota, 31 ff., 44, 46, 48, 52, 82, 249
Roehampton, 79–80, 124, 140
Rooksdown, *see* Basingstoke
Roper, G. F., 175
Ross, Sir James Paterson, 253
Rothesay, 15, 50
Royal College of Surgeons, 22, 43, 49, 181, 235–7, 239–45, 251, 253, 256–61
Royal Masonic Hospital, 87
Royal Society of Medicine, 86, 90–91, 98
Russian Embassy, 174–5
Rycroft, Sir Ben, 234, 254
Rye, 117

St Albans, 80, 84
St Andrew's and St James's Hosp, 65
St Bartholomew's Hosp (Bart's), 52, 56, 62, 65, 71–72, 97
St Clement Dane's Church, 259
St Dunstan's, 185
St Francis' Convent, Rochester, 32–33
St John's, Wellington, NZ, 18
St Mary's Hosp, Rochester, 33
St Paul, Minnesota, 32, 38
'Saints and Sinners,' the, 258
Saline Bath Unit, 83, 185
Saline treatment for burns, 84, 102
Salmon, Flt-Sgt, 185–6
San Francisco, 29
Seaman, Owen, 244
Seymour, Robert, 50
Shepherd, E. W., 240–2
Simpson, Bill, 138, 176
Slessor, Sir John, 185
Somme, Battle of the, 58
Spectator, 240
Spriggs, Squire, 244
Standen, Mrs Ann, 248
Stern, Douglas, 246
Stewart, Ross, 208
Stoke Mandeville, 79
Sunday Express, 176, 243
Surgeon, 241
Swiss Red Cross, 209

Tagliacozzi, Gasparo, 57–58
Tait, Lawson, 34
Tanganyika, 196, 216, 252, 260
Tannic acid treatment for burns, 87–90, 101, 109
Taylor, Tubby, 247
Tilley, Ross, 137, 144, 160–1, 178, 181–2, 184, 187–8
Times, The, 238
Tollemache, Tony, 100
'To Sir Archibald McIndoe' (Anon), 232–3
Towers-Perkin, Bill, 136
Trulah, Frankie, 178, 180
TV Times, 239, 241

United States, 30–47, 82, 190, 248–9, 257
'Uplift' (Anon), 204–5

Valadier, Sir Charles, 56

Waitako Hosp, Hamilton, NZ, 26–28
Ware, Dr, 202
Warlow, Squadron Leader, 167–8
Warrender, Sir Victor, *see* Bruntisfield, Lord
Washington, DC, 41, 47, 126
Webb-Johnson, Lord, 237–8
Weekes, Peter, 136, 139, 153
Wellington, NZ, 24
West, Maisie, 84–85
White's Club, 258
William White Travelling Fellowship, 41
Wimereux, 56
Windsor, Duchess of, 218
Wood, Michael, 225–6
Woollard, Professor, 52
Wright, Dickson, 237
Wright, James, 172–4

Zumbro River, 31, 32